"Give Me Fifty Marines
Not Afraid To Die"

IWO JIMA

by

John Keith Wells

Major United States Marine Corps
(Hon. Retired in 1959)

In 1945
Lieutenant, platoon leader
3rd Platoon Easy Company 28th Marine
5th Marine Division

ISBN: 0-9644675-0-X
LIBRARY OF CONGRESS: 95-94054

ACKNOWLEDGEMENTS

Many thanks to: RICHARD WHEELER, historical writer
In 1945 he was a Corporal, First Squad, 3rd Platoon Easy Company
28th Marines

Also: Survivors of the Third Platoon and Easy Company
God bless you all

PHOTOGRAPHS BY UNITED STATES MARINE CORPS
Also Personal

DR. LAWRENCE R. CLAYTON
DEAN, COLLEGE OF ARTS and SCIENCES
PROFESSOR of ENGLISH
HARDIN-SIMMONS UNIVERSITY

KATHRYN WELLS
(Wife, Supporter, Monitoring Every Page)

WESLEY WELLS
(Son, Supporter, Monitoring Every Page)
(Many ways)

****

INTRODUCTION:

FOREWORD

COLONEL BRADLEY MACDONALD, USMCR

DEPUTY DIRECTOR, MORALE, WELFARE
and RECREATION SUPPORT ACTIVITY, H O M C
QUANTICO, VIRGINIA

****

AFTERWORD

DR. LAWRENCE R. CLAYTON

DEAN, COLLEGE OF ARTS and SCIENCES
PROFESSOR of ENGLISH
HARDIN-SIMMONS UNIVERSITY
ABILENE, TEXAS

"How do you remember that far back?" several have asked. That is not the problem, I tell them. The problem is how do I forget? If some of your family or close friends are disemboweled and had their heads blown off in front of you, how long do you think it would take for that to become dim in your memory, especially if you were directly responsible for their actions and well being.

How do you remember?

"Try your best to forget and you will remember."

CONTENTS

Foreword

"Uncommon valour was a common virtue," this book describes the very details of this famous quote by Admiral Nimitz as he peered from ship to witness the Marines fighting at Iwo Jima. Major Wells, USMCR retired, captures our minds as he describes how he is successful in persuading men to do even more than they believe they can perform against an enemy that would rather commit suicide than surrender. His leadership inspired his men to become the most decorated platoon to come out of a single engagement in United States history. The awards included 1 Medal of Honor, 3 Navy Crosses and a Silver Star, and more than 100% Purple Hearts because of multiple injuries suffered by him and his warriors.

The author portrays small unit tactics and heroic actions by his men that leaves the reader with lessons learned that can be adapted to many situations in life. The writing and publishing of this book honors those Marines who made supreme sacrifices for our great country and helped shape our country's history. What a most opportune time to release this writing than at our 50th Anniversary of World War II.

As the President of the Marine Corps Reserve Officers Association I am delighted that our organization is represented by heroes such as Major John Keith Wells, USMCR retired. I have known him for more than ten years and am familiar with his work with the Boy Scouts, which covers some forty years, and his civic leadership accomplishments. These are character traits that are admired by all of us. I urge every officer and reader of military history to read this writing by a platoon leader of Marines.

Col. Bradley T. MacDonald,
USMCR

i

THE MOST DECORATED PLATOON TO FIGHT
IN A SINGLE ENGAGEMENT IN THE HISTORY OF THE
UNITED STATES MARINE CORPS.

Third Platoon

Easy Company, 2nd Battalion, 28th Marines, 5th Marine Division.

BATTLE Of IWO JIMA ISLAND
February and March of 1945

Private First Class Donald J. Ruhl, 3rd Platoon Runner.
Received: CONGRESSIONAL MEDAL of HONOR, Purple Heart, and Regimental Citation.
****
First Lieutenant John Keith Wells, 021592, USMCR
Received: NAVY CROSS, Purple Heart, and Regimental Citation and Bronze Star.
Lieutenant Wells entered the Marine Corps as a Private First Class in March 1942. He served (3) years and (10) months active duty, a total of (17) years in Marine Corps, before retiring as a Major in the Marine Corps Reserves in 1959.
****
Platoon Sergeant Earnest I. Thomas
Received: NAVY CROSS, Purple Heart, Regimental Citation and a Field promotion to SECOND LIEUTENANT before his death on Iwo Jima.
****
Pharmacist Mate Second Class John H. Bradley, Hospital Corpsman
Received: NAVY CROSS, Purple Heart and Regimental Citation, also on IWO JIMA MONUMENT in Washington D.C.
****
Corporal Charles W. Lindberg, Assault Squad Leader Received:
SILVER STAR, Purple Heart, and Regimental Citation on Iwo Jima, also in the picture of the First Flag Raising on Mount Suribachi, Iwo Jima Island.
****
Of the original forty-five enlisted men in the Third Platoon that fought on Iwo Jima, fifteen were killed and all but four were reported wounded one or more times. Kenneth D. Midkiff, the last Sergeant of the Third Platoon, was killed on the last official day of battle soon after talking with Lieutenant Wells.

Lieutenant Wells fought and remained on the Island for all but part of three days at which time he was on the flag ship USS Eldorado. General Holland M. Smith, commanding the Marines on Iwo Jima; Admiral Richmond Kelly Turner, a Naval Commander; and Secretary of the Navy James V. Forrestal were also on the ship.

Sergeant Thomas was brought to the Eldorado to talk by radio to the United States. He visited with Lt. Wells and Cpl. Wayne C. Hathaway.

ii

Prologue

THE FRONTAL ASSAULT
21 February 1945

A faint glow of light in the eastern sky announced the coming dawn and the United States Marine Corps' third day of attack on the island of Iwo Jima. The chill of the morning air matched the cold that lay in the pit of my stomach. My mind worked razor-sharp, the way that I suspect the mind of a cornered animal's would. I searched for any means to attack and destroy the enemy facing us. No one could pray harder than I prayed for God to show me the way to do just that. Many men in the Third Platoon would be wounded and killed in the next few hours. I knew it, and the men knew it. I was their platoon leader.

The coming frontal Marine Corps assault on the mountain fortress facing us had all the earmarks of the Marines making one of their famous suicidal attacks. My fortress confronting the Japanese was a full five-gallon G.I. water can turned on its edge. While we waited for more light and while I tried to think of what in the hell we were going to do and how we were going to do it, I cleaned my weapon.

Warlike sports like football, hockey, and other combat games are pure child's play. Cheerleaders work themselves and the cheering crowd into a high pitch frenzy in expectation of the coming conflict. The players feel the energy flowing from the playing band and yells from the orchestrated crowd. On Iwo Jima no crowds were cheering, no bands were playing, and no flags were waving. We felt the cold dark truth of death staring us in the face.

The atmosphere was much like that in the cattle butcher-house I knew as a boy. When the door closed and the cattle smelled the blood, they knew instantly what was about to take place. In the same way, after two days of fighting on Iwo Jima, every man in our platoon and every man on line facing the Japanese at the base of Mount Suribachi that morning knew that Marines' blood would flow that day and many men would die.

Human electricity, vibrations, or whatever we call the substance that saturates the air surrounding a life and death struggle was so thick we could smell it and taste it. Here, death hung in the air like a gaseous shroud.

Dim outlines began taking shape near the base of Mount Suribachi. I threw the white wool Japanese Navy blanket off my shoulders and laid my Tommy gun on top of it. The captured warm

1

blanket that our platoon runner had literally risked his life for would be of no use in today's battle; it would be left behind. Nothing-I mean absolutely nothing—home, mother, wife, girlfriend, hometown, cold, heat, hunger—had any meaning. Nothing mattered except today's forthcoming battle, and it would commence very soon.

The ground immediately in front of the platoon and between the enemy and us was generally flat with a few old death-trap bomb craters and three rolls of interlocking barbed wire. We could not use our platoon's reserve to support our morning attack. They could not fire from our flanks because other Marines were there. They could not fire over our heads, and if they could, what would they fire at? The enemy remained underground. Their mighty defense around the base of Mount Suribachi was an awesome sight.

A place of protection from the enemy firepower did not exist. The ground we lay on was the battle ground for Easy Company's First Platoon yesterday. Our company had lost an officer and several enlisted men there. Our Third Platoon replaced the First Platoon after their great loss, but before we could dig in, we had sustained a heavy artillery barrage.

I had studied the enemy defenses. We knew what the Marine Corps expected from the Marines. I lay there, heartsick. It would take the maximum effort of every man and more for tomorrow's attack. If we had twice as many men, it would not be enough, and now this enemy artillery barrage was descending on us.

The concentrated enemy artillery fire had been deadly accurate. I watched it landing directly on the far end of the Third Platoon defense line and coming toward us on the other end.

That deafening concentrated fire coming down the defense line meant to me that they would kill or seriously wound one half or more of the men on line. The way I looked at it, we did not have a chance. "How on earth would we be able to attack in the morning?" I asked myself.

The enemy observers pinpointed their fire directly on top of us. Their artillery fire was so accurate that the shells came within feet and sometimes inches from where we lay. Volcanic ash, driven up by the explosions, rose into the air until we could hardly breathe. With my mouth open to help equalize the pressure change coming from the deafening explosions, I lay flat on the ground. There was not a way for us to fight back. We could do nothing but lie there and take the battering.

The barrage moved into the Marine Company on our right flank and gave us a breather. Before we could count our losses and get a breath of clean air, the artillery barrage came back through us. My mind was whirling: where were our air forces, where was our Navy, why are they letting this happen to us? What a nerve-racking experience it was!

The barrage lifted, and the silence was almost as loud as the noise. A machine gunner in "I" Company on our immediate right flank yelled, "Hey, Wells, I wonder what your dancing girl is doing tonight?" He had worked in the officers club in the States, and my girlfriend, an exotic dancer, performed there often. I yelled back, "By God, she had better be thinking of me." Some men laughed, and then others began yelling to each other to break the tension. Our platoon lost only one man in the enemy artillery barrage. The loose volcanic ash had absorbed the concussion and shrapnel from the enemy shelling.

That was last evening; now it was morning and the Third Platoon did not have a single weapon that was effective against the enemy at this distance. Despite our best effort the Third Platoon situation was comparable to a little boy attacking a cornered tiger with a toy pistol.

Help would not come from company level; at least we could not depend on it. Company Headquarters had nothing that would pierce the concrete defenses from their distance. If they did, they would force the platoon to take men off the battle line to go back and get it. In two days of fighting the only thing Company Headquarters ever brought to us was a telephone and a roll of telephone wire.

The evening before, I had looked back and seen the company communication man running toward me. He ran bent over by the weight he was carrying and also the fear of becoming a target. As he drew near, he threw the heavy roll of wire and telephone toward me and ran back to the safety of a bunker in the rear. I did not blame him; the enemy shells buzzed around us like bees, and the area sounded and looked like the target zone it was.

The man's action, however, pointed me out as the leader. The Japanese killed every Marine leader they could. If there had been any doubt in the Japanese's mind who was in charge of this group of men, there was none now. Our company telephone man directed them when he threw the telephone and wire at me.

When we hooked up the phone, Company Headquarters said they had two shaped charges and two five-gallon cans of water for our platoon. A man on the telephone wanted to know if we would send men back to get these?

Send back? Send back? I was so God damned tired of hearing that command! The mortar platoon and one squad from the first platoon were at Company Headquarters. They had never been used,

3

and company headquarters always asked us to send someone back. Why in the hell did not somebody bring something? I had already sent someone back for barbed wire and trip flares. The only reason the Japanese were not killing and wounding us at the moment was that they were tired. They had thousands of targets over the past two days, and tomorrow they would have thousands more.

I looked around me to see whom I might send and saw the men lying in scooped-out trenches. Following the artillery attack, they piled the sand around themselves even higher. They did not want to move out of their semi-safe positions. The young ones were asking their sergeants for food and water, and we had none. I had the feeling that the young ones had done enough for the day. The sergeants were in full control, and the platoon defense looked as good as we could make it. I gave them what food I had and took another man from the assault squad with me. We would get the shaped charges and water. To accomplish this mission we would be working our way through and around other Marine positions after dark. We had to make sure that they knew who we were.

As we walked back letting the world know that we were Marines, I let our telephone wire slide through my fingers; that was the only sure method to find my way back to Company Headquarters. I cursed so loudly I think the men could have heard me across the island. I found that cursing was the best password the Marines could invent. No one, I mean no one, could curse like a Marine. I cursed all the way there and then cursed all the way back to our line. I did this for a good reason. In the fading light, the Marines were more dangerous to me and my helper than the enemy. The Marines normally did not move after dark, so they killed everything that moved at night. No one used the bathroom outside their sleeping spot. Some did, and they were killed by their own company men.

We lay there in the open in front of the Japanese all night. There were loud explosions on the beach and scattered explosions around us, but their night attack had not come. Now, dawn was breaking and the platoon must prepare for our morning attack.

I crawled to a prominent spot some distance in front of our line, squatted, and studied the enemy's defense. I was looking for any weakness to improve our chances in the frontal attack that I knew we were about to make.

My eyes were continually searching for the enemy in the early morning light. I saw the dark gray shadows, ghosts of the enemy, behind each mound of dirt. Suddenly, movement caught my eye and centered my attention on the trenches that joined the huge concrete

4

blockhouses and other pillboxes.

The enemy appeared to be moving their men in a unique way. I had seen them do this two nights before but thought it was a matter of convenience. Each man held onto a piece of equipment belonging to the man in front of him, and the group moved single-file without losing men or having any lag behind. Ten or twelve would be bent over and moving train-like one way and then another in the shallow trenches. This appeared to be an excellent way to move crowded combat men. We could do very little about this because only direct gunfire down those trenches that were perpendicular to our direction of attack could greatly affect the enemy there.

With shrubbery and camouflage blasted away from the base of Mount Suribachi by our Army Air Force, Navy Air Force, Marine Air Force, and Navy weapons, we could see the ring of interlocking concrete pill boxes, blockhouses, and connecting trenches. They looked like a string of beads around an old lady's wrinkled neck.

Their defense was interlocking and protected. Men in the principal fortifications could call machine gun, mortar, and artillery fire on themselves and be in very little danger. The Japanese stayed underground in the daytime.

The morning light grew brighter, and the Japanese defense looked stronger. If there was a weakness in their defense, I had not found it. Our Army Air Force, Navy Air force, Marine planes and the large shells from our cruisers and battleships had exposed but not destroyed a single huge concrete emplacement.

How could we possibly destroy them? The Marine Corps expected the absolute maximum effort from its officers and men. Instinctively, I expected in return the utmost in coordinated support weapons in our morning ground attack.

Suddenly, a form took shape in front of me. There, in a shadow, not more than fifty or sixty yards away, squatted a Japanese officer looking straight at me. He was studying our lines, the same as I was studying his. I had left my Tommy gun on the blanket behind me, so I turned to the men and yelled, "Get that son-of-a-bitch." The Jap officer stood up and showed all the teeth he could with a big grin and quickly stepped behind a large bunker a short distance behind him. He did this before anyone could act. This bunker had a damaged roof. I made a special mental note of that. The officer's grin appeared to be the grin of confidence. He must have thought he had us just where he wanted. I was not sure he did not.

The U. S. Navy had dominance of the sea. Not one enemy weapon had fired against our Navy's big gun ships. Our ships could move in close to the island and pulverize the part of the mountain in front of us and maintain the fire. This type of action would prevent the many caves on the side of the mountain from being effective.

We expected Marine tanks to lead the morning attack. The tanks would flatten the rolls of barbed wire in front of us and silence any large enemy weapon they could see, then blow holes in the concrete defenses. We could then use our efficient flamethrowers.

The Marine Corps' large artillery could help with the larger caves and do their best, along with the Navy, to neutralize the enemy's artillery that shelled us last evening. Our smaller artillery, like the 37 millimeter, that were positioned just back of our left flank could be selective in knocking out newly opened small caves. They would be firing at point-blank range.

I must have been living in a dream world to expect this much help. Even if we did receive most of it, I could not see how we could cross the open ground, cross our own barbed wire, breach, and then destroy their defense without a great loss of Marines.

The OLD MAN (God) had not given me a clue, and it was getting late. He always gave me a clue. I depended on it.

The time was drawing near to attack, and I had received no information or help from Company Headquarters. I picked up the sound-powered phone and asked for help. Their reply was that the tanks were back in a semi-protected area refueling. Well, the tanks had been behind the line all night; I thought, "How long does it take to refuel the God damn things?" Company Headquarters went on to say that the only artillery piece on the island was facing the wrong direction. The captain reported that we had no eighty millimeter mortar ammunition; it had not reached them from the troop or ammunition ships. They would not be effective anyway; the enemy was under ground. The battleships, cruisers, destroyers, and other Navy ships had not returned from their night's rendezvous, which was some distance away.

The very thought that we were attacking without help from anyone was a sobering and deep concern of mine. The enemy would slaughter the men in the platoon. At a time like this the leader almost hates the commander ordering him and his men to their deaths.

I asked Company Headquarters just what help we could expect, and they thought that they could call in an air strike. Dive bombers would come in at a low altitude to bomb and strafe. This sounded good, but this action would only distract the Japanese long enough for us to get out in the open, where they could massacre us.

We got the air strike. We were on top of the ground or slightly dug-in. The Japanese remained underground and well protected. To

6

avoid hitting any of the Marines, the dive bombers made their strike too far up the mountain to help us. If we could kill Japanese or scare them to death with noise and ground vibrations, that air strike would have done the job.

We had stretched coils of barbed wire with trip-flares some distance in front of our lines. We did this to give us warning and to slow an enemy night attack. The wire was far enough in front of the platoon that it would be difficult for the Japanese to be accurate with their personal weapons. This barbed wire entanglement can be a real hazard to the attacking force.

The expected enemy night attack did not take place. Now, the barbed wire night protector that we had so boldly laid the evening before had switched sides in the battle. We could not destroy the coiled barbed wire without tanks or help from our big weapons. The wire entanglement had become part of the enemy's defense. We had nothing to attack with but our hand weapons and nothing to protect our bodies but the clothes on our backs.

It was time to attack. Over the phone came orders to attack that fortification directly in front of us. So help me God, our orders were to do just that - ATTACK. I asked Company Headquarters if that was all the help we were getting, and they replied, "You should have jumped off one minute ago."

Our situation looked so hopeless that I could not order the platoon to follow me. I stood up, pointed my Tommy gun toward the enemy, and took off running straight toward that grinning Japanese officer's bunker, the one with the hole in the top. I did not know anything else to do. Only God could help us now.

Alone, my God, how alone! Never did I feel so alone in my life as I did when I ran toward the barbed wire entanglement, the Japanese line, and the bunker the Japanese officer disappeared behind.

Insanity! The attack was unreal, like something out of the movies. To me, I thought it was a great waste of life.

I thought I needed to see better, so I ran standing almost straight up. I fought off the urge to look back to see if anybody was following.

Out of the corner of my eye, I saw our platoon sergeant pulling one roll of wire out of the way, and then I saw our platoon guide and our platoon runner following close to me. I felt sure the others were coming behind.

The machine gunner in the other company that yelled the night before, called out, "Lieutenant, I'm going with you." He left his company and brought his machine gun and ammunition bearer with him. A great surge went through my body—what a lift their volunteer presence made. We jumped the other roll of wire and continued to run straight toward the massive enemy military might in the best tradition of the United States Marine Corps.

The military charge and the mental make-up instilled in me to make it was a culmination of a path set years earlier at my home as a boy, later as a student at the Agriculture and Mechanical College of Texas, and the very make-up and tradition of the Marine Corps. There was no decision to make, once I received the order. It never entered my mind to do anything else.

In American Heritage for June 1964 Richard Wheeler recounted the event:

"As the last group of planes droned away from the target, Sergeant Snyder, beside me in our shell hole, stood up and looked toward the rear. 'Where is our tank support?' he asked with a frown. It turned out that the tanks had been delayed by refueling and rearming. Lieutenant Wells decided not to wait for them.

A few minutes later he launched our platoon's attack. Climbing out of his crater he signalled with a sweep of his Thompson Machine gun for us to follow him, and began to trot toward Suribachi. By this time we had learned that Wells' courage was not just talk. As we forced ourselves to rise from our holes and imitate his example, I could feel the fear dragging at my jowls. We seem to be heading for certain death." (201)

Wheeler also wrote; "Wells was an enthusiastic Marine who once told us in training: "Just give me fifty men not afraid to die, and I can take any position!" (56)

THE ATTACK HAD BEGUN!

8

Chapter 1

THE JAPANESE ATTACKED PEARL HARBOR
TEXAS A. & M. MILITARY COLLEGE
Sunday, December 7, 1941

"The Japanese attacked Pearl Harbor Hawaii." I bolted upright. The announcement over the radio must be true, we had read about nothing but hostilities building between our countries. Quickly, I ran into the hall knocking on doors to make sure everyone knew. I heard yells coming from other stoops in Puryear Hall.

Radios developed the drawing power of magnets. Young cadets began gathering around or paused to listen to any government announcement. The President of the United States, Franklin D. Roosevelt, soon after, announced, "A state of war exists between the United States and the Japanese Empire."

War was no surprise to some of us. We had direct contact with the military, but the Sunday morning sneak attack was a surprise. The rest of the first day and most of the night our radios stayed tuned to the news.

War! Me? Kill someone? At nineteen years of age my teenage mind raced through the possibilities of actual warfare—not play warfare. My school and military coaches said that I played and fought with the killer's instinct, but I understood the school contests and war games we played were not real. I knew deep down in my heart I could not kill anyone.

The United States Government remained secret about the part played by our leaders in being surprised at Pearl Harbor. They also went silent on everything that was "The Military." No one had television, and many people in the United States did without radio and newspapers. Most of the United States was still in the depths of the Great Depression.

Any day, we expected the Japanese to shell and make landings on the West Coast of the United States. It crossed my mind to go home and help defend that part of the country when the time came.

Our nation reminded me of a lazy fisherman taking a Sunday afternoon nap in the shade of a big oak tree. A nest of ants, living at the base of the tree, suddenly attacked him. The ants covered his body before the first sting. They stung him again and then again every time he made a move. What decision should he make? Should he get his clothes off quick, then jump into the water, or jump into the water

9

clothes and all? Our country soon realized that a full scale war was descending on it. The United States went to war unprepared and completely outclassed by its enemies.

The American people soon learned that most of the United States Pacific Naval Fleet lay on the ocean floor at Pearl Harbor. Japanese bombers sank the fleet as it sat anchored like ducks on a pond with no way to escape. Allowing our ships to be trapped in this manner was a disgrace. Our peacetime Navy officers lost not only men and material but respect as well.

All civilian organizations including our military school were straining to do their part in the war effort and to display their love for their country. The school wanted to do something extra. Before showing a feature movie, theaters showed newsreels of happenings around the world. Only two years before, we watched Adolf Hitler's young people doing precision exercises on large playing fields.

These accounts must have impressed someone in our school system, and they introduced an exercise program to the students. I think in somebody's mind the exercise showed the spirit of getting ready for war.

Exercises that the school sponsored were not strenuous, but doing calisthenics in the early morning hours was unpopular. Bugles and whistles blowing and gruff and demanding voices could be heard all the way to the parade ground. For a short time, the school took on the appearance and atmosphere of a training camp. The program failed miserably.

My physical condition was tops, and so it was with most of the young men at school. I had lettered in all four sports-football, basketball, track, and tennis-my senior year in high school. At Texas A&M, fencing and wrestling were my sports. I lettered in fencing and won second in school wrestling (169 pound) class.

John H.(Jack) Irving and I roomed together in 1941 and the first semester of 1942. Jack was older by two or three years, and he treated me like a younger brother. One of Jack's brothers attended school with us at Texas A&M. His only other brother was attending school at West Point Military Academy. Jack's father was a regular Army officer in the Horse Cavalry stationed at Ft. Bliss, El Paso, Texas.

Following World War I, the United States reduced its armed forces. Because the officers were few in number, Jack, a colonel's son, personally knew most of the Army's ranking officers and their families. For some of these officers, he gave high praise. For others, he expressed doubt about their ability under the pressure of warfare.

"Military brats" was a term given to children who were born and

10

raised in the military. Jack and his brother earned that name. The family kept the two boys well informed on military action throughout the world. The family received their news through the military grapevine (word-of-mouth), which was faster and more accurate than the newspaper or radio. I respected the two brothers' judgment on military matters completely.

Warfare stimulated my mind, and Jack found me an enthusiastic student on the subject. He did enjoy teaching me. I read and studied the lives of Genghis Khan, Jeb Stewart, T. E. Lawrence, and other warriors.

Before the Japanese attack and after, we spent endless hours studying strategy and tactics. These studies started with the individual as he attacks and protects himself from man or animal, using hat, coat, bare hands, feet, and deception. Because I was a fencer and wrestler, the body maneuvers became almost natural.

We then developed our knife fighting and the use of pistols. Jack had a few pistols with ammunition. They were illegal at the school. He and I practiced on the Brazos River bottom land. If the school pulled a raid, looking for weapons, the Colonel's daughter would know beforehand. She would back her car from the road to the dorm window. We would load the incriminating evidence into the trunk of her car until the raid was over. Her father was our Cavalry instructor at school.

While the other roommate read or slept, Jack and I made it a part of our daily life to enter and leave the dorm room without being noticed by the other roommate. Walking down the hallway near the wall presented a poor silhouette. We would find our way to important places blindfolded or in total darkness and climb and descend wooden stairs by walking near the edge to prevent the boards from creaking.

We allowed each other limited observation of a given terrain and then asked the other to attack an imaginary enemy defending the high ground. The defender and the attacker would have specified weapons. If conditions prevented outdoor observation, then books with pictures served as quick studies to be questioned later. The old trick of keeping the sun at your back and in the enemy's face was always good, if it could be managed.

We spotted birds, squirrels and other wild animals by walking slowly with long stops. Early in the morning and late in the evening was the best time. With the sun at our back, we could see them well. By standing still in plain view near a well-traveled pathway or sidewalk, we observed the number of people who would notice us. Non-movement, we found, is the best camouflage. We thought that in enemy country, it would be wise to stand still where plant foliage breaks the body silhouette, to travel after darkness, or move in bad

11

weather. If exposed, we moved quickly in a zig-zag manner. If you can fool wild animals, you can fool most untrained people. I knew the odds were against us ever using this training, but it was a good confidence builder.

Cavalry officers from World War I and friends of Jack and his family taught us young cadets advanced military science. Every other week we spent an afternoon in the field as infantryman and every other week as cavalrymen on horseback.

William G. Harrell and I were in "D" Troop Cavalry. "D" Troop was the Honor Troop and rode on horseback in all parades. The school military forced the other cavalry troops to march like infantry when parading at the school ceremonies. If for some reason our weekly drill or parade time changed, dorm cadets would get the word. Young cadets living away from the school would show up for drill out of uniform. A few times we were forced to quickly dress or hide Herrell. This sounds bad, but it was not. Herrell was a good man, and his heart was in the right place. We became good friends at school, and our friendship continued in the Marine Corps.

"Texas A&M furnishes more officers to the military service than any other school," the school paper informed us. Over the loudspeaker at meal time we heard our school news spiced with war news. With all their problems, our school remained on top of things.

Many country people were leaving the farm to go to cities and work in war plants. Everything indicated that we were at war. Still, the war raging in Europe and the Pacific see med unreal; it was much like watching a movie. We learned that a group of military personnel escaped to the Island of Corregidor in the Philippines. I learned later that they were Marines. With a group of Colonel "Skinny" Wainwright's men, they fought off the Japanese for another month. The radio news told us that the men with Colonel Wainwright made great sacrifices to give us more precious time to move relief troops to their aid.

We followed day and night the epic four months of resistance made by the defending American troops. The Philippine Islands finally fell to the enemy. That was a serious blow to the school and our Nation.

"Attention!" The military-sounding voice on the loud speaker in the school mess hall demanded attention. Clanging and rattling of dishes came to an immediate halt as the stern voice of the announcer said that "Silver Taps" would be held at midnight. We would honor the alumni of Texas A&M killed in the Philippines. Older cadets and relatives gathered in groups anxious to obtain information and hoping their friends and loved ones were not on the death list.

Midnight came, and the chilled night air made a light robe

12

comfortable. Cadets moved quietly like shadows in the very dim light to a specified place near the bugle stand. Not a word was spoken. With lights out, each man stood in the darkness, alone with his thoughts, listening to names with rank and graduating class read aloud.

The names were read one at a time with a long roll of the drums ending with a loud boom of a drum following each name. The list seemed endless. When the last name sounded and the last roll of drums beat, a silence fell on the school. Not even a whisper could be heard. Then the mournful notes of "Taps," played slowly, sounded clear and distinct in the noiseless night air. We made it back to our rooms in silence. No words could express the depth of feeling and thought.

The death roster brought to life and made real the struggle that existed in a far off land between our country and her enemy. Our students' "ESPRIT de CORPS" was never higher for school and country.

Texas A&M drew attention, and Hollywood sent a crew to make a short propaganda movie, <u>We Have Never Been Licked</u>. Wallace Berry's nephew Noah played a leading role.

The movie people mixed and mingled with the adults of the school and drank beer with the Cadets at local joints. They decided to use the horse cavalry to get some action in the picture. Jack, my roommate, landed the job of machine gunner in the picture, and he rode a fine cavalry horse. I became his assistant and drew a regular line horse with a pack-horse carrying a machine gun and ammunition. The term "pack-horse" was incorrect; the pack animal was a mule. They asked us to make brush jumps with these animals. My part with the pack mule should have been the comedy. I do not think the school cared much for this movie. I never did see it.

Our government asked foreign students to register for the draft and fight for the United States or go home. The foreign students migrated to our room, some to talk to Jack but others to talk with me. They were mostly from Mexico and South America, and one was from Palestine.

Large numbers of foreign students were packing and leaving school. I noticed a group of older men walking down the company street. They escorted young Aggies. The group drew more than normal attention. Cadets were running out, shaking hands, and then raising their hand in farewell to the young Cadets who walked with the older, civilian-dressed men.

The young escorted men were American boys with Japanese ancestry. Someone in the group watching them pass said that the young cadets would join their families in concentration camps. I did not

13

understand that then, but I did later. I shook hands with the Japanese boys; after all, they were Aggies.

Jack and I often discussed the roles we wanted to play in the war to come, and we both decided we wanted to lead men in combat. We did not want to fly a plane, sail a ship, or handle tanks. The paratroops or any other special infantry troop might be the answer.

With different nationalities and many countries fighting all over the world, it was interesting to watch the varied fighting strengths of races and nations. I asked Jack's opinion about the best fighting military organization in the world. He quickly said, "John, if you don't count the German Army, the best fighting organization in the world is the United States Marine Corps." What a shock that was to me! It was a shock and a surprise. He never mentioned this before now. He was Army, and the people he knew were Army.

The United States Marine Corps? I thought about this. As I said before, I trusted this man's judgment on military matters. Did I truly want to be with the best?

Draft board registration notices arrived daily. Cadets must register for the draft. I did not wait to register. On March 12, 1942, I joined the United States Marine Corps. They accepted only volunteers. My whole being swelled with pride. The very thought of the Marine Corps giving me the opportunity to become an officer built a fire inside me.

The recruiting Marine officer informed me that the Marine Corps accepted college graduates as prospective officers. They pushed them through Officers School and Reserve Officers School and then shipped them out to war. We were aware that other military services did this, but I did not know the Marine Corps did. The public called officers with this type of training "Ninety-Day Wonders."

Many men, including myself, thought that a ninety-day crash course in officers school did not provide enough basic training for officers expected to handle men in combat. I might have understood other services doing this, but the United States Marine Corps? Never! They had a long history of having well-trained men.

Marine Boot Camp had the reputation of training both educated and uneducated raw recruits into first-class fighting men. There were not many Marines, but the few that I had met or observed demanded and got respect from all.

The length of time it took to train these young officers was not important. Confidence gained by the young officers knowing that they had basic Marine Boot Camp training before officers' training could make a big difference in their ability to work with the enlisted men.

14

I wrote a letter to General Thomas Holcomb, the Commandant of the Marine Corps. I told him that I thought all prospective Marine officers should be required to go through private's training in Boot Camp before going to Officers Training School. That was what I wanted to do. Now, I cannot imagine my writing the letter, but I did.

In December 1942, with only three years of college, I received orders to report to Parris Island, South Carolina, to the Marine Corp's Boot Camp. I would join a group of college graduates expecting to go to Marine Officer's School at Quantico, Virginia after finishing Boot Camp.

Texas A&M College 1942
Advanced R.O.T.C. Horse Cavalry

15

Chapter 2

MARINE BOOT CAMP
PARRIS ISLAND, SOUTH CAROLINA
Called to active duty 17 December, 1942
Finished Boot Camp 10 February 1943

I am not sure what effect, if any, my letter had on General Thomas Holcomb, the Marine Corps Commandant; however, here I was joining the second platoon of college graduates ever to go through Marine Private's Boot Camp at Parris Island (P.I.), South Carolina. Our destination was Officers Candidate School in Quantico, Virginia. The first platoon to go through this new program had arrived one week earlier.

There, on the train station platform at Port Royal, South Carolina, a Marine sergeant stood looking his best. He had razor sharp creases in his uniform, and his shoes had a mirror-like shine from spit and polish. What a reception! With his cap snapped down over his face, I could hardly see his eyes. They were almost swollen shut. He had evidently been in a fist fight, and his face looked like a baseball team had used it for batting practice.

"Are you a Marine recruit?" He asked. "Yes," I answered. He said, "Follow me." Those were the first and last words he spoke to us that day. I am sure his punishment for fist fighting was picking up recruits at the train depot on Christmas Day. This was Christmas Day, 1942.

I arrived two or three days late, which could have been the reason they were so inhospitable. Christmas holidays did not cheer these people. However, I think it was their normal attitude. The base Marines had to give the impression of being mean. Three years in a tough military school had conditioned my feelings to ignore this type of treatment.

Christmas dinner was over when we reached the base and checked in. Moppers, pot wallopers (scrapers), and pearl divers (dish and pan washers) paused just long enough to scowl at the prospect of serving and cleaning up after me. My new escort stood and watched me try to gulp down the leftovers. The food became hard to chew, and it entered my stomach in wads.

Soon after eating I went through the ritual of being searched, much the same as if I were a criminal. Neither the county sheriff nor any city police had ever arrested me in my life, but I saw them do it in the

16

movies. Marine searchers took my pocket knife, and they sent everything else home. Later the men told me that the searchers kept knives, condoms, and alcohol and divided the spoils. The men claimed to know this beforehand and punched tiny pin holes in the condoms. I doubt this was true.

In a barn-like building separated by stalls filled with old clothes and old equipment, the base Marines outfitted me completely. They handed me an old out-of-date enlisted man's uniform with no belt. All Marine uniforms had belts, but this one did not. Next came a bolt action rifle from wars past, then blankets and other equipment from World War I or before. Worst of all was a pair of secondhand shoes with the leather turned wrong side out. The smooth leather was on the inside, and the rough side was turned out. I learned later that issuing secondhand shoes was normal. It was a Court Martial offense to wear shoes beyond repair. A Marine would receive a pair of repaired shoes when he turned his old ones in.

The Marines that issued equipment continued handing and throwing equipment at me until I had more things hanging on me than decorations on a Christmas tree. As we left the building, they handed me a bucket containing a bar of soap, scrub brush, and a sack of toilet articles. I paid for the bucket and the articles in it out of my first pay check.

Another harsh and determined young Marine escorted me, with my equipment, to an old tin quonset hut. The issued equipment I carried, partially in a large sea bag, partially in my arms, and the rest hung on and off me in every direction.

The Private First Class Marine escort informed me that Parris Island, South Carolina Training Center had the toughest training in the Marine Corps. He said it was tougher than any other training anywhere. He insinuated that college students, such as myself, likely would not make it through the training. I did not say anything. I thought that if he and the others I saw around us made it through the training, I could make it.

The quonset hut that we entered was a metal building without a definite roof or walls. It was a half circle of metal with a makeshift wooden floor. Moisture-laden air from the ocean near by added to the moisture built by the breath, and bodies of the confined men plus humidity from an old kerosene stove hung in the air like a shower stall in a high school gymnasium.

Wet, cold, and miserable men huddled around the stove. In today's world even the Marines would condemn it as a health hazard, a pneumonia hole. Our metal hut sat with others in the middle of a large

17

sand pile.

Because I was the last to arrive, a metal cot some distance from the stove was my living quarters. The men huddled around the stove and watched as I unrolled my thin cotton mattress and laid out my gear. I immediately liked these men. We were young men from most of the colleges and universities in the United States. The Marine Corps pulled us together to train and do a job.

In a side pocket of a small hand bag was a partial one-half pint of bourbon whiskey that the Marine scavengers had overlooked when I checked in. The Marine searchers did not ask, and I did not tell them anything. I had purchased the whiskey to get acquainted with a young South Carolina girl on the train. When I placed the whiskey on the floor, the reaction was almost like an explosion from the nearby officer recruits. The three days of training under the Marine Corps had put the fear of God in them. They quickly voiced their opinion. They said that the Marine instructors would treat me severely when they found out that I did not report the whiskey.

We were Boot recruits like the others on the base. At this point in the eyes of the Marine Corps we might or might not be prospective officers. I could not say or think anything bad about the men in the hut wanting nothing to do with me and the whiskey. The Marine Corps did not allow alcohol at their training base, and I knew it.

I sat wet and cold on my cot. I knew how to get rid of the whiskey; I drank it. The bottle was the problem. Relentless drill instructors did not allow a Boot to open the door of the hut until the D.I. (Drill Instructors) called the Boots to come out. The reaction of these men suggested we were in real trouble, because of my actions and their failure to report me. Apparently, nothing escaped the eye of the D.I. when he inspected the hut.

Our Marine D.I. must have delegated one man to report anything out of line in the hut. I slipped outside in the dark and worked the bottle under the hut. We soon had more pressing things to do, and that problem was forgotten.

I looked at all this seemingly unrelated equipment and wondered how I would keep it and take care of it, much less use it correctly. I learned later that they expected the Boots to keep all the equipment spotless and wash and dry their own clothes.

Outside, in the dead of winter, on a metal-covered wash table and with cold water and soap, we brushed our clothes clean with heavy brushes. We tied the clothes to the wire clothesline with pieces of cotton cord. This eliminated clothespins. Learning the Marine Corps way of handling these problems did take a little time, not much. There was no time for long lessons on routine matters.

Being a 100% percent male institution and out of the public eye, the Parris Island Training Depot dealt mental and physical abuse with their daily training. They trained the future officers and future privates in the same area and at the same time. The future officers received the identical training as the enlisted trainees.

"Fall Out and Fall In," came the orders from our instructors. Designated squad leaders echoed their orders. Immediately, with our rifles in hand, a mad rush was on to be the first in formation and knock down anybody in the way.

Our Drill Instructor's objective was for each of us to get to our assigned place in the platoon and be standing at attention in the shortest length of time. We must move faster than everyone else in the platoon if possible. God help the poor son-of-a-bitch that was last to get in line. No matter how fast we moved, they would degrade and verbally abuse the last man to find his place. This training went on time and again, day and night, until we achieved some exactness in timing and order.

Close order drill in ankle-deep sand continued hour after hour, day after day. Before dawn and after dark, we marched with orders: "To the rear march!" "To the rear march!" "To the rear march!" Men fell to the ground, right and left; others marched into each other. We marched over or around fallen men.

At first we seemed to have men with two left feet, and they were out of step as much as they were in step. Three years of Military School saved me from much of this harassment.

The Drill Instructor yelled day and night and seemed to enjoy the sound of his voice. Each of us would be on constant alert, because we might be the next one picked out by the D.I. to be stripped of any dignity. A fine young man marching behind me had trouble at first. His name was Gilman O. Wales. Because of the similarity in last names (my name being Wells), I would stiffen every time they called his name.

Instant response to orders day and night could be a problem to those who lived a sedate life before coming to Parris Island Training Depot. If I had not known the purpose of the harassment, I am not sure how I would have taken it. I knew that there must be discipline and quick reaction to orders, and I knew all parties involved must work as a unit.

Marching to the chow-hall was show off time for the D.I.s. Every D.I. used a different cadence call. With his own corrupt marching cadence, each D.I. displayed the improvement of his platoon. With no trick maneuvers, the platoons did their best each day.

Banging of the pots and pans and the typical galley noise

worked as a muscle relaxer to the recruits in the chow line. For a few minutes at least there was no emergency. This was a welcome relief from the tensions of the day. A relaxed atmosphere in the chow line would be short lived. The struggle would be underway for extra food that was already placed on the table.

No civilians lived on the Island. Parris Island was the private domain of the Marine Corps. They ran the island much the same as a dictatorial government. The only place besides the head (toilet) that the Boots could manage any control over themselves was at the dining hall table.

Everyone could have enough basic food and a balanced diet. The fight was over fruit, milk, and sweets. It was not long before these future officers were fighting for food and acting as uncivilized or worse than the regular enlisted Boots.

We would go to our tables from the serving line. Lying on the table would be one piece of fruit for each person and one quart of milk that we were obligated to divided three or four ways for cereal. At noon and evening meals we might have cake cut in flat squares or bowls of pudding. I could have drunk the quart of milk in one gulp—some did. Individual pudding rations were three, maybe four tablespoons per man. The first food hog to the table would scoop up these tasty tidbits for himself and his buddies. These small groups took advantage of individuals who might protest. This was not right, and the hogging of food was about to change.

While talking to the other Texans in the platoon, Amos Walley from North Texas and J. Olan Reed from West Texas, I got the feeling, if only temporarily, of being at home. We grew up near each other but had never met until we arrived in this platoon. The focal point of our conversations always ended with our platoons problems. From our common background, we naturally understood each other. Olan Reed, Amos Walley, and I became fast friends.

In one of our conversations we decided that each Boot at the table had a right to eat, trade, or give his food away. Our decision was for each of us to take a table, sit in the center, and divide the food on the table. Each man could do with his food as he pleased.

We did not discuss this decision with the others. It was not voted on. We did it the Marine Corps way; we laid down the law. The food hogs showed signs of fight but soon gave way. They saw that hogging the food was not going to work.

After that, the only food problem we had was the food habits of a young Jew who sat at my table. He would not eat the regular food. In 1942 the Marines did not serve Kosher food. The young Jew ate only the fruits and sweets. The sweets were usually three metal bowls of pudding that should be divided. He wanted more than his share, which he did not get. Unless he traded or someone gave him theirs, he did without. I felt sorry for the little guy.

He claimed to be a Russian Jew and could do the Cossack dances that a few of us tried to learn. In officers school his family sent food, and the Marines allowed it. He did not graduate as an officer.

I am not a psychologist, but my experience in the Marine Corps led me to believe that the D.I.s and the brig (jail) personnel had more than their share of sadists or men with personalities turned in that direction. Before we left Parris Island, the Marine Corps brought a platoon of Texans to the island for

PFC. John Keith Wells USMCR
Marine Boot Camp Parris Island,
South Carolina 1942

training. Texans normally went to "Dego" (San Diego, California) for their boot training, but "Dego" had become overcrowded. The Marine Corps sent the platoon of Texans to Parris Island. These were raw recruits and perfect targets for the type of people who get their thrills by hazing people under their control.

The D.I.s who took over the platoon from Texas either hated Texans or worked under someone who did. I suspect the latter, and volumes could be written on what the drill instructors forced these poor recruits to endure. They quartered them in huts only a few feet away from and facing our huts.

We heard screaming and yelling of their D.I.s at all hours day and night with loud noises of someone slamming metal beds against metal walls and the wooden floor. We heard the doors crash open in what seemed like the middle of the night as men rushed to get out. Our platoon would be marching near them at daylight. We saw that they had every piece of equipment issued to them, and their sea bags filled with everything else they owned, including their bedding, on their backs or dragging behind.

Sometime later, while we were in Officers' school, word reached

21

us that when this platoon of Texans graduated, they allowed them their first liberty in town. The new graduates took over the town. They either beat up or ran out of town all Marine base personnel, Marine M.P.s (Military Police) and the Navy's S.P.s (Shore Patrol) included. We received word that it took all night for the combined police forces to get this group under control. If the Marine Corps wanted men who were mean and fighting mad, they had them in this group of Texans.

Even under these trying conditions some humor survived. One of these humorous events involved an Ivy League graduate whose name was Private First Class John B. Green. The D.I.s made him responsible for the platoon's Head. "Latrine Green" was his unofficial name.

The Head, a bath house and toilet combination, had community showers of the crudest nature, with community toilet seats that were even cruder.

Large groups of men invaded the Head at the same time. They did this without the piercing eyes of the D.I.. Many toilet seats were cut out in a long piece of wood. They were cut as close as the carpenters could cut them side by side. The buttocks lapping over on one side of the seat might almost touch the overlap of the buttocks sitting on the adjacent seat. This long board with the cutout seats sat on top of a huge pipe that was open on top. Salt water from the ocean flowed continu-

ously into one side of the long pipe, under the chain of seats, and out the other side. Any type of privacy was unheard of, or thought of.

Early one morning, when all the seats in the head were full and the occupants were seated in deep meditation, one or two men wadded up a huge ball of toilet paper, not too tight, and lit the top of the paper ball with a match. They dropped the flaming ball into the first seat. The water carried the fire under all the seats. Recruits popped up like pop corn as the fire went under their seats. No matter how bad things got after that, the thought of this prank always brought a grin— even today. Some blamed Private Green for the stunt, but I cannot give

Pvt. Mike Gayles & Pvt. John K. Wells
Parris Island, South Carolina 1943

22

Private Green total credit. I am sure it was handed down from one platoon to the next.

Another thing happened about that same time that caused one hell of an uproar on the island, but I did not see it. This was the gossip (scuttle-butt); the platoon in front of us was having short-arm inspection. Each man was to step in front of a Navy Doctor or Corpsman and D.I.; he would pull out his penis, and "Milk it down." To do this, a Marine would place his thumb and forefinger on the opposite side, top and bottom, of his penis, pinch the thumb and forefinger tight, and move the thumb and finger toward the tip end of his penis. If the Marine could strip out any discharge, the corpsman would take a smear culture, and test the culture for venereal disease. They did this to see if any of the recruits had Gonorrhea. This procedure is what they did to the regular recruits. Consequently, this is what they did to the first officer platoon going through Parris Island Marine Recruit Depot.

The first platoon had two movie stars, Robert Taylor and Sterling Hayden. The drill instructor of the first officers platoon made a bad mistake. When Sterling Hayden walked up, reeled out his penis, and milked it down, the drill instructor commented out loud that he always wanted to see the dick that screwed Madeline Carrol. She was the movie star to whom Hayden was married.

Hayden "decked" him (knocked him down) on the spot. You can imagine what this did to The Parris Island Training Depot. I know one thing for sure; our platoon did not have to suffer this indignity. Later, word reached us that Hayden received no punishment for his act against the Drill Instructor. Madeline Carrol did come to officers school in Quantico, Virginia while Sterling Hayden was there. She worked at a jewelry store. Many young officers went by to look at jewelry.

We finished Boot Camp, and the Marine Corps put us on a blacked-out train headed for Quantico, Virginia for training at Marine Officers School. All windows were closed, and not one speck of light was intended to be seen from the outside. Lights were extinguished on the coast because of enemy submarines. My life and my relationship with the Marine Corps and "The War" moved on and left Parris Island behind.

Chapter 3

CANDIDATES' CLASS
MARINE CORPS SCHOOLS
MARINE BARRACKS, QUANTICO, VIRGINIA
11 February, 1943

A good breath of fresh air welcomed us when we disembarked at the train siding in Quantico, Virginia. The three enlisted men acting as our reception committee put on an air of superiority and gave us a look of disgust. On the blacked-out train we had no light, no place to sleep, no place to wash, and no fresh clothes. I lay on the floor most of the night just to get a breath of air.

You can imagine how this group looked when we disembarked from the train. There was an old saying back home that fit the situation, "We looked like something the dogs drug up and the cats wouldn't eat."

Because we had spent the worst part of winter taking whatever they gave out on Parris Island, we were in no mood to take any more of the superior acting "bull shit" of the so-called Old Marine Corps. Especially, we would not take it from Marines who had never been in combat.

Looks are sometimes deceiving as our "spit and polish" reception committee soon found out when they directed us to our barracks. I do not remember the precise words, but Olan (Tex) Reed let the reception committee know that they could not haze us around like some people do animals. The rest of the platoon members supported him in Marine Corps language that the reception Marines understood. When they turned and looked us in the face, and sensed our mood, their attitudes changed quickly.

I believe Boot Camp achieved its purpose. I could see it in the confidence and attitude of these men. Most of the men survived well in basic training. A few men did not make it and left for home or another organization. The confidence gained in this training was worth its weight in gold. It always pays to build a good base from which to grow, and I felt we had one.

Our credentials for war received at Parris Island did not help us in fighting the prejudices and bureaucratic war of Washington, D.C. I learned this fact the hard way on my first liberty trip into Washington from Quantico, Virginia.

Liberty! The announcement came over the mess hall speaker. This would be our first liberty in about two months. From the moment

24

of the announcement, the push, jostle, and rush continued until the barracks almost emptied. To rush was understandable for those who lived or had friends nearby. For the rest of us, it would be a new experience we would never forget, Washington, D. C. in wartime.

While I stood steam pressing my uniform with a huge pressing iron and a wet cloth, my mind told me that my appearance would be shabby at best. The old belt-less, misfit uniform and the World War I overseas cap looked bad enough on the Marine base. I was almost ashamed of being seen in Washington, D.C., where the absolute pinnacle of our nation's military power worked and displayed themselves.

This sounds as if I am exaggerating, but I am not. I wanted to go on liberty bad, so I continued pressing my old uniform and cap. My shoes were no better than my clothing. They had gun oil, bacon grease, and butter rubbed into them to protect my feet from the cold, wet weather at Parris Island. The toes of the shoes stuck up at almost a 60-degree angle. Firing on the rifle range with the right knee in a kneeling position and with me sitting on the heel of my right foot turned up the toe of my right shoe. These shoes collected dirt. They always looked like hell in public. The cadets could not buy new shoes without a government stamp.

Shoes and many other things that we used daily headed the nation's list of rationed goods. Upon graduation from officers school, we would receive stamps to buy shoes, but until that time, we would wear the combat shoes on liberty or stay on the base.

The cap did not look bad, but it was not a showpiece. I had used it to clean my rifle several times at surprise inspections. I am sure I used it to wipe my eyes and nose when I was firing on the rifle range. Priorities change in war time. I might add that having my hair cut off to the scalp did not add to my appearance or self esteem.

I caught a train for the weekend liberty in Washington, D.C., with only a few dollars in my pocket. Most of us in Officers School were Privates First Class in rank, one rank above the bottom. We would stay that rank until we finished school. We drew less than thirty dollars a month in pay.

Washington, D.C., overflowed with politicians and their helpers, as well as businessmen looking for war contracts. Ranking officers and politicians would party on the weekends. Things moved at a rapid pace.

Under wartime conditions you might think desirable goods and services would be expensive, but they were not. They were cheap or unavailable. Ten dollars a night would get me the finest hotel room in Washington, D.C. Factories were making war goods. Congress froze the price of almost everything for the duration of the war.

In war time the military's needs were great. The military had considerable power in the civilian world and was excessive at times. When they demanded, they usually got what they wanted. Consequently, the top men in the military and their friends controlled most of the hotel rooms and everything else in Washington, D.C.

It was vogue to be in military uniform in Washington, D.C.. An officer in uniform was the absolute top of the high government officials and their women's fashion-conscious social world.

What rank we were and who we knew were the trick. The color of our skin counted also. My father and I had a good bank account at my home, and I could draw money from it. With these shabby clothes, However, I would feel out of place in a decent hotel if I got a room in one, so I did not try.

With the availability of hotel rooms, we understood with amusement the story told about a civilian in town on business. His search for a hotel room proved fruitless. He then called a major hotel and said he was with General Mills. They quickly furnished him with a first-class room. The clerk did not realize that General Mills was a food processing firm and that the caller was a salesman in Washington to sell food to the military. The story may not be true, but it reveals the condition that existed. My high school girlfriend, Lou Alice Adams, let me sleep on her couch. She was working as a secretary in Washington, D.C.

I walked around town looking at the sights and looking for a good place to eat. On the front door or entrance sign of the fine restaurants in town, I read, "No Negroes or enlisted personnel allowed." I was not yet an officer, so I could not eat in the better restaurants. I never felt so lonesome or out of place in my life. My thoughts wandered far and wide about the inequities in our country; however, I kept my total commitment to the Marine Corps and the United States of America.

Politicians in Washington, D. C. gave officer commissions to all their friends, and to each other - at least it looked that way. Later, I met a young Marine officer that received his commission through politics. He worked for Wendell Wilkie, who was a pre-war presidential candidate. He gave a talk about his experience to those who were interested. I did not stay for the lecture. We were told that he later decided that the Marines were not for him and changed to another branch of the service. Never before or since have I seen so many officers in one place and with each trying to out-rank the other in importance.

I wanted to get away from them and to a place where I would feel more comfortable. A poorer section of town seemed to fit my condition and my spirit, so I walked toward one. I found out later that the Marines called this area Skid Row. I looked at the signs and just walked. Truthfully, I did not know one part of the city from another. I did notice that in this section of town there were no signs banning enlisted men from establishments.

As I walked down the street, I saw a crudely printed sign on a door that declared " U.S.O." This was not an official U.S.O.; that was plain to see. The official U.S.O. (United Service Organizations) became well known as the war progressed. All branches of the service used the official U.S.O. The volunteers that worked at the official U.S.O. intended to make the servicemen feel at home, while he was away from home.

The crudely printed, not very inviting, little U.S.O. sign would appear as a strange and doubtful harbor might appear to a ship lost in a stormy sea. I had all the confidence I needed that I could protect myself. I looked inside the open door and found a dark stairway with a drop cord light at the head of the stairs. It contained a very dim light bulb. Soft music floated down, and a little scuffing noise came from the room or rooms at the top of the stairs. I climbed the stairs, opened a door, and stepped inside.

The bright lights almost blinded me at first. Women came in a rush from every direction. As many as ten or fifteen women served and entertained three or four service men. When I realized the predicament I was in, my thoughts were to get the hell out of there quickly. The women appeared to be whores, ex-whores, and women from the very dregs of society.

I found that these women had formed their own U.S.O. They obtained this room, brought food and soft drinks, and put on their best clothes. I soon saw they were not drumming up trade. They loved their country, and all this food and soft drinks came from their hearts. They apparently wanted to do something for their fighting men. When I realized what these women were trying to do, I would not leave quickly, even if a spotlight shined on us for the world to see. These women had patriotism, whatever their status in the community. Wartime seems to bring out the best and worst in us.

When I returned to school at Quantico, I vowed that I would not return to Washington until I was an officer. There was no point, as I felt very uncomfortable there. I did not have time or the ability to change the inequities. Instead, I set my mind on doing my part in fighting the war.

Officers' training in Quantico was much the same as officers' training anywhere else, with one or two exceptions. In Officers Training School at Texas A&M. College, we spent one afternoon a week in the field training. In the Marine Officers' School in Quantico, we spent as much as three and four days a week in the field. We did this regardless of the weather conditions.

We trained in damp, cold, and biting air with the ground frozen or partially frozen. Everything we touched was cold, and this made the weather conditions more of a consideration than the training itself. On still nights, I remember the mournful sound of a train whistle in the night air and the cracking sounds of frozen tree limbs. It was a lonely time.

Many officer candidate's hearts were in the right place, but their bodies were not accustomed to this harsh treatment. Some Cadets had been out in the business world and had grown soft.

I was fortunate in this regard. When I was a small boy, a young man in my home town trained many of us to exist outdoors in cold weather. He taught us how to take advantage of any protection from the weather and to make camp in places out of the cold north wind and driven snow. He also showed us how to take care of each other and our equipment. In 1933, '34, and '35, Howard Weatherby, now from Shamrock, Texas, taught several of us North Texas boys how to cook on an

11-12 yr. old John Keith Wells rodeoing with Howard Weatherby

Howard Weatherby, Shamrock, Tx a great influence in John Keith Wells' life.

open fire, hobble our horses at night, and wrangle them the next morning.

In North Texas, we had very little material to make a fire with, except dried cow-chips (dung). We camped in the mouth of the Palo Duro Canyon at the head waters of the Prairie Dog Fork of Red River, near Amarillo, Texas. There were no mountains and very few trees for protection. Because of the extreme cold wind and, at times, wind-driven snow, the older people would say that the only protection from the cold wind between the North Pole and Amarillo, Texas, was a barbed wire fence.

Every Christmas, Howard and several of us young boys would take a ranch wagon with a chuck (food) box on the back, and we would cut Christmas trees (Cedar, Juniper) for the school, churches, and the boys' homes. We rode our horses and carried our bed rolls in the wagon. Several ranches invited us. Howard's brother's ranch was one of our regular stopovers. As young boys, we learned the hard way, but we learned. This experience was valuable to me in the sub-zero Marine Corps problems where the instructors did not allow fires.

On one of these training sessions the Marine instructors made camp in a clearing where formerly had stood a farm house, barn, and other wooden structures. The only things remaining were the spots they occupied. I noticed a small unnatural mound of snow where the barnyard should have been, and with some digging under the snow I found the remnants of a hay stack. I took my poncho off, piled on it all the hay I could find, and returned to the camp ground. There was just enough for myself. The Marines referred to this selfish act as, "Semper Fi" meaning, "I got mine Mack, how are you getting along?" This is a play on the words Semper Fidelis, (Always Faithful).

I put some straw under me, some on top of me, and between my poncho and blanket. Still, I did not sleep warmly. To avoid freezing to death, some men walked and stomped their feet. Moans, groans, cursing, and the noise of stamping feet continued throughout the night as men did their best to stay alive.

On another training experience, the instructors expected us to travel by compass, in patrols, and at night through a thickly wooded area with undergrowth adding to the darkness. The cold and dismal night closed in on the little group huddled close together. We were trying to decide the best way to follow the compass course out of that God-forsaken place. After our eyes adjusted to the darkness, we realized that we could not see each other although we stood only a few feet away. The patrol's objective was not a great distance away. Busses were waiting, and it was warm and dry there.

29

Navigating even at night was no problem to our patrol. In high school, I had worked with Mr. Dunlap, the school agriculture teacher, and Mr. Hooser, the County Agent, in surveying our county for terracing and contour plowing. We did this work with a transit, a glorified compass. My father let me run my own life, and his standing in the community opened many doors for me. I had come to the Marine Corps with a wealth of experience that added to my military training.

The patrol improvised a system to travel in this darkness and be sure of ourselves. We tied a white handkerchief around one man's neck, and then we moved the man out in front of me until the handkerchief was almost out of sight. I would then have him move right or left until he was in line with the compass heading. The rest of us would then move up to him. We advanced very slowly at first, only a few feet, but it was not long before we cleared the trees and brush and entered the open country. I got a compass shot on a bright star. It was clear enough, and we were not traveling far, so we could use a star. We soon made our way to the bus. Our group spent the night in the bus, because one of our patrol groups stayed lost the entire night, and we had to wait for them.

I remember one man who spent the night in the woods because his patrol had become lost. When daylight came, we traveled a mile or more from our pick-up spot to load his patrol. The totally exhausted man fell asleep instantly when he collapsed in the bus seat. His window was open, and his helmet rolled out the window. He never knew it. The Marine Corps forced him to pay for the helmet.

Near the end of our training, we participated in another night project. Our orders were to "man" rubber boats and paddle down the Potomac River close to shore. At a certain point we would leave the rubber boat and river and go inland to a specified spot. To do this we must travel down the river and through enemy territory unnoticed. The enemy consisted of a regular Marine company dressed and acting as Japanese. They would do any and everything to make us look foolish.

Our rubber rafts, half in and half out of the water, rested on the muddy river bank. We extinguished all lights, and total darkness engulfed us as we began loading our equipment. We used only one partially-hooded flashlight. The hood prevented the light from reflecting on the water. Our instructors looked on in amusement as we awkwardly tried to finish loading and launching our rubber raft. The small paddles seemed inadequate, but finally we worked in unison and moved down the river near the bank.

Struggling to keep the rubber raft near the bank one minute, and then striving to keep it from hitting the bank the next, took all the attention away from our mission. Flashing lights caught someone's attention, and we immediately made ready to land. "The signal is wrong," someone whispered, and we pulled away from the bank just in time to keep the enemy from capturing us. Once or twice more the enemy tried to trick us before we received the correct signal and landed.

If loading and manning the rubber boat was a problem, unloading in total darkness on a strange river bank presented even more of a puzzle. Some men got wet, but we soon unloaded and dragged the raft ashore. We collapsed and hid the raft. We did this in the darkest of night, and without practice.

Judging distance at night is almost impossible. Sound and smell are the only quick ways, and they are not always reliable. Sky-lined objects may be ten feet or one mile away.

Judging direction and distance when we have limited vision is something everyone should practice, especially, if he or she plans to enter a unknown environment at night. My friend Tye Williamson and I learned judging distance in the dark the hard way. When I was twelve years old and Tye was eleven, the two of us spent ten days on a lake, ninety miles from home.

The women in our area gave our fathers a good tongue lashing, trying to change our fathers' minds, but our fathers carried us to the lake and left us. Tye and I checked in with the gate keeper every two or three days to pick up groceries and report our presence. We motored in a small outboard motor boat to a spot near the gate keeper's store and quarters. After reporting our presence, we tied the groceries on a paddle between us and returned by boat to the cabin.

The Game Warden checked on us occasionally. On one of his visits he told us that a good panfish was being caught on another part of the lake, and they were plentiful. He directed us by pointing his finger. It would take at least an hour to get there, and that much time or more to get back, so we began to collect food for ourselves and small fish to use for bait.

Our fathers had left us a seine (net) and a sack of cow feed. Small bait fish filled the small protected harbor where we beached our boat. We would throw cow feed on the water and wait for the bait fish to start feeding, and then we circled them with the net. Getting ready took more time than we thought. We reasoned that we had plenty of fuel for the boat, food for ourselves, and a lake full of water to drink. We had confidence, and we were proud of ourselves.

The familiar humming sounds of a well-tuned outboard motor on the small boat caused our confidence to rise. We motored across a larger part of the lake in a light afternoon breeze. The wind usually calmed down even more in the early evening hours.

Tye circled a small island just off a point of land, and turned back into a very quiet section of the lake. A large tree lay floating upside down in the water. A storm had evidently washed the tree into the lake, and some fishermen towed and anchored it to make a perfect bait fish sanctuary which would attract larger game fish. We eased up to the tree.

Before I could tie us to the tree trunk, Tye had a fish on his hook. We each caught and strung fish until darkness settled over us. Everything seemed peaceful as darkness closed in and the night noises floated across the water from a great distance. Lights began to pop on and could be seen for miles. When we decided to return to the cabin, I started the motor. Tye untied the boat, and I flipped the motor all the way around and backed into smooth open water.

Tye laid down on the bow of the small boat to be my guide and keep us from ramming the shore. We did not lack confidence, but we soon learned that we could not judge distance at night by eyes alone. We cleared the point of land and saw lights and what appeared to be open water. I made the turn and picked up speed. Suddenly, I felt a jolt and heard the loud banging noise as the motor almost came into the boat with me. I did not consider the island we circled before tying to the tree. The water was shallow between the mainland and the island, and we had rammed the shallow bank.

The motor remained attached to the boat, and when I started the motor it ran. Tye slowed me down and almost stopped me, two or three times. He thought we were about to ram the shore, when actually the shore was across the lake a considerable distance away.

Finally, we spotted a campfire near our cabin and reasoned there would be no land between us. That same reasoning got us into trouble before, so we motored slowly. We knew that a day or two before, a group of men from Oklahoma made camp near our cabin. We visited with them and saw that they cooked by open fire. This was our guiding light home.

During the next two days, the wind blew, and there were whitecaps on the lake, which slowed our fishing. Tye and I decided to catch a ride into Vernon, Texas, the nearby town. We could buy some things that we could not get at the gate entrance and have a short sight seeing adventure. You must remember, he was eleven and I was twelve years old. By that time the lake people knew us, and most of the day fishermen did also. We soon caught a ride into town.

In town, we met some town boys who lived much the same as we did. Their families let them do about anything they wanted. Tye and I liked three of them immediately. They returned to the lake cabin with us. We decided to stay up most of the night and play cards. Upon checking we found that we were short on fuel for the lamps, and we would need a lamp to play cards. It was getting dark, the waves were still high, and there were no boats on the water.

Across the lake was another completely furnished cabin, and our fathers had left us a key. It had lamps full of fuel. Tye and I decided to make the trip. I am sure we wanted to show off a little before these city boys. With a partial tail wind going over, I had no-problem checking my speed and riding the waves. We made sure the lamp was full, and we found an old jacket to protect it on the way back. I rode in the bow to guide us and to hold the lamp.

By throwing my weight forward to get the bow of the boat down when it was too high, and leaning back to allow it come up when we headed into a trough, we had very little water enter the boat and soon had things working for us. We would not hit the steep shore near our cabin, but we soon reached the quiet water protected by the bank, and made our way to the cabin. This impressed the young boys from Vernon. Our guests stayed, and we played cards most of the night.

Two or three years ago—fifty years later—I flew my plane into the Vernon, Texas, airport. I was killing time waiting on the airport attendant to fill out car rental papers. He looked about my age, so I asked him about the two Chaney boys and found out that the two cousins were killed in World War II. Vernon veterans named one of their veteran's halls after them. The other boy, named Key, I think, became an officer in the military service, and after the war, he ran for political office and won. I am proud to have known those young men. They were great people. The experience on this lake with these young boys was helpful in preparing me for the current and demanding situation.

We needed all these boyhood experiences and more to reach our objective, which was to move on a compass heading until we reached the enemy's lines. The instructors expected us to move through their lines undetected. After we passed through the enemy's lines, they instructed us to realign ourselves with our previous compass heading and continue to our objective. This is what they expected, and it was a tall order.

Our enemy patrolled the river bank. We made an effort to deflate and hide the boat, and then move away from the river as fast as we could. I disliked the man who insisted on leading us on the compass course, and he disliked me. I did not blame him for wanting to lead. After all, the others were not learning anything with me always doing it. If they held back even a little, I would do it. Deep inside me, I knew this was going to be a long night.

It was a black night; I do not remember a star shining. The leader moved out fast with the patrol following in almost lock-step, one man behind the other. I made my way back to the tail end of the line, and then dropped back a little farther. The leader did not dodge anything. He either knocked it down or stomped over it. Our patrol was making so much noise that we were sure to get caught. I thought that if the enemy caught our patrol, I probably could get away if I stayed far enough back.

I was not afraid of losing the patrol. Every few minutes, the leader would take a compass shot. He did it on the move. Back near the river the leader had charged the luminous dial on his compass with a flashlight while we hid him under a poncho. We tucked the poncho around him, so no light showed. The dial was so bright that I think I could see the compass for fifty feet or more.

My senses told me we had been traveling for an hour or more, but in actuality we had been traveling for possibly twenty or thirty minutes. I was lagging back and waiting for the leader to take another compass shot. The compass flashed, and then I thought I saw the compass fall from our leader's hands. He did not drop the compass. He walked off a high creek bank. We heard the noise when he hit the bottom. After a few seconds we heard a long string of curse words uttered loud and clear from about ten feet below us. Most of us laughed; at least I did. If he could curse, he would live. This is the attitude you can develop in wartime. Because other accidents were happening, the instructors called off the problem, and the men's wounds were treated.

The Officer Candidates' class, while on an outdoor training problem, got food poisoning, and all but a few of us became deathly sick. Men were vomiting and having bowel movements everywhere, including on themselves. They were hanging out of trees in the most ridiculous positions. Sick Marines were trying not to mess on themselves or anyone below them. They were hanging their butts over rocks and fallen tree trunks, and some took off their pants, held on to tree branches, and spread their legs. Many were too sick to care for themselves, so they laid in their own filth.

Our instructors told us that the class filled the infirmary, and that included the hallways. Food poisoning was a serious thing. I was fortunate that I never suffered this illness in the Marine Corps, although many did.

I felt sorry for the poisoned men, but I truly felt sympathy for the ones that were forced to live in an outdoor environment that was completely foreign to them. Many of them would be forced to fight an enemy, the Japanese, who seemed to flourish in the outdoor surroundings.

34

The Officer's School separated the men alphabetically. These Marines came from all over the United States, and a few men from other countries were also attending school there. Enlisted men that showed leadership potential joined us at school.

Some of these young men thought the food served in the mess hall should be fought over here the same way it was in their boot camp. In the mess hall, we had no assigned seating arrangement. One morning at breakfast I saw an arrogant young man run to the seat at the end of the table where the mess men placed the platter of food. I guessed we were going to have trouble with him. The rest of us, mostly from the Parris Island Platoon, walked to the table and sat down like civilized people.

That morning, we were served pancakes. The waiter placed a platter of hot pancakes on the table, enough for each of us to have one. The cooks would quickly send more. By using that system we could be sure that the pancakes were hot. Ten or twelve of us sat at the table. The arrogant bastard that seated himself at the head of the table took the entire stack of pancakes and started buttering them. The very thought that he would commit such an act, in Officers School, just flew all over me.

I was the last one to seat myself and that was at the far end of the table. I quickly rose and made my way to the end of the table and picked up the food hog's plate of pancakes and divided them among the others. I sat and ate my own and the stranger's pancake. There was mumbling at the other end of the table, but that was all for the present. The men divided the rest of the pancakes when they were served.

Tex Reed sat across the table from this crude man, and Tex told me what all the mumbling was about. After I seated myself and started eating the pancakes, Reed said the stranger asked in a low voice, "Who is that son-of-a-bitch?" Reed answered, "If you say that louder, you will find out who that son-of-a-bitch is." This standoff would not end here.

It was only natural that there would be some personality conflicts in our class. The high pitch of training would bring even more conflicts. Each man was a volunteer and knew he had a total commitment to the Marine Corps. It is hard for people living in peace time to understand a total commitment to professional killing. This group of men would play a major role in the forthcoming battles, and some of us did not back off from a confrontation here.

The man I had trouble with at the breakfast table, whom I so delicately named <u>Bastard,</u> had some friends. They were always mumbling something when I walked by, but nothing out loud. None of them would directly confront me.

35

Then one day while the class was doing body building exercises, I saw this unfriendly group and several other candidates building a human pyramid. I began running. By the time I reached them, the last one, a small man, was about to reach the top to finish the pyramid. From the shoulders of one man I vaulted almost to the top. The whole human pyramid came down in one mass of tangled humanity. The ones on the bottom, which included my enemies, had a rough time of it.

Where I had a few enemies, now I had many more. I am sorry the others got mixed up in this, but I reasoned that it was time to bring this festering boil to a head. To be truthful about it, I was ready.

The instructors marched us back to the barracks and dismissed us. I noticed the instructors were staying around for some reason. One of my enemies, a large one on the bottom of the pile I had just demolished, confronted me. He challenged me to a wrestling match. We knew nothing about this man, but I knew that he had unknowingly picked my game.

We were facing each other and standing on concrete. The men and the instructors formed a ring around us. I am not sure what they expected to see, but all they saw was that large man hit the concrete so fast and so hard that his body shuddered. It was all over in seconds. I had no more trouble from that group. My actions did not help me in the eyes of the instructors or some good men that got caught up in this, but that is the way it happened.

Our schooling and training was a never-ending process both day and night in every type of weather. We had little time left for study and sleep. The strain was on, even for men twenty years old. Once, I thought I might have made a serious mistake.

The class sat in a warm room listening to a dull speaker. On this day, one or two young Marine officers stood in the back of the room and kept an eagle eye on everyone. These young officers had completed Officer's School with good grades and other credits. The school assigned them the duty of remaining with the school to help train the cadets. These young officers taught classes and assisted other officers in teaching. They were good men; however, they were often a little over zealous and anxious to show off their newly found authority.

The warm, still air in the room, the complete quietness of the cadets, and the low pitched voice of the speaker made it easy for us to prop our heads with our hands and drop off to sleep, or sit there in never, never land, somewhere between sleep and almost asleep. I heard very soft, almost soundless footsteps approaching. The noise stopped immediately behind me. I turned and looked up. The young officer could not stop. He was coming down hard on my desk with a swagger stick to wake me up and, I guess make an example of me. I was looking him in the eye when the swagger stick made a booming noise. The swagger stick noise was nothing compared with the noise made by the sleepy men in the room. They jumped and almost tore their seats and desks apart. I did not move a muscle; I laughed and others laughed. That was a mistake. The young officer was very proud of himself, and he did not intend to stand by and be a point of laughter for the young candidates. When the class was over, another young officer instructed me to report to the main office.

In the office, I was left standing at attention for a long time. The officer in charge handed me a book, a large one, which he was having trouble carrying. I am exaggerating, but the book looked big to me, especially, when he ordered me to memorize it. The book, I discovered, was <u>Rocks and Shoals,</u>" the governing laws and bylaws of the non-criminal acts in the U.S. Navy. The impossibility was evident; I guess they thought I would quit and return home.

I took the book back to the barracks and began memorizing it. The next day they called me to the office. When I entered the office, I handed the large book to the officer in charge. I told him and the sergeant instructors standing there that I was ready to recite the first paragraph. They looked at me in an unbelieving way. They took the book from me and ordered me back to school. I do not know what happened, but I heard nothing further from the incident.

Some people get so involved in their day-to-day environment that they lose sight of the big picture. The United States was at war, and we were not winning in a big way. We had no time for this petty bull-shit. War is not a social event. It was easy to forget that we were in school training to kill people.

On April 7,1943 graduation day came. I accepted appointment and oath of office on the same day . At the graduation ceremony, the same old uniform and shoes were uniform of the day, but for the last time. Lou Alice Adams, my high school sweetheart and friend, came down from Washington, D.C., for the graduation. God bless her heart. These were the dark days of the war for the United States. How grateful I was to get a tailor-made uniform and a shoe-stamp to get a pair of shoes. Things were going my way. Some say, a good-looking uniform does not make the officer; but, I say, "It surely helps."

Assigned to: RESERVE OFFICERS SCHOOL
Military Records: April 7, 1943, Joined the 25th Reserve Officer's Class, Marine Corps Schools Marine Barracks, Quantico, Virginia.
We were now officers. In the weeks to come, we would receive

special officers training and would accept positions of leadership in the Marine Corps. We began with two hundred sixty-seven (267) men in the Twenty-second Candidates Class. Two hundred and thirty (230) successfully completed the course.

Out of the class, only four would go to the Marine paratroops. The commanding officer of the Marine Paratroop Regiment sent Sergeant Everett W. Lusher and Corporal Edward Tomasian to Officers School. They graduated to Second Lieutenants, and they would return. This left only two positions open for men in our class.

The class of young officers had other choices. They were Sea Going, Raiders, Tanks, Artillery, Ground aviation, Engineers, Line Company, and others. I thought the Marine Paratroops were the best of the best. I wanted to go to the Paratroops so bad that I could think of little else.

One evening while we were awaiting assignments, and as we were dressing and preparing ourselves for cocktails and dinner at the Officers Club, a young man walked up and introduced himself. Of course, I recognized him. It was Edward MacDonald Carey, known by his professional name as MacDonald Carey. He came from the other end of the dormitory. It was our only meeting. He said he wanted to talk. We moved to the library at the Officers Club. He had come to me of all people to ask advice. Carey was deciding what part of the Marine Corps he should try for. This, of course, was a compliment of the highest order. Carey said that I seemed to know what I was doing.

I am sure he realized later how wrong he was. I knew what I was doing all right—that is, I knew what I was doing for "Old John Keith Wells." Yes, I was as single minded as a tight-wire walker. My type person should not be advising anyone.

I did enjoy the evening with MacDonald Carey. He had played the role of pilot in the movie <u>Wake Island</u>. The movie was about the Marines defending Wake Island soon after the Japanese started the war. He played in this movie before he joined the Marines. We only talked about the Marines and the assignments we wanted. After the war McDonald Carey was in several movies and in the last few years he has played in the daytime show, <u>Days of our Lives,</u> on television.

In their new uniforms and with a feeling of pride, the young officers talked of nothing else but what they wanted, or what they thought their assignment might be. Only a few weeks ago most of these young men were privates; now they were Marine Corps Officers. The instructors handed out individual papers to fill out and list five assignment choices in the order of preference. I listed # I. Paratroops 2. Paratroops. 3. Paratroops 4. Paratroops 5. Paratroops. I admit this sounded juvenile, but that was the way I felt.

I thought then, and I still do, that the Infantry is the only true combat unit and that the Paratroops were the ultimate Infantry. I thought that all other units, no matter how sophisticated, fell into the category of being the suppliers and tools of the rifle platoons of the infantry. Generals have tried to win wars with other branches of the service, but they never work against a determined enemy.

At this time, I was courting a young Navy nurse from the Navy hospital. One evening I walked her to the nurses' quarters and waited for her to dress for dinner. As I sat in the waiting room, a nurse and a young man dressed in tennis clothes entered the waiting room. The young man appeared to be the nurse's little brother. He looked about seventeen and his sister, or whom I thought to be his sister, was at least

a half-head taller and older by three or more years. I guessed the teenager to be a military brat.

The teenager came over and sat by me while we waited. We did not introduce ourselves. I told him I was in school, and he asked me what Officer's class. When I told him, he also wanted to know what part of the Marine Corps I planned to enter. I tried to impress the boy that I was sincere and that I thought I would go to the Marine Paratroops. He seemed intelligent, but the military brats always seemed to know more than the rest of the base personnel. My date came back, and we left without introductions.

Look sharp, be sharp, and collect our wits; it was interview day. The School Commandant or his assistant would interview each young officer before the day was over, and the assignments would come later.

"Officers on standby" came orders from a staff officer. The

commandant was on-board (in his office). A tense atmosphere settled on the Officers class gathered in the waiting room. We formed in groups by the assignment we chose. When each group was formed, we formed a line in the hall outside the commandant's door. He would interview us one at a time.

The Sea-Going group was the first called. Men chosen for this usually came from the top of the class. Robert K. West from Great Falls, Montana, was in this group. His assignment was to <u>The Salt Lake City</u> (a Navy Cruiser). Bob West is a medical doctor in Fresno, California, now, and we have been friends all these years. The <u>Salt Lake City</u> participated in the Battle of Iwo Jima.

The instructor asked the third group to line up and wait in the hall. I was nervous and in the restroom and ended up last or near last in line. This was the group seeking the two vacant Paratrooper spots.

About thirty men lined up. A sinking feeling settled over me when I looked to my front. There stood the finest men our nation could produce. Their physical fitness, their attitude, and their loyalty to our country were unquestionable. My chances of being a paratrooper looked hopeless. How could I beat all these excellent people out for one of the two assignments?

The two lieutenants selected from this group would draw captain's pay after they passed parachute school. Jump pay added to second lieutenant's pay would equal captain's pay. I would do it for nothing. In my way of thinking, the two chosen would be among the elite of the elite.

My turn came. I gave the military rap (one loud knock) on the door and received permission to enter. I opened the door and stepped inside. At a desk in front of me sat the school commandant, Brigadier General C. B. Cates, or his assistant Colonel John W. Beckett USMC. I do not remember which. On my left, at a desk, sat the boy I had met at the nurses quarters. Only this time, he was in uniform, and with highly polished, First Lieutenant bars on his shoulders. I advanced and stood at attention in front of the Commanding Officer. He asked two or three regular Marine Corps questions, and then he looked at me straight in the eyes and asked if I would jump from a plane in flight. I answered, "Yes sir," so quickly I think it startled him.

He dismissed me. I saluted, and did an about-face. As I walked out, I saw a faint grin on the lieutenant's face. He recognized me. I was not sure if that was good. When I returned to the waiting room, I found out that the young officer sitting with the Commandant was brilliant, a real force at the school, and only loosely controlled by the school Commandant. I had not only thought he was a teenager but had treated on. I quickly made my way to a reading position near the board. There in front of me, printed in GOLD, at least my eyes saw it that way, PARACHUTES: Arthur Keefe, John K.(Keith) Wells. After ten days delay-in-route, Keefe and I had to report to El Cajon, California for training. My whole body sang. Two hundred and thirty from a total of two hundred and sixty-seven graduated. I took time to look on the bulletin board and saw that McDonald Carey went to Marine Aviation. I never saw him again.

The ones I remember in the class were Maurice S.Dampier, William H. Scully, Robert K. West, Everett W. Lusher, Jay Olin Reed, Eugene J. Adams, Jack P. Stone, John B. Green, Max M. Mills, Jack J. Wallen, Gilman O. Wales, Arthur D. Keefe Jr., Tom J. Thompson, Amos N. Walley Jr., Frederick L. Stone, Harry H. Wesselman, Robert C. Williams, Robert E. Wollin, Jay P. Wade, Edward McDonald Carey, James I. Wallover, Edward Tomasian, James A. Warren, W. W. Worsley, James W. North, Joseph A. Weber, Milford C. Miles, Clayton Y. Vogel, B.A.W. Young, George G. Wells, David P. Torrey, Arthur I. Weingerg, Carlos L. Pate, William C. Stiles, George H. Waterhouse, W. L. Willson, M. E. Wilcox Jr., H. W. Vaughan, Jordan E. Ege, John Vickers Jr., Robert K. Williams, and Michael Gales.

New 2nd Lt.
U.S. Marine Corps

41

NAME: WELLS, John Keith   2ndLt., USMCR

DATE OF PHOTO: 20 April 1943

SIGNATURE: *John Keith Wells*

Promotion to 2nd Lt. U.S.M.C.R.

Chapter 4

MARINE CORPS
PARACHUTE TRAINING SCHOOL
Camp Gillespie, San Diego, California
EL CAJON, CALIFORNIA
14 July 1943
Joined Company "A" Parachute Training School

The Marine parachute training base at El Cajon, California, looked like a movie model of a school. It appeared that the men stationed there polished, shined, and freshly painted it almost daily.

Not one piece of trash or cigarette butt spoiled the landscape. The Marine enlisted personnel wore their dungaree and dress pants legs tucked into their highly polished jump boots. The creases in their uniform looked razor-sharp. They wore gold wings with a parachute in the center over the left shirt pocket, and they drew extra pay for jumping. I am not exaggerating. No man left the base without a personal inspection. Training here would be an experience never to be forgotten.

I reported to Lieutenant Colonel Charles E. (Skin Head) Shepard, Jr. His head looked as slick as a billiard ball. He commanded the base with rules and regulations as G.I.(government issue) as the Marine Corps Manual.

The school furnished ironing boards and large pressing irons in all barracks. The men looked militarily sharp. They pressed with a wet cloth and in minutes their uniforms looked fresh. A totally wet and starched shirt could be ironed dry in seconds and looked as crisp as fresh lettuce.

All personnel, officers included, washed their clothes immediately after their work day. Then, we dressed for the evening meal. If I wanted to join the evening gossip group with the usual negative thinking, it was there. They would discuss and re-discuss all the bad things that happened or could have happened that day. Thank God, I avoided it.

The school permitted one sergeant to have and use a small steam presser. He pressed uniforms for all enlisted personnel, especially the ones who were just back from the South Pacific. He also pressed uniforms so that they would pass inspection at the gate. In minutes, the odor disappeared from months of storage in sea-bags. This little presser worked overtime for the men returning from overseas. I am not sure that this close attention to dress and personal hygiene made a better

43

combat Marine. I am sure it created a better atmosphere for training men.

Nothing then and nothing in today's world that I see comes close to the physical and mental strain we endured at that school. In the first place our laws today would not allow it. The students schooled, exercised, and ran for hours. If a student showed one sign of weakness while we were outside training, a jeep ambulance picked him up, and the school moved him out fast. He simply disappeared. Nothing remained to remind us of him when we returned to the barracks.

We finished each day of training and exercise with a long run. In cadence and almost lock-step, we ran. The never-changing rhythm of the cadence and the momentum allowed many men to endure. Any slight change could cause someone to fall; this put others in jeopardy.

Regardless of how exhausted we became, we remained sensitive to the men struggling in front and on each side of us. If they showed signs of breaking step or falling, we made quick decisions to avoid falling.

Because of the extreme physical strain and fatigue, most men could not get up after falling. If they did, they must show inner strength by regaining the momentum and cadence. We made large circles, a practice which everybody hated with a passion. The circle would bring us up behind stragglers or downed men trying to regain their momentum. If they could stay ahead of us, they could stay in school. If they could not stay ahead, the training sergeant would shove them down and yell, "Run over the Son-of-a-bitches." We would move aside ever so slightly and leave them lying as we passed. The meat wagon (ambulance), which followed us everywhere we went, picked up the fallen men and whisked them away.

If a man knocked down by someone else tried hard enough to get up and start moving, we might circle him twice to give him every chance but no more. Most of the men could not recover their momentum. We did not know what became of the fallen men. They just quickly disappeared from school. The school seemed to work on the theory that the same weakness was in all of us and that the best thing to do was remove it quickly.

Exercises of every description, multiplied over and over, especially leg exercises, occupied our every waking hour. Deep knee bends, seventy-five to one hundred times, duck walk for one hundred yards— on and on for hours with short breaks to work in other schooling and training.

Once our physical conditioning began toughening and hardening our bodies, we experienced the rigors of things more related to

44

using a parachute. One event was an opening-shock torture device. It dropped us from a great height. When we reached the end of a piece of webbing, it stopped us just before we hit the ground. We were snapped like the end of a whip.

In addition to this training, we jumped fully equipped from a series of platforms, each one elevated higher from the ground than the last one. We jumped from heights that we never dreamed we could without breaking bones. In this way we gained experience on how to hit the ground.

In another training device we dangled under pre-opened parachutes. They were snapped into a metal ring to hold them open. The instructors pulled us up by a cable to the top of a high tower. After experiencing a nerve-wracking short wait before the operator tripped the release, the small men free floated to the ground in the large practice chutes. The large men, which included myself, hit the ground hard. This experience was telling us what to expect from the smaller chutes that we would use in the actual plane jumps.

We learned how to enter, position ourselves in a mock-plane, hook-on with a static line, and simulate diving out of a plane. The Marine Corps dived. We were told that the Army paratroopers jumped out feet first. I am sure it made no difference as long as we cleared the plane.

The training demanded the best of our bodies. No one smoked or drank alcohol on the week days. Our trainees sweated and trained so hard for a week that when the weekend came our body systems were so clean that we had the experience of learning to smoke again. We suffered the same experience with alcohol. Most students refrained from both until they finished school.

The school expected injuries, some serious. They gave no extra time to the injured. The injured would either drop out of that class and start from the beginning again, or they would leave the school for other duty. Serious injury usually came when jumping from an airplane in flight. They constantly reminded us that in combat an injured or wounded person is a drag, not an asset, to the combat unit.

In addition to the many training exercises, each man learned to pack his own parachute. The small twenty-eight foot Marine Corps silk parachutes breathed as if they lived. Fid-bars and lead-pellet weighted packets held the silk until we could put it in its place and keep it there. An initialed card in a small pocket sewed on the back of the parachute identified the man who packed each chute. Men that were normally careless about other things took great pains in packing their chutes. Their lives depended on it.

When the students are jumping, the school's jump master does not jump. He stands near the open door, and he clears the plane of men as quickly as possible, actually throwing some jumpers out of the plane if they turned the wrong way or hesitated at the door. Shifting wind currents caused some jumpers to cross over or under and circle other jumpers. As they drifted down, the jumpers controlled their parachutes to a limited degree. When two parachutes accidentally bump together while descending, it could easily dump the air from one or both of the jumpers' chutes. If the accident happened high enough the chute or chutes might reopen before the jumpers hit the ground. With the many things that might happen, it is easy to guess the tenseness and keenly awareness each man felt.

After we jumped, some men would lift themselves and their legs as high as they could as they passed over someone else. They wanted to prevent knocking the air from the other person's parachute. We could hear warnings, threats, cursing, and screaming as men passed near one another on the way down. People on the ground could hear us cursing for miles. A church, near by, asked us not to curse on Sundays. Nothing blocked the sound coming from the open air. To my knowledge, no one stopped. We would laugh and say, "We were trying to save them, and they were trying to save us."

Because I was the officer, I always jumped first, and equipment would rain down on me for several minutes after the men left the plane. The opening shock would often snap off helmets, canteens and weapons. Fid-bars and lead-weighted packets that were used to pack the chute were sewn into the chute by mistake came down also, and believe it or not, candy bars. Some smart asses tried to eat a candy bar before they hit the ground. Our chutes would shield us from most of the small falling equipment. Smaller students, because of their light weight, had danger also; their chutes would swing them. Their oscillating sometimes caused their chutes to hit the ground before they did, and they would hit flat on their back or on their hands and knees. At that time, the meat wagon came flying to pick up the injured. Meat wagons stayed in constant attendance, for both training and jumping. They quickly picked up the injured men and hauled them away.

I never remember having an easy parachute landing. We large men spoke of our landings as "semi-controlled crashes." My jumping weight exceeded one hundred and ninety pounds. The daytime air in southern California always moved toward the sea, and the air was dry and thin. I jumped, and for a few minutes after the opening shock, the world seemed to be floating in space, but then the ground rushed up to meet me.

46

It was about this time that I got a chance to talk to one of the pilots and his co-pilot. They showed me pictures that the Navy pilots took flying over the West Coast. The American Japanese farmers had plowed arrows in their gardens and small fields. The arrows were pointing at American camouflaged factories. Our West Coast had been extremely vulnerable soon after Pearl Harbor.

Regardless of our physical fitness, dexterity, and mental capability, there remained the accident, the miscue, the many small unexpected things that might cause mistakes. We jumpers saw it happen to others, and they did not have a chance. They were not with us any more, washed out.

Thinking about the unusual, the accident, could build tension and pressure. This mental state could cause more problems than the actual training itself. The Colonel once looked at me and said, "John, you think you are going to pass this school, don't you?" I did not know if he was teasing or not. I think he enjoyed leaving me in the dark. It was fifty years later before I knew how high he rated me.

Being injured was a serious problem for any student. A slightly injured officer, let us say with a broken leg, might read books or play cards while recuperating. He would grow soft for weeks and then commence his training from the beginning. Many injured enlisted men continued working at their profession. They used walking cast and arm slings. The dread of starting their training from the beginning haunted the waiting injured.

We had a doctor with a broken leg, and he worried day and night about starting over. I am sure it became a mental problem to overcome. He and others talked of nothing else. The school instructors and doctors said that a student might break a good leg by favoring a hurt one when he jumped. Colonel Shepard and the other school officers did everything they could to prevent slightly injured students from jumping.

Each time before entering the jump plane we walked in a circle around the jump master. He looked for limps and never allowed a student to jump if the man favored a leg. They forced the student to drop out of that class and pick up another class.

I listened to these injured men talk about the dread they had in starting their training again. I had to make the same decision. On my fifth jump I broke my left leg between the knee and ankle. As I said before, I hit hard every time I jumped. I heard a "thud" sound when I hit the ground, and the pain and shock rippled through my body. I did my prescribed body roll, collapsed my chute, and tried to get to my feet. A telltale limp gave me away to the Colonel and his judges. After several miles of running back to camp, the Colonel and his staff ordered me to the hospital for x-rays.

I needed only two jumps, one daylight and one night jump, to graduate. I quickly calculated that if I could, in some way, get by the day jump, then nothing else mattered. If I broke one or both legs on the night jump, I would graduate anyway. It was war time.

The Navy Chief giving me the x-rays worked with a walking cast on his leg. He had broken his leg in a school jump, so he had to wait to enter a new class. He knew my situation. The film of my leg showed two large cracks in the large leg bone. The cracks, wide apart on one side, ran together on the other. A triangular piece of bone looked as if it might fall or fly out. This piece of bone had a hairline fracture in the center of it. Despite the break, my leg did not swell badly.

Dr. Swartz left his office early and would not look at this film until morning. Luck or my guiding angel seemed always by my side. I asked the Navy chief who took the x-ray if we could fake the picture. He looked me straight in the eye, and said "Too many people around." His answer gave me hope, and I sent word to a sergeant friend of mine to pack my chute. Ordinarily, every man packed his own chute. It was against orders for anyone to pack someone else's parachute. The packer must initial a card and put it in a small pocket on the back of the chute. We broke the rules.

I thought the night would never come. I inspected my hurt leg every few minutes. The swelling increased very little. Darkness finally came and the hospital had lights out. My eyes remained wide open as I lay there. I must have dozed off; when the chief woke me, the hospital lay quiet. He motioned for me to follow him. We went to the X-ray room. The Navy Chief informed me that the only way a doctor or anyone else could tell the right leg from the left leg on a X-Ray film was the lettering taped to the film.

I think the lettering was made from lead. The Navy chief arranged it and taped it to the wrong side of the film. He then shot a picture of my right leg. I know this sounds as if we had this all worked out, but we did not. As I said before, he was in a walking cast and knew my problem.

Dr. Swartz's leaving early helped us, but if he came in very late the next day, he would not be able to release me in time to jump. His signature and his alone determined whether I jumped or not.

The doctor arrived late the next morning, and I would normally be pacing the floor. Instead I sat in a chair facing the door. When He came in; I quickly got to my feet. He began seeing other patients and left me standing. I never let him see me sitting. My friend, the chief, finally caught his attention and brought him to me. He looked at the film,

48

walked me around, and sent me on my way.

I laced my boot tight. The swelling was not bad. I ran as fast as I could to the parachute loft and looked for my chute. The students had left for the airfield only minutes before I got there.

There on a packing table lay my parachute. The sergeant had packed and left it. After scooping up my parachute, I ran out the back door. The truck that carried the students to the jump field sat there, and the driver stood near by. I commandeered the truck and driver, and he rushed me to the jump field.

When we arrived, the students stood at the outdoor trough, taking care of the nervous piss before boarding the plane. If they did not, some wet their pants. We walked in a circle, around the Colonel's inspection team. Officers jumped first, so I boarded the plane last, and I felt the eyes of the inspection team zeroed on my walking and climbing into the plane.

We sat on the floor, and I sat next to the door and watched them carry the loading ladder away. I did not feel safe until the plane left the ground. I thought the colonel might order me off. He kept everyone guessing.

In 1943 the United States was short of pilots and even shorter of navigators that were not in combat. The inexperienced plane crews jumped our students everywhere in the countryside except on our school jump field.

The jump school hired a farmer with a breaking plow to deep-break the ground that outlined the jump field. The freshly plowed border was 20 or 30 feet, maybe wider, around the pasture, so the pilots and navigators could see the outlined jump-field for miles.

We were soon airborne. The men sang their song about the paratrooper whose chute did not open, "blood on the chute, blood on the ground, and guts all around." Their nervous voices cracked above the roar of the plane. I sat thinking about what I needed to do to prevent breaking both legs. If I jerked down hard on my lift-webs just before landing, I could slow down my fall, and that was all I could do.

The plane slowed to about 90 knots and we stood up, hooked on, and prepared to jump. I jumped first, so I stood in the doorway and waited for the tap on my shoulder. The jump master tapped me, and I dived. I no sooner cleared the prop wash than a freak wind caught me and off to one side I went. Before I knew what was happening, I found myself moving fast and away from the other jumpers. I quickly grabbed for my lift webs to deflate part of my chute and stop the fast drift.

Suddenly, I realized the drift was carrying me away from the men and jump field, and straight toward the plowed-up soft dirt border. I landed in the soft dirt, collapsed my chute, rolled it up, and ran to where the other men landed. I knew then that I had probably made jump school, even if I broke both legs on the night jump.

We ran back to camp from the jump, and as we passed the hospital, I saw the Navy chief. He stood, with the help of his walking cast, on the small front porch of the hospital. We smiled at each other as I ran by.

Now, I needed to prepare myself for the night jump. To protect us from enemy submarines, the United States established a coastal "Black-out of all lights." We could not light the jump field for our night jump, and Colonel C.E. Shepard, Jr. did not trust the plane crews to navigate for the night jump. He said that too many students would be hurt and scattered across the countryside.

The colonel decided to use another plan. The school would use the jump towers with the lights turned out. Total darkness below, and not knowing my relationship to the ground, made this jump different. I was feeling good inside, because no matter what happened, I would graduate.

I remembered when I was a teenage boy. Tye Williamson and I talked the night keeper of the Memphis, Texas, city swimming pool into letting us do a night dive. The night dive would be from the twenty-foot tower with the lights turned out. When we looked down, it was into total darkness. Our bravado would not allow us to go back down the ladder. Our dive was not bad, but we did not do it again.

I thought of this boyhood adventure when getting ready for this jump. Darkness gave the jump an added risk. I prepared for the worse. The release came, and I floated down so easy I could not believe it. The heavy night air came in from the ocean, and I landed standing up for the first time. I graduated!

Twenty-two graduated. With the help of Johnny Arview from Whittier, California I will try to list a few: Johnny Arview, Lieutenant Arthur Daniel Keefe Jr., Lieutenant John Keith Wells, Robert E. Radenbaugh, Joe Gragurich, Jack D. Stewart, Kenneth Smith, Don Heim, James Farrell, J. Felco? Koonce ? Elofsen (red head),Sisk??, Twenty-two men were awarded certificates of completion of pre-scribed course in parachute packing, ground training, and jumping from a plane in flight. We were designated as Parachutists, effective 21 August 1943.

At twenty-o ne years of age I took charge of my first platoon of Marines—about thirty-five men. No one could be prouder. Truthfully, the platoon took charge of me. My Platoon Sergeant, Earnest L. De Fazio, already a veteran of the South Pacific and highly respected,

50

brought the platoon and me along nicely. He taught me the workings of the combat Marine Corps.

On Iwo Jima Sergeant De Fazio won the Silver Star and two Purple Hearts. Years later in Korea he won another Silver Star and another Purple Heart. In Vietnam 1965-66 they awarded him the Bronze Star and South Vietnam's Cross of Gallantry with Palm Leaf and Gold Star. He retired from the Marine Corps as a Lieutenant Colonel. I do not believe I could have found a better teacher in the Marine corps. With my background, we fit like a glove.

Weeks later, I brought the platoon to the hospital for a short-arm inspection, and I felt a tug on my sleeve. The Navy Chief stood there with a grin from ear to ear. He still wore the walking cast. He said that Doctor Swartz had left for the day, and he wanted another look at the broken leg bone. We x-rayed the leg and found the bone had healed and had grown a large rim of calcium on the outside of the breaks. He thought the movement of the bones in the breaks caused the extra accumulation of calcium. The Chief said, "It won't break there again."

The men in the platoon exhibited intelligence far above normal.

Seated left - Lt. Col. Ernest L. DeFazio U.S.M.C. Ret.
and John Keith Wells, Denver, Colorado 1982
In 1943, he was Wells' first Platoon Sergeant - 1943

51

I learned later that many men that volunteered from Boot Camp had high I.Qs. When you add that to the enthusiasm of parachute combat, it created a good atmosphere for training.

De Fazio and I held class on all Marine Corps weapons. The platoon attended Scout and Sniper school, Tank school (I drove a tank and loved it), Defense school (which I hated). I dug about one half of a fox hole, and that was the last time I ever dug even a spoon full of dirt for shelter. Last, we attended a live ammunition school, which included throwing live hand grenades.

After a forced march for ten miles, we crawled under rolls of barbed wire with live ammunition firing above the rolls. Small land mines exploded around us. We then jumped into shallow fox holes, and armored tanks ran their treads directly over the hole. We did the forced march to the training site and back hours faster than any other platoon. The men paid a price, and I learned a lesson. I think the men learned one also.

On a field problem the next day I saw several men limping, and we called a halt for foot inspection. Most of the men's feet looked as if they had suffered hot-water scald. They did not report to the hospital for my sake and their own ego. The corpsman doctored their feet, and we hid out for the day in the warm sunshine with their boots and socks off.

On a forced march, the men bringing up the rear always had a hard workout. They either stopped to wait or ran to catch up with the platoon. After that experience, I periodically switched ends with the platoon when we were on a forced march. We also allowed them time to change socks.

The weekly Paratroop School inspection was so thoroughly done that every man on the base, I mean every man, turned out on the parade field. Hospital personnel and patients, and brig personnel and inmates had strict inspection also. Colonel Shepard always graded our platoon number-one.

On one particular inspection day, I was not the one to be inspected. Lieutenant Wells (green as a gourd) received orders to inspect the base personnel. Colonel Shepard normally assigned this job to an older base officer. I did not know what the Colonel had in mind, but I knew one thing—the base personnel would be inspected.

These were older men (Old Marine Corps - pre-war Marines). I found only a few minor things, with one exception. The hair of one sergeant measured too long. This may sound minor to someone else, but it was not, especially with Lieutenant Wells under the watchful eye of Col. Shepard.

Col. Shepard's orders were no hair on the neck, no hair on the side of the head, and the length of one-half of a kitchen match on top. The Colonel handed me the piece of match to measure with.

The long-haired Sergeant's uniform and shoes looked near perfect. His hair looked long but well-groomed. I guess the sergeant looked handsome by women's standards, or he thought he did. His long wavy hair did not grow in one week. I told him to cut his hair off to the length of that short kitchen match and handed him the match. I expected to take his word that he would.

He told me the older officers, of much higher rank than I, inspected the weeks before and said nothing. He did not intend to cut off his hair. His attitude and his speech in front of the other men flew all over me. I told him to present himself at the parade ground for a personal inspection in one hour, and I expected the hair cut off to the measured length.

One hour later I went to the parade field. The long-haired sergeant did not show up for inspection. There was a deep meaning to this. Here was an enlisted man who was not going to obey my orders. Yes, I would have given anything for the opportunity to rearrange that man's facial features, and tear him a new ass-hole with my jump boot. I thought I had no choice but to report him to Colonel Shepard. This is what I thought, but I soon learned better.

As I turned to walk back to the Colonel's office, I heard my name spoken. Sergeant De Fazio and his friend Sergeant Ladicio briskly walked toward me. They had found out about the problem and wanted to know what I intended to do. I told them the long-haired sergeant left me no choice; I must report him to the Colonel. They said that if I would wait just a few minutes they would take care of the problem.

It was not a long wait. Soon out of the door they came the long haired sergeant between De Fazio and Ladicio. They marched him to me. All three sergeants saluted smartly. The long haired Sergeant removed his cap and turned slowly around. His head did not need a close inspection; he had very little hair. The sergeants had cut his hair to the scalp. I dismissed him. He placed his cap on, stepped back one step, did a smart salute, then an about face, and marched away. He showed me all the respect due an officer in the Marine Corps.

The news of this happening spread throughout the camp. One day I was a green second lieutenant, and the next day men intentionally walked by to salute. If Sergeant De Fazio respected me that much, then they did also. There is no way I can tell you how much this act did for me and to me.

Not long after that, I heard that an officer gave Sergeant De Faizo a hard time. I hunted the officer out and told him in Marine Corps language that if any of my sergeants needed disciplining, I would do it. The officer had me to confront if I heard of it again. That was the end of that. Sergeant De Fazio and I became close friends and went on liberty together often. Fraternizing of officers and enlisted men was accepted in the Paratroops.

I knew that officers could threaten or give a Court Martial (trial), and the use of the brig (jail) had its power. However, that power shrank to nothing when compared with being backed by good Marines.

The Paratroop men drew fifty dollars a month more than other Marines, and officers drew one hundred dollars more a month. Money had ten times the buying power in 1944 that it does now in the 1990s. We drew the extra money and spent it. I was a poker player, five-card stud and five-card draw. I knew the odds in those two games, and I knew the odds of us coming out of this war in one piece, and so did most of the others. We lived only one day at a time and trained for the day we would engage the enemy. The Marines destined for immediate combat with the Japanese worked hard and played hard. Some civilians (feather merchants) found it hard to understand us.

Mrs. Roosevelt, wife of the President, returned from the South Pacific on a fact-finding tour. She did this for the President of the United States, Franklin D. Roosevelt. We were told that she suggested isolating the Marines when they returned to the States from combat. She thought they needed to be segregated until they learned to function as human beings. She should know: she had a son with the Marines Raiders in the South Pacific.

We received our shipping orders. A sergeant that I did not know gathered money from men and officers alike. The money was for a big party at the Grant Hotel in San Diego. Excitement grew, especially for the younger set. They could not buy drinks in town until they reached twenty-one years of age. The military controlled the party, and the teenagers hoped to share in the fun they normally only heard about. The women gathered where the money was, and they were as wild as the men.

To isolate this wild bunch from the people on the street and the people in the lobby, the hotel previously blocked off the top rooms and roof garden for this boisterous party. The class before us, a drunk young man held his handkerchief over his head, yelled "Tally Ho" (Our jump yell) and jumped off the hotel roof. This time the management decorated the basement and isolated a portion of the stairs and an elevator for our use.

The sergeant who gathered the money to pay for this brawl,

54

blew (spent) it on a wild party of his own. This forced us to gather money again. This money went to the hotel. We had our party!

Before we shipped out, I was in an isolated tent area looking for a sergeant when I heard mumbling noises coming from one of the tents. I stuck my head in and the low talk went silent. There were at least ten or fifteen senior sergeants in the tent. They began coming to attention when I gave the order "At ease." A senior sergeant vouched for me, and they continued talking.

I could understand their anger at the sergeant who stole the money. If they wanted to beat him up often, make him pay back the money with interest, I would go for that.

They went further. They swore to throw him overboard when we were at sea. All of the sergeants stood up and swore. Killing Japanese I understood. Killing one of our own was completely foreign to my way of thinking. I did not report them; we were not yet aboard ship.

We were trained and mentally conditioned for fighting the Japanese who respected no rules of warfare. We left for combat in the South Pacific.

The thieving sergeant came aboard ship and a heavy guard gathered around him and remained around him until we made anchor in New Caledonia, South Pacific. The military flew him away from us. I know this is unbelievable but true. I heard that he was a Mason (a secret organization) and members of the group protected him.

U.S. Marine Corps Parachute Training School

Certificate of Proficiency

This is to certify that SECOND LIEUTENANT JOHN K. WELLS, U.S.M.C.R. has satisfactorily completed the prescribed course in parachute packing, ground training, and jumping from a plane in flight. He is, therefore, entitled to be rated from this date, 21 August, 1943 , as a qualified Parachutist in the United States Marine Corps.

C. E. Shepard Jr.
C. E. SHEPARD, JR.,
Lieutenant Colonel, U. S. Marine Corps.

DofP-18—1141—M.I.N.Y. 11-23-42—5M

FILE - SELECTION BOARD CASE

55

Chapter 5

THE 32ND
PARACHUTE REPLACEMENT BATTALION
SAILS TO THE SOUTH PACIFIC
3 December, 1943

We sailed from the United States to the Pacific War Theater on the M. S., Weltervreden, a Dutch ship belonging to the N.V. Roderdamsche LLoyd Line. Their home port was Rotterdam, Holland. The captain's name was Rammel. The Dutch ship had sailed away from its home port before the war began, since Germany had overrun and occupied their country. The ship and crew had been away five years and would not return until the war's end. They turned themselves over to the United States and now served as a troop carrier for U.S. Forces.

Dutch officers ran the ship. Javanese seamen served as partial crew and did all the servant's duties. The United States had installed anti-aircraft guns around the ship and put a three-inch gun on the fantail. Men from our Navy manned the guns, and Lieutenant Commander L.B.(Bolton) Outlar from Wharton, Texas, a U.S. Navy Doctor, and his corpsmen staffed the medical quarters.

As we sailed away, on shore a small band played patriotic tunes, and a group of wives and girlfriends stood near them waving flags. Some dock workers paused to look up but were more interested in the women flag wavers than in the troopship moving out to war.

You might think this scanty show of patriotism insufficient for sending men off to do battle, but, after all, we were going to war and not off to play some opposing team in a ball game. For me, they could leave the band and flags at home. Just a friendly wave was enough.

Why should I gripe? There was no one there to see me off. I went below deck to look over the new quarters. In other words, I was ready to get on with the show.

Many changes had been made in an effort to protect America. On the coast, the United States camouflaged all factories, airfields, and military bases for daylight protection from the enemy. The cities tried to do a total blackout at night and avoid being targets for enemy submarines. Commercial airplanes had curtains over their windows. Travelers could not look out over coastal cities, because there might be a spy among them. Thousands of military men gathered on the West Cost to train and ship out to war. This automatically caused a buildup of tension among everyone involved.

We sailed out into the great Pacific Ocean alone to travel without a convoy of protective war ships. The minute we cleared the harbor entrance, I expected enemy submarines and our ship dodging torpedoes. I am exaggerating, but I was nervous as hell until we were well out to sea, and off the beaten path. After all, I was a country boy and unfamiliar with the sea or sea warfare.

Our ship, traveling without protection of a ship convoy, made a wide circle to the south. The ship traveled in a straight line only for short distances. It zigged and zagged. By moving southeast of the regular shipping lanes and by never traveling in a straight line, our ship would be hard for the enemy to locate.

"Slip of the lip will sink a ship" was the warning in the States that followed us out to sea. We heard this statement constantly over the radio and saw it acted out in newsreels at the theaters in the States. Our ship's captain and crew never mentioned our location at sea. Do not ask me the reason for all the secrecy; we never knew. We Marine officers on board the ship thought that the Japanese would know where they were if they sank us, so why all the secrecy?

The Dutch officers were an interesting group. They did not speak English. They dressed in white uniforms for dinner, and they lived well aboard-ship. The Javanese servants worked continuously. When cleaning close quarters, the Javanese sat on their haunches. With their toes turned outward, they waddled like a duck. They walked with ease with their butts less than an inch from the floor. With a table top brush they could clean in, around, and under anything in minutes. This was my first experience with Dutch and Asian people. The ship sparkled with cleanliness because of their efforts.

I attempted to make friends with both Dutch and Javanese, and neither one made friends quickly. I tried to speak Dutch, but I mixed it up with German; "Ja wohl" or something like that is "Yes" in German, "Ya" is yes in Dutch. They would correct me on the spot, and not in a friendly manner. This may sound casual to you, but it was not to them. They hated the Germans with a passion.

The ship's doctor and I became friends quickly. He had books describing the diseases among the tribes living on the South Pacific Islands. I found one book more informative than the others—A Yankee Doctor in Paradise by S. M. Lambert. The writer had previous experience in other backward countries where he had observed many things besides diseases. The world knew very little about the South Pacific Islands. Detailed maps were not available. I gathered all the knowledge I could and enjoyed the companionship of the ship's doctor.

Our Marines scouted the ship, and before many hours went by,

I knew where everything was on board the ship. This information included the ship's beer-catch. The Dutch galley crews were trusting, and they kept the inside passageways below the galley open, except in storms. Their daily activities were by the clock. We could depend on it. Their pattern of work allowed us a chance to steal some of their beer. We did it only once. The Dutch never reported it. We sat on the fantail of the ship one night, in the moonlight, drinking Dutch beer and some Tequila that I had bought in Mexico. We drank and talked about home and the enemy.

Four or five beautiful, peaceful days went by. The Dutch cooks were professionals and served the best food. As a country boy from Texas, at my Grandmother's house, I expected hot biscuits, ham and eggs, with red-eye gravy for breakfast. Often, pork sausage with brown flour gravy substituted. We topped this off with wild plum jelly or sorghum syrup. Many country families started or ended their breakfast with a bowl of oatmeal, but my family never did. I only ate oatmeal when I went visiting.

For breakfast, the Dutch cooks had the center of the table piled high with fish, several cheeses, freshly baked bread, and sweet rolls. These were on rotating trays. They also served fresh fruits from the States, and many other things-I wish I could remember. A large bowl of oatmeal sat on the table; it looked out of place. The ships United States' Navy personal may have asked for the cereal. I would not eat it; it was too slick for me.

Besides our good food, the troop officer's quarters were on the top deck with a small sun porch overlooking the world and the bow (front) of the ship. This was heaven to an adventurous soul.

The sun shone brightly with scattered clouds and a steady south head wind. The ship moving south may have caused the light south wind. We waddled around on the deck to develop our sea legs like the "old men of the sea." "Sea legs" is a term describing the leg action of a person walking on the deck of a moving ship. The human body finally learns to accept the rise, fall, and tilting of the deck as the ship moves and rocks with the ocean waves. To a landlubber this is hard to believe and understand. We were told that when a sailor goes ashore after experiencing several days of rough seas, he walks much like a drunk man.

One pretty and calm day the sailors scurried about tightening down and securing things that were already secure. The Dutch officers routinely checked everything. Now, they double checked. We soon learned that a severe wind storm lay on the horizon, and it was headed our way.

58

Everyone stood on deck watching and waiting in an atmosphere of anticipation, and then the first wind and waves hit the ship. The ship shuttered and began to pitch. In minutes, everything shifted backwards; we grabbed for hand holds on anything. The next moment, we were almost stationary on top of a large wave. It took all our strength to hold on as the ship plunged downward and rammed its bow into the base of the next wave. Weight of the water on the bow-deck held the bow down as the water rushed off to release it. The bow then lunged up the next wave, and the whole process repeated itself.

There was no place to go to avoid the punishment. The storm had us in its grip. Each man explored every remedy for seasickness. We stayed outside and away from the rooms with the dancing walls. We breathed deep, closed our eyes, and thought of something stable, but nothing helped.

With the storm raging outside, all passengers were so sick they could hardly take care of their necessities. Some of us kept trash cans between our legs whether we were lying in our bunks or sitting around. Officers who were late in getting trash cans used helmets and other ingeniously selected containers to keep some order and sanitation.

We were ready to try anything. Someone said, "Eat something and keep it down." That was the answer to our seasick problem. I made my way to the breakfast table on the second morning of the storm. I staggered and grabbed a hand hold on anything I could. None of the Marines had bathed, shaved, or changed clothes in two days. I am sure I smelled bad and looked worse.

I pictured myself as looking like a sick dog. I found a seat and sat across from a freshly dressed Dutch officer in a white uniform that showed attention to detail and custom; he looked at me in disgust. The Dutch cooks served their variety of foods on the breakfast menu. I knew that I could not eat it. The dining room, spotlessly white and tightly water-sealed, danced to the tune of the outside waves. Before I could brace my legs and unseat myself, I recognized the big bowl of oatmeal.

Boiled oatmeal would go down easily. I hoped that if it had to, it would come up just as easily. It did! The Dutch officer sitting across from me jumped back so fast he almost tripped over his chair, but too late. Before I could catch it in both hands, the oatmeal splattered over his fresh uniform. His face had the well-known, universal expression of disgust. Someone opened the door, and I staggered out with both of my hands full of oatmeal and looking for a head (toilet). These remedies may have worked somewhere else, but they did not work here. We decided that the only solution was to try to outlive the storm.

On the second or third night of the storm, the ship rose high on a monstrous wave and then it came sliding back and hit the bottom of the wave on its side. There was a loud boom when the ship struck the bottom of the wave and crash-like sounds followed. The first blast sounded louder than several pieces of artillery going off at once. The ship shuddered, floundered, and wallowed around for a few minutes before it righted itself. Thank God, smaller waves followed. A crippled ship sailing alone in war time, and not allowed to use communication, would have been in serious trouble.

The Marine officer's quarters at the top of the ship, three decks above the water, were not above the threat of the storm. All officer's gear not stowed away, safe and secure, and many officers themselves, sailed from their bunks to the deck. Our personal gear, including our weapons, lay awash in sea water. The water came through port holes and other openings thought to be water-tight.

While trying one of my experiments in staying alive, I sat outside in a semi-protected area. I was sick and wet; but I was breathing fresh air, and not the stale, stinking air of the junior officers quarters. I sat there almost hypnotized, and for a few minutes I forgot my condition as I watched a seasick cat.

We were told that only humans got seasick, and animals did not. A common house cat lived on-board the ship, and it was so seasick that it could not walk. The cat moved on the wet, tossing, windswept deck by sliding on its belly. She twisted from side to side, similar to a traveling snake. By holding her head just above the deck, and with her eyes glazed, she gave the appearance that she could not see. The cat paid attention to none of the outside elements as she worked her way toward the galley. Maybe she was like many of us, surviving.

On the day the storm slacked off, Doctor Outlar invited me to watch him and his staff do an emergency appendectomy. I could hardly walk, but I would not miss that experience. The ship was still rocking badly.

He knew that I was interested in medical practices. At twelve years old I attended a short course in animal medicine at Dr. Salsberry's laboratory in Lubbock, Texas. I did this with a man named Whitey Wallace from my hometown. We were the only acting veterinarians in the country. We tended to farm and ranch animals.

When I entered the small, spotless, white operating room, I saw a man tightly strapped to an operating table. The table did not move; bolts held it to the floor. A tube ran from the bottom of the table, and a small shield stood up in front of the patient's face. The shield prevented his inquisitive eyes from watching the operation. I was told that the doctor had done a spinal block to kill the man's pain. All the normal sickening hospital odors caused my whole being to rebel. The sea waves were still rough, and that small, white box-like room seemed to dance to the rhythm of the outside waves. The condition was rough enough to make any land-lubber sick. I did not see how I could be any weaker or more sick, so I saw no reason to worry about it.

Doctor Outlar wanted me to stand next to him. I stood so close we almost touched. His corpsmen needed room, and there was very little space left. I had not bathed in three days, and he put nothing over my mouth and nose. I just stood there, bent over, and watched him make a small incision. On the first grab with his forceps he missed what he was looking for. He stuffed what he pulled out back into the small hole. On the second grab he brought out the inflamed part. He quickly tied off and removed it. He stuffed the remainder back into the stomach cavity and started sewing by layers from the inside out. I felt weaker and asked to leave. I appreciated the invitation to watch, but I was in poor physical condition because of the storm.

We had no fear of the Japanese submarines as long as the storm raged; they would not try to operate in this weather. Now with the waves becoming quiet, and with us possibly moving near the regular shipping lanes, our Dutch officers became extra cautious. Ship's regulations did not permit lighted cigarettes on deck after dark. The ship had extra blackout curtains on all openings that men passed through. The ship attached three curtains on alternate sides of the doorways. Men passed through them as they would a maze. The curtains parted without allowing any light to be shown to the outside world. When the sun went down, total darkness existed outside until sunup.

We filled these days with activities to keep skills and mind sharp. Every evening just before dark we stood submarine watch. We were told that this was our most vulnerable time of the day. The ship's officers divided the outside rail into sections and assigned their men and our enlisted men to these sections. I joined their ranks.

Our U.S. Navy Officer in charge of the guns allowed me to form a gun crew from a few Marines. When the ship had gun drill, he would declare one of his Navy gun crews destroyed, and we would man a twenty millimeter antiaircraft gun. After we jumped into the gun tub, I would belt the gun to my body as two men snapped on the large drum of ammunition. Our targets were gas-filled balloons and black balls of smoke fired by another gun. Once the officer allowed us to fire at a small "drone" target plane.

Most of the Marine officers and men read or played cards, but for some reason I could not. I was tired of reading and playing cards. I wanted experience in tools of war. Luckily there were others like me, so

61

firing weapons was a big relief from the monotonous ship activities. The Dutch officers would never think of firing weapons or participating in this type of action. Work of any kind was beneath their dignity.

Only once did we spot a flickering light. We did this on our evening watch. Men from our sector spotted it. There was a small reaction from the ship, but nothing more. Our officers received word that it was one of our own submarines.

Land Ho! The yell was heard above the ship's noises. We were at sea a week or more when a ship's crewman spotted land. Without thinking, I announced at the evening meal that we were passing Christmas Island. The Dutch officers at and near our table stopped eating. Quietness settled on the room of men. The Dutch officers could not speak English, but they understood the English name, Christmas Island. I was asked to report to the captain of the ship when we finished our evening meal.

I approached the Captain's quarters, rapped on the door in a military manner, and heard the order to enter. In front of me sat a stern-looking man, middle aged, and heavy jawed. His head was hairless and shiny, and at his side stood an interpreter. Someone had told me that the captain's beard and what was left of his hair was shaved daily by a Javanese worker. He looked like the captain of a ship.

There was no sign of friendship on his face when he and his interpreter questioned me. It disturbed him because I knew where we were. He thought there had been a conversation leak from one of his officers. I did play chess with them; we did not need to speak to play chess.

After racking my brain for a few minutes trying to reconstruct, I assured the Captain that none of his men were responsible for what I knew. I explained to him that the doctor aboard ship was from my home and that the doctor and I were friends. Also, he had one or two books describing the islands to which we were going. I visited this doctor's room often. On his wall was a map of the Pacific Ocean with latitude and longitude marked. Someone had marked the longitude lines with thirty minute time changes. Each visit I made to the doctor's crowded stateroom, I sat in the same seat that was close to and facing this map. It was only natural that I checked the time changes going west.

Over the ship's loud-speaker, someone announced the time change each time we crossed a longitude. Everyone changed his watch because we had schedules to make while on-board the ship, especially chow call. So by these time changes, I knew how far west we were. I noticed, by looking at the doctor's map, that little or no land mass existed in the direction we were going. One exception was a small group of islands sticking out into the water wasteland. The lead island was Christmas Island. With the longitude fixed and a rough estimates of the travel time, it was easy to guess where we were, and that was all, a guess.

The reason I studied the map was not to know where we were, but I was interested in the islands lying just to the west and southwest of our route of travel. If we were unfortunate enough to be torpedoed and fortunate enough to launch life boats, we would drift in that direction. I learned later that he appreciated my thinking.

After that meeting, the ship's Captain and his interpreter gave the Marine officers a detailed tour of the ship, which included the navigation room and quarter deck. With two exceptions, I noticed that the ship and its major equipment were made in Holland. The ship's motors were made in Germany, a source of embarrassment to the captain and Dutch officers. Also, they had recently added an American-made instrument.

In front of the helmsman hung an old-time American manually wound, alarm clock. It was strapped and wired to the instrument panel. Strange and out of place, the clock with the two large bells on top occupied a prominent spot. Its face was open, and had electric wires attached to the hands. It would ring every few minutes as the hands made contact with other wires and the helmsman would steer a new course. I spoke of the zig-zag course earlier. The ship's unusual action was its anti-submarine protection. Later that day the Dutch Captain asked me to give the same tour to the Marine enlisted men. I knew then that the captain liked me, although he gave no other indication of doing so.

We dumped our garbage at night. We were told that our enemies could obtain valuable information from the garbage of a ship. None of us believed that.

The sea quieted down as we neared the equator; I would lie on deck near the bow and watch the flying fish. They do not fly; they sail. Disturbed by our ship, they sailed from one wave cap to another. If larger fish foraging for food chased them, groups of flying fish would sail by touching the tops of consecutive waves to build gliding power. Once I thought our ship would ram two large tree trunks out in the middle of the ocean; two large sharks parted and let us pass.

We moved into the Equatorial zone. Some of us went to the head (toilet) often to circulate water. We were told that water circulated counter clockwise south of the Equator. This was true, but the change was not that fast.

The new men on board were also told that the Equator was the

"Domain of Neptune Rex" and that we land-lubbers would be honored by the presence of NEPTUNE REX, RULER OF THE RAGING MAIN. After initiation we would become a Trusty Shellback who has been gathered into the fold and duly tested into the Solemn Mysteries of the Deep. During the ceremony, I was required to wear a gun belt with a towel for a loin cloth and hold a piss-pot with a handle. Then I was doused with sea water and other imaginative things. I still have a water color picture of me done by an enlisted man.

On the Equator there was very little wind, and the days were pleasant out on the ship's deck. The men gathered there playing cards, talking, and washing clothes. To wash clothes, they would tie their cloths to a rope and throw them over the side. If they thought of it, they would rearrange them once or twice and then dry them on a makeshift line. If the men's clothes stayed on the line and dragged in the ocean too long, they disappeared or only threads were left. The clothes dried with the ocean water's salt in them. The ship did not allow fresh water to the enlisted men unless it rained; then we all went outside to rinse out clothes and take a fresh-water shower.

Customs aboard ship were similar to the ones at home. It was Sunday, and we had a chaplain on-board the ship. I do not remember ever talking to him. He was out of place here among this wild and boisterous bunch. The parachute chaplains we knew back home chased women, and the Catholic chaplains drank at the bar with us. This man was different. He was a modest and pleasant man. He sailed from San Diego with us, and I only observed him in passing.

One beautiful Sunday, this Chaplain attempted to hold church services. He stood on the main deck of the ship near the bow, and four or five men were trying hard to listen to him. Boisterous card players, some only a few feet away from them, covered the deck. I think the card games were pinochle and poker. The loud, unruly players showed no consideration for the worshippers. The attitude the card players displayed caused a small explosion inside me. I raced down to the main deck and cleared the whole deck, and I did it in action and words that the men understood. The men knew they were doing wrong, because they moved quickly with little or no reaction.

I did not stay for services; however, when I looked down from an upper deck a few minutes later, I saw this picture: the sun shone brightly in the crystal clear air, and a light breeze caused a gentle rocking motion to the ship. The chaplain and men stood with heads bowed in prayer.

On 21 December, after three weeks at sea, we drew near the French-controlled islands of New Caledonia. The waters of the open sea became quiet as the land swells from the nearby small islands gently rocked the ship. Land birds filled the air. Soon we entered a waterway between two rows of small islands. The waterway led us to the harbor at Neumia, the capital city.

Each small island looked like a lovely picture. White, well-kept government houses lay on a beautiful carpet of blue-green water. Each house sat in a blanket of flowers, and palm trees surrounded them. Houses, gardens, and small islands stood connected by white sea-shell walkways and white, arched foot bridges. The bridges were high enough to allow small commuter boats to pass underneath. The surroundings were in sharp contrast to what we left behind in the United States. It was difficult to believe that these people's home country was in the hands of one of their enemies.

The ship's horns, bells, and other forms of communication brought harbor officers, dressed in spotless white uniforms. They scurried from the buildings and down the pathways to the harbor. By the time we dropped the ship's anchor, darkness had settled in. The harbor lights, city lights, and lights on all the adjoining islands dazzled us. The ship lowered a spot light over the side, and lashed it a few feet above the water. Tropical bait fish drawn to the light became possible meals for larger fish. All this light made me nervous; I had become accustomed to the feeling of security that darkness gives.

Before we left the ship, the Dutch captain gave me a handwritten letter that stated that I was to be given some consideration by the Rotterdamsche Lloyd Line if I chose to sail around the world after the war. I had expressed that wish in his presence. This letter was written on the ship's stationery. I was impressed with the Dutchmen.

No one informed the dock and transportation people of our arrival date. Evidently they thought the Japanese might find out; I am just being sarcastic. It was the weekend. Our truck transportation arrived at the docks late, and we arrived at the Marine camp much later. The sergeant in charge of billeting assigned us to tents.

With no ropes or with slack ropes, the tents were hanging on the center pole. Without tent lights, and lying on a bare cot, I neglected to put up my mosquito net. I awoke in the middle of the night, my head felt twice its size, and my left eye was swollen shut. The rest of my swollen body felt as if it belonged to someone else. The mosquitoes were having a feast. It is a wonder the doctor did not order me to the hospital.

After wiping mosquitoes, blood, and other body juices from my face and body, I tried every means to avoid the determined pests. I crawled under, and tucked myself in with my waterproof, mosquito-proof poncho. I could hardly breathe, and it was stifling hot.

65

The draw string at the head-opening left a small entrance, and the pests, in my mind at least, grew into monsters. Each time I moved or tried to get a breath of air, a small crack would open, and in came the enemy. There was no use. Quickly I wrapped myself in the poncho, and walked to the only light in the area. I spent the rest of the night sitting up in a lighted, screened-in cook shack.

I think it is worth mentioning here that the galley Marines told me that the mosquito that spreads Malaria did not exist on this small group of islands. They also told me that a tree, called Paper-tree, growing on this small group of islands was responsible. They did not say how. I have often wondered why someone did not look into this further. If growing a tree would prevent malaria, it would save many lives in Africa and other countries.

The battle for the Japanese-held airstrip on Bougainville Island was on and the Marine Corps needed two young officers there, fast. The Marine command ordered Lieutenant Smith, a young Jewish man, from Dallas, Texas, and me to leave our units and sail with the Army on an Army transport ship to the island of Bougainville. Before we left, the Navy Chaplain that I had cleared the deck for while on the Dutch ship joined us. I was ready; I would rather fight the Japs than the mosquitoes. On 22 December, 1943, we sailed on an Army transport ship. I do not remember the name of the ship, and it is just as well that I do not.

I was not aware that the Army had its own transport ships. The minute we stepped aboard, a depressing mantle of gloom closed in on us and the ship. The Army officers expressed no goodwill toward their men or us. They quickly segregated and isolated themselves. They took with them special food and many other things not allowed to the men or others aboard ship. A recreation area below deck separated the officers from the enlisted men. The officers would leave their area for movies shown in the recreation area; the rest of the time they isolated themselves.

Our sleeping quarters were on an open rack at the very bottom of the ship with the bilge water from thousands of small leaks, no air circulating, and stifling equatorial heat. Rotting filth that had been there since God knows when lay untouched.

Salt water showers were permissible if we would wade through the filth getting there and back. The salt water did not evaporate, but stuck to our bodies, and in no time we would be totally wet with saltwater and sweat. The shower was useless.

The body odors and the stench coming from the bottom of the filthy ship were bad. Worst of all was an open urinal with poor drainage that slopped over with each roll of the ship.

66

An enemy torpedo almost anywhere in the ship would be the end of the three of us. We would not have time to climb the ladders, open the water-tight hatches, and escape. Sweat ran from our face and arms, and there was nothing we could do. The water we drank was hot.

The Army allowed no one on the open deck after dark. I would slip out, but there was no place to hide. The night guards would catch me and order me below. When I would ask, "Why?" the guards would say, "Orders."

The ship's officers claimed another ship had rammed their ship recently and destroyed the ship's refrigeration unit. At least that was the excuse they gave. Primitive dehydrated food without bread or crackers was fare for the day. The Army enlisted men did not have bread or fresh food of any kind, but their officers did. We ate with the Army enlisted men, if we ate.

We went to get food on the second or third day. The ship was near the Equator, and the heat was stifling outside the ship. Inside the metal ship with no air circulating, the heat must have risen over 120 degrees. We went below deck to the chow line. The sight was something to make a pig happy. With each roll of the ship the scantily dressed men in the chow line were slipping and sliding along in other seasick men's vomit. The stink and revolting sight were overwhelming; we turned back.

Our ship finally joined several others and moved into a convoy. Destroyers (small combat ship) and Destroyer Escorts (smaller versions of the same) protected the ships by continually circling the convoy of troop ships. We moved slowly toward combat.

One evening the Army officers made a mistake by all going to the recreation deck to see a movie. Lieutenant Smith stole two bottles of their best whiskey and one loaf of their precious bread. I searched through my sea bag and found a small can of turkey. After moving to the fantail of the ship and out of sight of the others, we divided the turkey, bread, and one fifth of whiskey three ways and consumed the lot.

Our bodies were dehydrated from the heat and lack of water. We were forced to drink hot water or dehydrate. We chose to dehydrate. Without water and because of only a small amount of food, our bodies had a violent reaction to the whiskey. Our chaplain friend suffered more than Smith and I. He could not get up and stand. I brought him water. I am sure he had never drank whiskey before this. How we survived, I do not know. I liked this modest and pleasant preacher, but I repeat, he was out of place here. I will never forget the last time I saw him. On Guadalcanal, we passed each other going in opposite directions in military vehicles. We were both standing up to absorb the shock of the rough ground. Our drivers did not stop. We waved to each other until we were out of sight.

The commanding officer of this gloomy ship was Mr. Gloom himself. The scuttle-butt quickly passed around the ship that the commanding officer spent most of his time in New Caledonia with an attractive French prostitute. Before we left, the island authorities had carried her to a Leper colony on the far side of the island. I am not sure it is true, but the men told us Mr. Gloom could worry for the next twenty years. The disease could develop at any time in that period.

To keep my energy flowing and my mind away from our hardships, I formed a substitute gun crew with some Army men. We would replace a gun crew on a twenty millimeter antiaircraft gun when the officer in charge declared the regular crew knocked-out. Their anti-aircraft guns stood aligned along the outer edge of the ship in shallow metal tanks; we called them tubs. This was not a new experience for me; I had formed a gun crew on the Dutch ship.

On the Dutch ship, the Navy officer checked our timing and the target for accuracy. The Army Gunnery Officer did not furnish targets; his interest was only timing. When called upon, our substitute gun crew would replace the regular gun crew and fire three short bursts . Where the shells landed did not bother the gunnery officer. It was the quickness in manning the gun and firing that impressed him.

Pieces of iron pipe were welded together and to the ship to block the gun barrel from firing on the mother (our) ship. There was one exception. A recently installed ship's compass occupied a spot near the gun, and in an unprotected area. The compass sat on the end of a standing four foot piece of pipe. The compass was only a few feet away from the gun. A direct hit on the compass by our own gun would demolish the gun and crew.

Normally, we squatted low behind a metal barrier and watched without exposing ourselves until we heard our gun number yelled. On one practice day while concentrating on speed, and without looking, I shot three bursts from our gun. Our shots burst just off the fantail of an escort ship.

The escort ship came alive with signal lights flashing and three burst from one of their guns exploded close to our fantail. Where the ship came from, I do not know. It seemed to appear there as I fired. I swear, I checked only a few minutes before I jumped into the gun-tub. The Good Lord stood by me again. Thank God; I did not hit the ship. No one said a word to me about the incident.

Our rush to Bougainville ended. The Marines took enough of the island to hold and secure the airfield. The Army replaced the Marines, and the Marines sailed back to Guadalcanal. My feet never touched the ground on Bougainville. All the rush was for nothing. On 29 December, 1943 we joined Headquarters Company; First Marine Regiment; Parachutist (with "K" Company at Guadalcanal, British Solomon Islands.)

On Guadalcanal, we were put on "Stand-by" because it looked as if the Army might be pushed off Bougainville. They held.

Chapter 6

GUADALCANAL
Solomon, Islands
North, North East of Australia and East of New Guinea
British Rule before the Japanese arrived.
29 December 1943, I joined Headquarters and Service Company; First Marine Regiment; Parachutist; Guadalcanal, British Solomon Islands.

The island bustled with activity. The Japanese concentrated their bomber and fighter groups at Rabaul Island. I was told that for them it was about fourteen hundred miles trip to Guadalcanal and back. Our newly acquired airfield at Bougainville Island cut the distance to the island in half for the U.S. Forces, but doubled the distance for the enemy planes coming from Rabaul Island. Formerly the Japs could use Bougainville Island as an emergency stopover to refuel and repair their aircraft after a raid on Guadalcanal and other islands, but no more.

A successful attack like the one at Bougainville Island always raised the spirit of everyone. U.S. air raids on Rabaul increased. From our camp we could hear the continuous roar and drone of airplane motors coming from our Henderson Field on Guadalcanal. Marine, Navy, and Army Air Forces were on the move.

Major Harry Torgerson, an enlisted man's officer, was in charge of the remaining Paratroops on Guadalcanal. His regulations provided for the men and not for himself. He acted in every way as a natural leader. He did not need the laws and bylaws of the Marine Corps to show that he was a leader.

"The enlisted men fight the wars," Major Torgerson would say. Richard Tregaskis spoke highly of Major Torgerson in his book Guadalcanal Diary, and so did Richard Wheeler in his book A Special Valor.

Marines coming back from Bougainville needed rest and relaxation, called R.& R. The sight of these men would have scared their mothers, especially seeing the running sores caused by jungle rot all over their bodies and the great loss of weight. Back on Guadalcanal, the men ate and slept most of the time.

Instead of allowing the war-weary Marines R.& R. in New Zealand or Australia, someone in high command ordered beer brought to Guadalcanal. By the time the beer reached Guadalcanal, most of the paratroops had left for the States.

70

Word came to "K" Company, First Parachute Regiment, U.S.Marine Corps that a ration of beer was at the dock waiting for us. Major Torgerson ordered me to take a squad of men to the unloading area and bring back our ration of beer, which he judged to be about two thousand cases. He told me where the beer should be unloaded, ordered some trucks, and that was all. I do not know what I expected, maybe some authorization papers and the usual blah, blah, blah the senior officers gave. To our knowledge, a beer bust after a campaign was something new. There was no set plan; we would play the game by ear.

Apparently there was no deep-water port on the island, or at least, not one that we could use. Barges brought supplies in to a small off-loading dock, and men or vehicles hauled the goods away. Occasionally native men waded out to the barges to bring in the supplies.

We did not expect an easy task, so we heavily armed ourselves. I carried a large knife in the top of my boot, a forty-five pistol in a shoulder holster, and a folding-stock carbine over my shoulder. The Japanese were not our enemy here. The enemy was our own Army and Navy stevedores (dock workers).

We arrived at the unloading area and made very little camp preparations. We expected to be loading trucks and getting the hell out of there. Our plans did not work out the way we expected.

After the first day of just waiting on the beach, I released the trucks. The men and I foraged for food and shelter while I watched the beer-ship sitting idle in the harbor. On the third day while I was forging for food, someone directed me to a beautiful little bamboo hut newly built by natives. Unassigned officers could get something to eat here and await transportation.

Sitting in the hut were two Marine pilots back from Australia. Sitting between them was a woman. I do not think I expressed surprise, but I may have. They introduced me to her; she was from Australia. They had sneaked her in by plane. She was the only woman on the island, that I knew of. Woman odors saturated the air. I tried being pleasant to the woman without looking her in the eyes. Thinking about sex can rob the mind of clear thinking, especially if sex is not available to everyone. Why wake up that sleeping monster. Without looking at her directly, I sat there while the pilots briefed me on the type of ship I was dealing with. They told me the ship with the beer cargo on board was not military and that the men serving aboard the ship drew extra pay every day their ship stayed in a combat harbor. I did my exit from them as pleasantly as possible and moved to another table with my back to them.

Guadalcanal remained listed as a combat zone. We suspected the beer ship crew was taking advantage of the situation to make more money. There was no more fighting on the island although Washing Machine Charley, a single Japanese airplane, whose motor sounded like its namesake, formerly made night raids here, and got away with it for a while. He had not visited us for some time.

The very thought that this ship and its crew would lie in this quiet harbor to get extra pay while our nation was at war caused a bad reaction in me. Why this made me so angry, I do not know, but it did. I told the sergeant to flag down a barge to carry us out to the beer ship.

When the barge reached the ship, we noticed that the boarding ladder was not down, but the ship's crew had left a cargo net thrown over the side. The beer ship crew seemed to be asleep as the ship rode on a quiet anchor. My sergeant and I climbed the net and searched for the ship's day-watch crew.

On the opposite side of the ship sat a seaman leisurely watching the water, birds, and coast line. I yelled to get his attention, and when he looked at me he jumped to his feet. Fear showed in his eyes, his mouth hung open, and he could hardly talk. I asked to see the Captain of the ship. The scared seaman directed us to the Captain's quarters.

I gave a loud military rap on the Captain's door. When I heard a noise behind the door, we pushed the door open and stepped inside. The Captain jerked upright, looked wide awake, and struggled to his feet as we roughly pushed open the door.

He did not know our rank, because paratroopers did not wear rank except on liberty. We showed him no papers or authority for coming aboard his ship. He did not have a chance to say a word. I told him that we had waited several days to take that God damn beer and I did not intend to wait any longer! The Sergeant and I did an about face and got the hell out of there. On the barge going back to the beach I looked back and noticed the ship's crew uncovering the hatches on the ship, and I saw the unloading booms swing out.

The sergeant hurried to get the Marine Corps trucks to the loading dock and lined up. I lined up the barges to bring the beer from the ship.

The first barge went up the river nearby and did not come back. Some of these dock workers and barge men were professional thieves. Saying that is like one donkey calling another donkey "Long Ears." The Marine sergeant working with me posted a guard on each barge and each truck. We sent back to camp for more men to help escort the beer.

At one point the beer came in faster than we could truck it. We made walls with cases of beer. The men threw a canvas over the walls to make a small shelter for us to live in. We posted a guard around the shelter. Military stevedores (dock workers) circled us like buzzards around a recent kill.

The army had a regular company of men to load and unload equipment from barges. I am sure the Marines did also, but I did not see any. These dock workers tried to trade me what looked to be stolen equipment for beer. They tried every trick. One fast talker continuously called me sergeant. I never told him any different. Nothing worked for them. That type thinking did not interest me.

No doubt existed in the minds of the thieving stevedores. They knew what would happen to them if they made a bold try for the beer. They would be dead men. It was that simple, and they knew it.

Two thousand cases of beer went to camp, and still the beer came. I sent word to Major Torgerson that the beer was still coming and that I did not know when it would stop. The truck drivers told me that Major Torgerson had a barbed wire fence built around a storage area. He posted guards, and they were stacking beer there.

I knew that before long the ship's captain would send a Bill of Lading for about six thousand cases of beer and expect someone to sign it. We did not have the full count; I was not signing release papers. The

Larry Hart, D.A. Carson, Johnny York & "Red" Graan, having a few from the stockpile procured by Lt. John Keith Wells, Guadalcanal 1943.

73

sergeant and I caught the last truck load for camp. I never did sign a Bill of Lading; I guess the ship's captain faked it.

Major Torgerson had the Rainier Beer issued daily to all men whether they drank beer or not until cases of beer began to stack up in some tents. The men tried to cool the beer at first. They buried it in sand near wave action, and they popped CO_2 cartridges from life belts, but nothing worked. Frost would appear on the cartridges when punctured, but not enough to transport the cold to the beer. The tide would wash away markers and hide the buried beer. So the beer went down hot, by the gallons. I am sure you can guess what happened in this situation. Whatever you thought would happen, did happen and more.

Life of a Marine in the first part of World War II was primitive with no thought of planned recreation. To prevent myself from growing stale and becoming bored, I looked for things to do. Only a few feet from our camp lay the ocean with a beautiful underwater reef. Lining the shore lay partially sunken Japanese ships, a residue from the battle of the Coral Sea. After their ships became mortally wounded, the Japanese Naval Officers rammed their sinking ships into the shallow reef that bordered the island. This action gave the Japanese sailors a better chance to survive. One of the ships had a gaping hole in its side, and the Marine swimmers would swim through the hole to the stairway on the other side. They would climb the stairs in almost total darkness and dive or fish from the exposed part of the ship.

Swimming around beached Japanese ship, Guadalcanal, 1943-44

74

Beached Japanese ship Kinuagawa Maru Guadalcanal, 1943
(Iron bottom bay)

Reef sharks by the dozens hid under the ships in the daytime. We knew nothing about sharks. In the past, sailors wrote scary tales about attacking sharks. I questioned the Marines that had spent the most time in the islands. They said that they knew of only one man eaten by sharks. In a port south of there they were loading ships, and some of the men went swimming afterward. The ship was ready to move and ordered all men to stay aboard. One man dived and was sucked into the propellers of the ship. The sharks did the rest. They said that the decision was made to move on. I knew that those were good odds, but it is hard to bury old fears. At first, I watched without tiring for sharks.

Swimming in that beautiful water remained the number one sport for me. No one thought of posting rules about swimming. The men would tell each other the rules: 1. Never swim alone. 2. Swim with your hands under the water in breast stroke, side stroke, or dog-paddle. We were told that slapping the water attracts foraging sharks.

Besides the reef sharks, we had large ocean-going sharks that occasionally cruised the outer banks of the reef. A Marine on leave in Australia stole a recreational diving mask, the same as the snorkeling mask used today, and to my knowledge it was the only one on the island. I paid twenty-five dollars for it. That was the cost of a fifth of whiskey bootlegged from Australia by the pilots.

This was the best money I ever spent; I broke the rules by

75

swimming alone. Only in recent years has the general population been able to see what I saw in 1943. I did not worry about the sharks. The thousands of small, colorful schools of reef fish acted as my watch dogs. When I saw them scurry for a hiding place, I knew a hungry shark was working the reef. Quickly, I would look and see the shark searching, and I had plenty of time to protect myself. I did not know it then, but I was never in very much danger from the sharks. Since then I have scuba dived around the world. One unusual sea shell on Guadalcanal Island attracted my attention, and I still have it.

One day in the jungle, I was in charge of a group of men cutting bamboo to improve our camp. I wore cutoff shorts and no shirt. The mosquitoes that roamed the island at night stayed in the jungle in the daytime. We soon entered the bamboo forest, and the pests covered me. As I brushed each swarm of mosquitoes away, a new group landed.

Regular mosquitoes stayed flat on their feet when they punctured us, but the female anopheles mosquito stood on her head. She was the Malaria-carrying mosquito, and she always found room to work. I identified her and her lady friends quickly. Their small dark bodies and their butts sticking straight up created warning flags that the female anopheles mosquitoes were dining.

I decided to return to camp to get more clothes to protect myself. As I neared camp, I looked out beyond the reef and saw a lone swimmer; it was Snodgrass, our cook. He used the overhand stroke and made splashes on the mirror-like surface of a wave-free ocean. I saw him turn and head back toward the reef. Behind him moved a huge dark object above the surface of the water. At first I thought of a floating coconut with its husk still on, but this was larger. Then I noticed it moving in a slow, rounded, zig-zag pattern. It was a shark, a large one, and it trailed Snodgrass without his knowledge.

I raised my hands to my mouth to call to him but decided against it. The shark closed in on Snodgrass, and any quick change in his swimming pattern might cause the shark to attack. I still thought the shark might attack when he saw the swimmer reaching the shallow reef. Snodgrass stood up on a small platform of a shallow reef, and I yelled for him to look behind him since he was not out of danger. The big shark made his turn and headed back to deeper water. If Snodgrass lives today, I bet he remembers that close call.

Native blacks on Guadalcanal and islands near by numbered close to a hundred thousand, as calculated by the British missionaries. The native black men were tortured and treated badly by the Japanese. They either fought against the Japanese or backed-off and stayed neutral.

76

L. Bernard Holly and Ira Hamilton Hayes (flag raising fame)
Guadalcanal, 1943-44

The Marines told me that the time the Japanese held the island, they tortured a black native man for several days, bayoneted him several times, and left him for dead. The man's name was Vousa. He served as a sergeant major with the British Police before the Japanese came. Vousa survived and lived to kill many Japanese. I was told that he helped the Marines endlessly. I read a few years back that this man still lives. He wears a near-regulation Marine uniform, and enjoys the title of Honorary Marine. Marines who knew him send gifts to him.

Many black native men helped the Marines. I heard that another native named Seni tried to join a band of native soldiers trained by the British to harass the Japanese. The soldiers refused him the honor of joining them because they had no weapon for him to fight with. They said that the next day Seni came back with a Jap rifle, a good one, with ammunition. When asked how he came by it, he just grinned. Almost every day after that he came back with another rifle. In pidgin English he would say, "Some more Jap rifle." In no time he had restocked the British-trained group with Jap rifles and ammunition.

Some Guadalcanal native men worked by helping unload barges.

John Stanton and William Peace with natives, Guadalcanal, 1943.

They waded out to the barge and came back loaded. When they had finished, they found their loin cloths hanging on near-by bushes, dried off with them, wrapped them around their waist, and walked off to collect their pay. With the money they bought cheap trading goods.

The natives loved coloring or dyeing their hair red. They shaded it with anything they could find. Someone, possibly the British, introduced peroxide to them. It turned their black hair red, and they traded almost anything for it.

Money had very little value to Marines because there was nothing to buy. The Marine command allowed only a limited amount sent home each month. For some big gamblers this became a problem. Paratroop Marines could not go to Australia or New Zealand, so many of them gambled their money away.

Some Marines, especially the ones who did not drink beer, thought they deserved liberty in New Zealand or Australia. In the past this was the custom. They knew that if they became sick beyond the scope of the island military doctors, they might be sent to one of these countries.

The men left their mosquito net off to let the malaria mosquito bite them. This act would bring a Court Martial if they were caught. Some men refused to take their Atabrine tablets. Our high command hoped that Atabrine tablets would ease the pain of malaria; however, some Marines thought the tablet also contained a substance that would kill their desire for sex and eventually make them impotent. The nearest source of Quinine, the only reliable medicine to fight malaria, was in the hands of the enemy.

Orders came for us to force the men to take the tablets. I could not believe this, but it happened. When ordered, each man stood in line with his mouth opened wide, like a little child. A sergeant would place a tablet on his tongue, wait for him to swallow, and had him open their mouth for inspection before passing on to the next man. An officer stood near to observe. Then my turn came to observe. Yes, I felt stupid doing this to grown men. I always walked down the line after the men left, and counted the tablets in the sand. How they managed to hide them, I do not know.

Some natives caught a dreaded disease (Elephantitus) that made them look horrible. An arm, leg, or some other portion of the body would grow larger than the rest of the body. I saw one or two with extra large legs, but they could still walk around. Someone had a picture of a native man that had testicles so large he had to haul them in a wheelbarrow. I saw the picture.

Scuttle-butt had it that if a Marine rubbed a copper penny on top of an exposed blood vein for a given length of time, the results would fool the doctors into thinking the Marine had the dreaded disease and send him off to Australia. I never knew this to happen.

Most of us planned to stay on the island, so we played poker and occupied our minds with other things. One day I won a large sum of money in an officer's poker game. Most of the money came from one officer. He was the high roller type. He either won a lot of money or lost it all.

This young officer lived dangerously in the States. He courted the wife of movie comedian Groucho Marx when they could sneak off. She came to visit him at Camp Pendleton, and we met her at the Officer's Club. Groucho could not come on the base, so they were safe there. One weekend, we heard that Groucho chased the two of them with a gun at the Beverly Hills Hotel.

A Marine officer asked Groucho if the girl was his daughter, and Groucho said "No, she is too young to be my daughter; she is my wife." I am sure this was for laughs.

The Marine officer gave Groucho's wife a beautiful ring. The other Marine officers who had seen the ring talked about it as a thing of beauty. Seven egg-shaped rubies with ten small diamond chips on each side made the ring outstanding. I do not know, and I did not ask what happened, but before we shipped out, the young officer got his ring back. He kept it in his locker box in camp. He wanted me to buy the ring, but instead I loaned him three hundred dollars ($300.00) on the ring, and gave him a certain length of time to pay the loan. I had won his three hundred dollars. He did not pay the loan, and I still have the ring.

Two of the native men saw me loan the officer the three hundred dollars. They had learned the value of our money quickly, especially the amount of trade goods it would buy. When the two saw the amount of money I handed the other officer, they began "chattering loud," and others came to look. They motioned that they wanted to look at the ring. They could not believe it. With that much money they could buy a boat load of trade goods. While they were standing there, I traded for one of their wooden war clubs, and still have it.

Some of these natives were Christians. They had worked for the British Government before the war and lived by the Christian code. There were other natives who lived the primitive way.

Most of the Japanese showed little or no sign of outward feelings toward any part of the human race except themselves. We thought that the attitude of the Japanese was a reflection of their top military leader. His name was Hideki Tojo. I was told that Tojo's son was killed and buried on Guadalcanal. When the Marines passed his grave, they would urinate on it. I did not go along with this, but I did not try to stop it.

This act of pissing on a grave might have more than one meaning to a Marine. The Marines had two sayings that anyone might hear day or night when one man thought another acted too cautiously: " Ha! Mack, what do you want to do, live forever?" Or "Don't worry about me Mack, I'll piss on your grave." This expression meant that the speaker thought he would outlive the first man.

On another break in routine, two other officers and I left camp looking for a native village. This was against high command regulations. The Japanese never surrendered and remained a potential danger. The natives moved to higher ground, and out of the way, so that the civilized people could slaughter each other.

We followed the native trail that ran beside the nearby river and through the jungle. Soon after making contact with the river, we heard singing. A Marine was perched on a tree trunk with his bare feet dangling in the water. He had a sack of beer in the cold water, and the sack was staked to the river bank. The Marine was fishing and he was alone. This could be dangerous. Roving Japanese were not as dangerous as the native crocodiles.

Soon after leaving the fishing Marine, we found the bone remains of a Marine's body in some undergrowth. His dog-tags (identification), and some of his clothes were missing. His helmet held his skull. Writing on the liner of his helmet said his name was Miller and that he was from Texas. I guess the natives took his dog-tags for jewelry. We notified the company office when we returned.

The other two officers and I continued to climb until we were almost out of the trees and thick undergrowth. If we followed this native trail far enough and high enough, we knew that we would find a native village. No one moves in the jungle except on a trail.

On this trip into the jungle, I noticed the natives did not plant food crops, but they would cultivate around wild food when they found it. Each food gathering area belonged to one group of natives. Poaching brought on tribal conflicts. The outside group must have their own or trade with those who did. They used large war clubs carved from mahogany wood, like the one I traded for earlier, to settle their trading disputes.

Because of the enemy and all the unknowns in the jungle, we became keenly alert to everything around us. We reacted quickly to any change in environment. We noticed all the areas where the jungle changed from the normal, and where the natives protected the wild plants. The fruits of the jungle were normal, but I saw a wild bushy plant

81

that the natives cleaned around, and gave special attention. When I studied it, I saw small, green hot peppers.

We came to a large clearing. Small black nude bodies swarmed around us. "Hi! Joe, Hi! Charley." These were the only words the boys knew. The Marines had taught them that. They ran up with eyes beaming like headlights on a car. They took time to skip flat stones on the river water just like little boys at home. One little boy wore a pair of Marine Corps underwear tied up under the arm pits.

The natives had built the camp in a large loose circle in what looked like a natural clearing in the jungle. The chief's lodging, with its four walls made of leaves, stood near the middle. Most of the others had only a quickly made roof of bamboo and leaves worked as shingles.

The roof made good sense because it rained daily. No wind blew unless there was a storm, and rain drops fell straight down. They needed no walls for their shelter. Natives that were caught in the rain would take two leaves from the same plant and hold them over their heads to escape the rain.

Some other huts may have had four walls. I remember the Chief's hut did because his young wives were sneaking a peak at us and trying to show themselves. The Chief thought he had the young girls hidden, but these girls, like young girls everywhere, found ways to look and show themselves.

Two older women, one large woman with bulging breasts, and a skinny one with breasts that hung down like a pair of socks on a clothesline, stood in an opening in the center of the camp. The women wore loin cloths, and the skinny woman nursed a small pig using one of her own breasts. I do not believe the pig got much milk. I understood they did breast feeding while preparing a pig for slaughter. The women only glanced once or twice in our direction and continued talking. Their faces had the same look as Mrs. Whitefield and Mrs. Yore, (two women back home) gossiping over a picket fence. As a boy, I saw these two women almost daily when I walked to school. The native women had the same expressions.

Wild pigs furnished the natives with most of the protein in their diet. Some areas had an abundance of wild pigs, while other areas did not. This fact brought native groups together for trade. The wild pigs stayed hidden in the daytime but roamed the entire area at night. This included our camp. The pigs, accompanied by large lizards and hermit crabs, scavenged at night. The weird noises kept us on edge. It could be roaming Japs.

Noise beneath one Marine who was sleeping in a jungle hammock caused him to ease up on his hands and knees and fire his weapon through the bottom of his hammock. Loud struggling and thrashing noises soon ended, but the Marine said he stayed on his hands and knees for the rest of the night expecting a knife or bayonet any minute. Daylight revealed a large land lizard lying quite dead.

Other creatures of the jungle included the deadly crocodiles. The women washed what little clothes they wore in the river. They washed on rocks and always faced the river. We were told that crocodiles were a menace to women and children.

Native men's eyes kept us pinpointed even though they pretended to be enjoying the sunshine. We made our way back as cautiously or more so than we did when we went up the trail. I could feel the tension in the air. The natives knew we were in the jungle and did not know our purpose.

Marines could have all the coconuts they could consume without depriving the natives, and we did enjoy drinking the juice from the green ones. We ate the meat of the ripe ones because drinking and eating the other way caused diarrhea. British companies developed and harvested coconuts in large groves. These large ripe coconuts with the husk weighed many pounds, and when the overripe coconut released itself from the tree, it hit the ground with a loud thud. We could thank God we were not under the tree when this happened. The loud thudding noise sounded day and night.

Even with the abundance of fish, I never saw the natives fishing. The paratroopers fished, but in an unusual way. They used concussion grenades traded from the Australians. When the grenade exploded, the fish came to the surface stunned, and the Marines gathered them easily.

Our own food was not too bad until the officers in charge of buying our supplies decided we should eat the canned mutton and vegetables from Australia. They called the mutton "bully beef." This was my first experience eating mutton. The odor and taste ruined the vegetables. I found some peanut butter at the galley and went on a peanut butter diet. I am sure, given time, I could learn to eat mutton. I have not yet.

Mooing (lowing) and bellowing could be heard in the late evening and at times in the morning. This was not a new sound to me. Even though it was mixed with the noises of the camp, ocean, and screaming noise of the parrot-like birds in the nearby jungle, I knew the sound well. Semi-wild cattle, formerly owned by the British, fed through the night and hid through the day. It was against regulations to kill them.

Open sores covered the neck and shoulders of the cattle. The cattle rubbed or hooked themselves with their horns to drive off the biting insects until their shoulders bled. This blood mixed with other juices of the animal's body to make an unappetizing sight. The island medical officer condemned the cattle as a food source.

A scouting party from the paratroopers killed a cow. After dark they brought the cow to camp. Our doctor examined it and found no disease; instead a parasite (insect) invaded the skin. Our cooks threw the pest-infested part of the meat away, and we ate the rest. We not only had fresh beef, but we had beef cooked in ovens made from limestone coral-reef material. Our metal oven grates were made from damaged pieces of portable airplane runways.

Word came to Guadalcanal that the Marine paratroops and the Marine Raiders would return to the States and disband. These were two specially trained groups that would become regular Fleet Marine Forces. I could not believe what I was hearing; I was stunned. I thought it had to be jealousy among the higher brass. This type of thinking would eventually destroy the Marine Corps, I thought.

It should be the other way around. The Fleet Marine Corps should have joined us. Every Marine should know how to attack the enemy from air, land, or sea. Marines should know how to fight every way there is to fight. Marines not able to see or do this should get out of the Marine Corps. Their only limitation is physiological. That's what I thought.

Our Marine Corps Headquarters was sending both Paratroops and Raiders away from the islands and jungles. They were being returned to the States to train for island and jungle warfare, I thought. I did not understand.

I wrote a letter to a general (General Biggs?), Head of Personnel in Washington D.C., to see if I could switch to the Army Paratroops; I was angry. He wrote back that they formerly allowed the switch, but not any more. I hoped the Marine Corps did not find out that I wrote the letter.

Another shock came. New replacements to the South Pacific area, which included myself, received orders to report to the 3rd Marine Division. Their camp on the island sat in the commercial coconut grove. This well-known and highly respected Marine Division consisted of the 3rd, 9th, and 21st Marine Regiments.

The day I reported to the 21st Marine area, I made friends with the Marine Warrant Officer in charge of transportation. He was older and had his feet firmly on the ground. He impressed me. I then reported to the regimental commander, and this was a different story. He glanced up at me with a deep frown on his face. I saluted, and he did not return my salute. He told me he did not like paratroopers or paratroop

84

officers, he did not like me, and I had better watch my step. While I stood around waiting for orders, I noticed that the 21st Headquarters area, where this Colonel lived and worked, had all the niceties of life— clothes washing machines, etc., and the companies under him had none of these. This reminded me of the situation we had left on-board the Army ship.

I reported to "G" company, and I never met a finer group of officers or men. When I reported to the officers tent area, I found the lieutenants on hands and knees playing marbles. Back home, a buddy sent a lieutenant in this company a sack of marbles for Christmas, because he jokingly thought the lieutenant had nothing else to do. The game of marbles was one of my better games, so I joined them.

The coconut grove sat in a large clearing with individual trees spaced and all vegetation cleared underneath. Many of the trees showed signs of shell and shrapnel damage, and many more had their tops completely blown away. They stood out, seemingly alone, in dedication to the men on both sides that had died here.

The tents in the paratroop's camp stood up like big umbrellas with the sides brought up and out about four or five feet above ground. There were no doors. This allowed the light ocean breeze at night to circulate through the tent area. We could come and go in any direction as long as we dodged the shallow air raid trenches beside each cot. The trenches were that close for convenience, easy to roll into from the cots on which we slept.

The only trouble with this convenience was that the trench would likely have six inches to one foot of water in it from the rain that day. It could also have one or more land crabs (hermit crabs) and large lizards. The one to two-foot long lizards looked meaner than they were. Many of the tents had parachutes hanging inside. This was like having a tent hanging inside a tent. It gave added insulation, and looked good. That was the way the Paratroops tents sat.

The tents in "G" Company sat according to regulation in the States. The men rolled the sides up about a foot. The daily rains flooded the camp, and water ran through the tents three to six inches deep. The men sat on their cots with their gear stacked around them waiting for the run-off to go down.

Two or three things were wrong with this camp site, but the most important thing was drinking and bathing water. Marines were forced to haul the water. The companies took turns checking out trucks and barrels from transportation and hauling the water for several miles. One time of this operation was enough for me. Back home, I had watched men dig water wells for my father and knew it could be done here.

I contacted my recently acquired friend, the transportation officer. He let us check out a truck to go to Henderson Field to get three or four barrels to make casing for a water well. We obtained the captain's permission but avoided asking the Colonel for his permission. We knew he would turn down the project.

Our battalion doctor knew what we were doing and suggested a place that might not be polluted by the daily run off. He told us to run the casing into the air above flood level. With the shallow well completed, the Doctor tested the water and found it good. We had plenty of water to drink and bathe with.

"H" and "I" Companies made a mad rush for trucks and barrels. The colonel came down to see what the commotion was about. When he found out what we had done behind his back, he looked mad as he marched stiffly out of the area. The look he gave me would have made the meanest Japanese look like a Sunday school teacher.

Just in time, I received orders directly from Washington, D.C. countermanding the island commander's orders that sent me to the 21st Marines. Without consulting the powers in Washington, the local island command transferred the recently arrived paratroopers to the Third Marine Division. My luck stayed with me. I returned to the Paratroops.

Major Torgerson announced that we were returning to the States as soon as a troop ship could be brought in. The supply airdrop part of the Paratroops was to remain intact and function in the same way. A Paratroop officer, Lieutenant Lusher from our Quantico class, wanted to know if I was interested in staying with the Paratroop supply unit. He said that we would continue drawing the extra pay and that our base station was Australia. I realized this was an honor, but I turned down the offer. Australia was absolute heaven on earth with all the wine, women, and song a man could stand, but I believed my place was in the line company. Something inside told me that I would function best there. My mind and heart were there.

On the 29 January, 1944, we barged out to the U.S.A.T. David C. Shank lying off shore for our trip back home. Young Marines who looked ten years older than their age, with eyes sunken, weight loss, and with deep pus-running sores shocked the young sailors on the ship. The fungus growth (jungle rot) on the young Marine's bodies looked like something from a scary motion picture.

Any small scratch or cut from the jungle or coral that lined the beach could start sores. Scratches washed with salt water from the ocean were safe. We tried everything to prevent the fungus. Marines cut their pants off near the crotch, and wore no underwear because they wanted air to circulate and keep dry in that area. They cut toes and heels from their shoes, and wore no socks to allow air to circulate there. Marines used anything that could be thought of that might prevent an area of the body from remaining moist and forming a place for the fungus to start. We had no effective way to fight these infected areas once they gained a foothold.

The sailors might forgive the loss of weight on the Marines' bodies. They would not forgive or understand the deep holes running pus and the jungle rot covering their bodies. Some Marines were helping other Marines who were having malaria chills.

Young sailors on the ship, fresh from the States, looked alarmed when they saw our Marines in the shower and rushed off to find their ship's officers. Their officers quickly isolated showers and head seats and quarantined the Marines to sections of the ship. Our officers assured them that nothing was contagious and conditions returned to almost normal.

Some time passed before the ship's crew came near us. They were the same age as our Marines, but the young sailors looked like young high school kids, flushed with health.

The trip back to the States was much the same as the trip down. The men played dice, pinochle, and poker, and the officers played poker, cribbage, and bridge.

Back in the States we landed at San Diego, California, on the 14 February 1944. On the docks stood the Marine Corps Band blasting the "Star Spangled Banner," "Marine Corps Hymn," and other marching pieces. By their side waving and smiling were the Women Marines. The men paid no attention to the Marine band, but yelled and waved to the newly formed Women Marines. Someone named the poor girls "Bams" (Broad Ass Marines).

Combat units did not have Women Marines, and I was always in a combat unit. I seldom had contact with the young women. The reports I got on our Lady Marines were good; they worked hard and had a good attitude.

We had trained so hard to get out of the States, and now we were back in the States to train. We had much to learn.

Chapter 7

CAMP JOSEPH H. PENDLETON
OCEANSIDE, CALIFORNIA
THE FIFTH MARINE DIVISION
Designation as Parachutist discontinued as of
29 February, 1944.

21 March, 1944, I joined Company
"E" 2nd Battalion 28th Marines, 5th Marine Division,
Fleet Marine Force as Company Officer.

There were those who said, "No one knows what they will do the first time in combat." I hope you do not believe that. I knew what I was going to do. I had made my mind up, and I told anyone who asked. For some reason many people interpreted this thinking as egotism personified; it was not. The Marine Corps' training and a good youth enabled me to make decisions fast and easy.

Tent Camp I, Las Pulgas(the fleas) Canyon , Camp Pendleton, California, was a Marine training base in walking distance of Oceanside, California. The camp was north of San Diego and south of Los Angeles. The Marine Corps created Camp Pendleton by dividing the newly

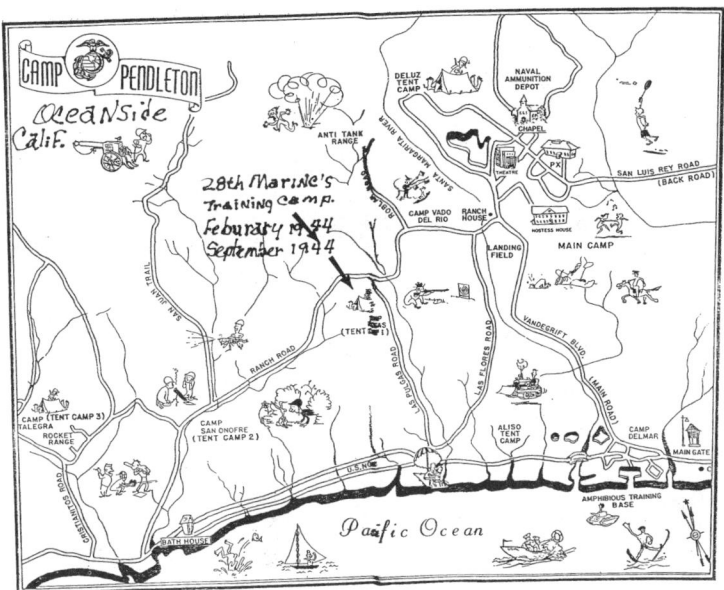

Conner, Howard M. *The Spearhead: The World War II D.C.*: Infantry
Journal Press, 1950.

purchased Santa Margarita Ranch into tent camps and training areas.

The Division, composed of the 26th, 27th, and 28th Infantry
Regiments, and the 13 Marine Artillery Battalion, organized here in
January and February 1944. The 28th Marines were assigned to Tent
Camp 1. Our campsite sat on dry earth with little or no vegetation.
Trucks and Jeeps passing through the camp created a constant cloud of
dust that settled on everything. Powder-dry grass on the open ground
was as volatile as gunpowder and was a fire hazard this time of year.
Rattlesnakes were almost as thick as the grass. What the snakes lived on
was a mystery to me. The area was a demanding training site.

Our best living conditions in the South Pacific was a tent with
sand or rock floor, an outdoor privy with no cover or sides, and an ocean
or river to bathe in. In Camp Pendleton the tents sat on wooden
platforms, with one light bulb hanging from the ceiling. Camp Pendleton
had outdoor screened-in toilets with cold water showers.

The Marines needed more liberty than training. This was not the
hero's welcome these men fresh from combat expected. However, they
did have a thirty-day leave when they returned from overseas. Afterward we gathered to form new fighting units.

A recently disbanded Marine Raider Battalion and a Marine
Paratroop Regiment formed the backbone of these regiments. Also,

89

Pfc. Gerald Smith having a bit of fun at the wash trough.
Camp Pendleton, California - 1944

men previously wounded in other battles and recuperating from their wounds re-entered the combat cycle. An equal number of Marines came from special training centers and boot camps. The Marine Raiders, a specialized group of volunteer Marines, had proven themselves in several combat missions in the South Pacific. The Raiders launched one attack in rubber rafts from submarines. Since the paratroops could not parachute-drop onto the small Pacific Islands, they had launched one of their attacks from fast-moving P.T. boats. Although the men were young in age, the Raiders and Paratroopers were old in experience.

I remembered what I thought about the Marine Corps breaking up the patchwork of Marines operating in the South Pacific. I was wrong. We could now see that a more sophisticated kind of warfare lay ahead for the Marine Corps.

Easy Company, 2nd Battalion, 28th Marines. Captain Dave E. Severance was the company commander. He was a picture post card of a Marine officer, tall, straight, properly dressed. He had military bearing. First Lieutenant Phil Roach, also an ex-Paratrooper, was our second in command. The company remained shipshape and according to "the book." The Captain and John A. Daskalakis, the company first sergeant, saw to that. They were both pre-war Marines and both ex-Paratroopers. They knew their jobs, and they knew the Marine

90

Corps.

My first command was the Machine Gun Platoon. It was much larger in numbers of men than the rifle platoons and was made up of a rich mixture of experienced Paratroopers and Raiders. I could never sing their praises enough. They carried their heavy, water- cooled machine guns and ammunition in their arms and hands.

Easy Co. Machine Gun platoon under 2nd Lt. John Keith Wells, March, 1944 Camp Pendleton, California

Gunnery Sergeant Nathan A. Lipscomb was platoon sergeant of the machine gun platoon. Nate reminded me of a school superintendent that knew his business and stood for nothing but the best. His brother was a school superintendent in Texas.

Combat Marines knew that their leaders and the men with automatic weapons would be prime targets for the Japanese. Because of the heavy weight they were forced to carry and the high casualty rate, it was hard to keep the Machine Gun platoon fully manned.

We trained with both light and heavy machine guns but soon discarded the light guns. Rapid firing would melt down the barrels of the air-cooled guns. The barrels on the heavy machine guns were water-cooled. The extra weight of water and the containers to carry the water was heavy enough, but the men must also carry extra heavy belts of ammunition and a heavy tripod. The creators of this weapon issued

91

a hand-pulled trailer to carry it and its equipment.

We schooled only one day with the trailer-mounted gun. However, to my knowledge we never used the trailers a single day in training or in combat. We carried everything on our backs, even in the most difficult terrain and on forced marches.

The men griped at first because I led the platoon on forced marches, carrying nothing but a map case and a carbine rifle. Then I loaded myself with the same weight that the machine gunners carried and tried to make the marches harder. These men were as tough as I was or tougher. They were soon challenging each other to individually carry a heavy machine gun and race up the hills in front of our campsite.

It was easy to see why the machine gun platoon was always recruiting. Besides, the danger, a man must have size, strength, and endurance. Captain Severance granted me the right to recruit from the three rifle platoons.

Lieutenant Phil Roach, formerly a football star for Texas Christian University, Fort Worth, Texas, fell the company in (company formation) for roll call. He turned the company over to me, and I asked for volunteers for the machine gun platoon.

I waited, looking for interest in the men's eyes; however, no volunteers came forward. I understood this; most of them had formed a loyalty to their platoon sergeants and officers. I would rather fight short handed than to have someone who did not volunteer.

When I walked back toward the machine gun platoon, I saw a small hand sticking up. At first glance, I did not see the raised hand at the end of the first squad. He was the end man of the Third Platoon. The hand was not much higher than the men's heads. The boy-like hand belonged to James (Chick) Robeson from Chewelah, Washington. The company had other men just as young but none that looked as young. He did not look a day over twelve or thirteen (12 or 13) years, and I will bet he did not weigh over one hundred and twenty pounds soaking wet. I bypassed the young man, but I never forgot him.

The company sent us to machine gun training camp for a week. I had forgotten my earlier training on heavy machine guns because we did not use them in the paratroops. These heavy guns had the capability of firing like artillery. We sand-bagged the guns to keep them stable and fired patterns for accuracy. I fired the gun a few times. My job was not to fire weapons but to conduct those who did. However, in the training period, I worked hard to see that the men understood the weapon. At the end of the week-long training period, the men fired their weapons in competition. Men with the two top scores would have a shoot-out for first place.

While they were setting-up and sandbagging their weapons, the men challenged me to fire against them. I encouraged them to challenge me in anything. They thought they had me here. The instructor helped me set up a weapon. My challengers could not believe it, but I beat them. The men did not know that I had fired the large machine guns aboard the two ships. It just confirms that any experience might come in handy later.

We were always short of equipment in the Marine Corps, and machine gun parts were scarce. We did not have spare parts. This forced us to cannibalize parts from two or more machine guns to keep the others functioning. One evening we were on a battalion problem, and the captain ordered the company to set up a defense for the night. Rolling hills to gently sloping flat terrain was ideal for setting up machine guns with interlocking fire at the slope's base. Our company's rifle platoons could protect the machine gunners from the same contour and from the military crest of the rolling hills. On top of the hills were observation points for the leaders.

Nate Lipscomb and I knew the platoon had only a few minutes to find our positions and set up the machine guns because darkness was already setting in. All we needed was one quick look at the aerial photograph map to see the company's assigned defense position; we would pick spots for our machine guns. The machine guns' positions and their fields of fire usually regulated the defense of the company but not always. In my youth I had learned to read aerial photographs accurately. I had worked for the U.S. Government correcting aerial photographs in the open field with two men working under me.

Sergeant Lipscomb and I designated each gun location, but at each location we found someone else's unguarded machine gun sitting there. Never before or since have I heard of Marines leaving their weapons unguarded. We knew we must report it, but first we field-stripped the weapons and took the parts that we badly needed. All of our weapons were again in top shape.

The report of this act never reached high command, which saved the officer and sergeant responsible for leaving them. The act could have developed into a General Court Martial for one or both men. The machine gun sergeant that lost the parts never forgave us. He was still mad when we left the States for combat.

I was back in the States for maybe a month when I remembered the air mattresses I saw in the South Pacific. Marine Paratroop officers owned them, but I think they came from the Australian Air Force. They were good. After inquiring through regular channels, I was told flatly that it was impossible to get one. I located a small factory in California that turned out a few, but the government had a tight hold on all of them.

A city bus carried me close to the factory, and then I walked. I approached the factory, entered an unlocked side door, and stepped out onto a large floor with several long tables. A few women scurried here and there, while others seemed intent at one place. Quickly, I noticed they were putting together the very thing for which I was searching.

Everyone seemed surprised that a Marine officer entered their all feminine domain. A second-in-command lady quickly escorted me to her superior's desk at the far end of the room. The young-looking female supervisor rose quickly and seemed as surprised as the others. I told her I was a Marine combat officer. I was leaving for overseas shortly, and I wanted an air mattress.

Work stopped and everyone heard the lady supervisor say that my acquiring an air mattress from them was impossible. She stated clearly and loudly that they had to account for every mattress and that every mattress went to the U.S.Government. I did not beg; I did not show anger. I told her that I was part of that same government. Surely, we could cut through red tape and I could get one mattress. She said, "Definitely not."

Eyes of the working women were fixed on the supervisor, then switched to me as I slowly turned and walked toward the outside door. When I reached the door, I felt a heavy, newspaper-wrapped, object as it slid under my arm. As I closed the door behind me, I quickly inspected the gift. In my arms was a beautiful, heavy-duty air mattress, just the right size. I never knew the woman or women who managed this. I wanted to think that the supervisor winked and they all shared in the crime. I am telling this because the mattress played a major roll later.

On a training exercise where the entire regiment was involved, we were firing live ammunition, and one of my machine gunners refused to carry the machine-gun. He said it was too hot. With my arms, I scooped-up the weapon and ran with it. By jiggling it in my arms, the machine gun burned me little or none. The machine gunner's ammunition bearer (helper) and I spotted the gun and put it into action. I did this because I wanted the men to know that I would never order them to do something that I would not do. The battalion and regimental commanders were watching this action without our knowledge. This helped me later.

Just as the machine gunners and I thought we were getting good, Phil Roach, our Company Executive Officer, made the rank of Captain and assumed command of another company. In June, 1944 Colonel

94

Johnson moved me into company executive officer's position. Sergeant Lipscomb, our machine gun sergeant, received a field commission as second lieutenant, and he took over the Machine Gun Platoon.

My tenure as Company Executive Officer lasted much longer than anyone thought. June, July , August and part of September went by. I was a new twenty-two years old and determined to make a fine Marine. My job included all company activity, from running the mess hall to live ammunition exercises in the field. The noncommissioned officers ran the company almost to perfection. I learned more from them than anyone could imagine. For a second lieutenant in the Marine Corps, this was the top in training.

By 1944 most of the Marines were in the Pacific, but Headquarters Marine Corps thought that too many Marines remained in the States. The Marine Corps wanted all Marines to be near the action. Marines in the States stayed either as trainers or base mountaineers. High Command ordered the Marines rear echelon to move to Hawaii. No Marines would return to the States until the war was over. We had a first class Navy hospital at Pearl Harbor, Hawaii, and the Navy on Guam Island was building one. Wounded Marines would return to combat units in the Pacific. Only seriously wounded Marines beyond quick repair would return to the States. Hawaii, of course, was not a state then.

Consequently, veteran instructors from Quantico, Virginia Officer's School, and other officers previously frozen in staff jobs arrived at our tent camp daily. The 28th Marines accepted few. These officers were good men, but some were out of their environment. It would take time for them to get combat oriented.

The drill instructors from Parris Island, South Carolina, and San Diego, California, arrived in groups. This change was not easy for many of them. Their stateside experience did not impress the Marines with combat experience. There were only a few instructors who made the transition with ease.

I am sure Colonel Liversedge wanted officers who had experience in the field. Most of the officers sent to us from training and staff jobs had advanced in rank because of advanced education or intelligence. They had little or no experience in the field.

I was the only second lieutenant Company Executive Officer in the Fifth Marine Division. None of these first lieutenants or captains sent to us from training centers or other similar State-side jobs could take my place.

The normal training period for the Army and Navy was five days a week with the weekend or part of the week-end off. The Fifth

95

Marine Division found that they could accomplish more by training ten full days without a break, and then take three days off.

At the end of ten days' training, we received seventy-two hours of leave. Command called it seventy-one hours to prevent the time from going into our record books. Seventy-two hours' leave would count against our regular leave time. Liberty could fall on any day of the week. We had time to travel to Los Angeles and be there when the city was not crowded with service men on weekend leave.

Mike Lymons at Hollywood and Vine, Beverly Wilshire Hotel, and the Paladium were my hangouts. The older civilian groups partied there. I did not have the time to play the teenage game. After days of turmoil in the training field, it was relaxing to be around the older men and women.

I met Dorine, an exotic dancer, in a middle-class restaurant. I had no idea she danced. She was a quiet, good woman in her late twenties, Her family was from South America, and she danced all Latin American dances, also Hawaiian Hula. She had recently started dancing at the Hollywood Canteen to entertain the service men. Besides being a good dancer, she was a good woman.

Soon after taking the job of executive officer, I returned to camp early one morning, after spending a seventy-one hour pass in Los Angeles. I found that the company had a live ammunition problem and that I was in charge. The problem would take most of the day.

Our camp was not awake when I reached the company area. Ott, a company cook, brought my breakfast in a cup - four raw eggs. He doctored them with spices to help me get them down. I needed energy fast. Klotts, Ott's helper, brought me a fresh mug of "JOE" (coffee) that he had made in a large G.I. can (today we would call it a garbage can).

I downed one gulp of coffee and the eggs rebounded; up they came. The struggle to keep any part of them down was useless. The coffee had a foul odor. We discovered that Klotts had made the coffee in a can that formerly held petroleum. My stomach finally settled, and I got my speech back.

The Company would be up and about soon, and Marines wake up on "JOE." I ordered Ott to make a new batch of coffee and marched Klotts to the company office tent. Captain Severance asked Klotts if he made the coffee in the dirty GI-can; Klotts said yes. Severance gave him five days "piss and punk" (5 days bread and water) in the brig.

"Piss and punk" allows one complete meal a day and the other two other meals consisting of bread and water. That small problem should have remained on a much lower level of authority. Ott was the one to take care of it, and it should never have gone above me. I am sorry

Klotts had to be part of my growing up. This was the first and only Marine I would run-up for any kind of discipline in my entire active duty career. My stomach settled, and we ran the company problem.

Soon after the Fifth Division was formed, the combat experienced Marines from the South Pacific were going over the hill or AWOL (absent without leave) at an alarming rate. If not caught, they would remain at large for twenty-nine days. They paid a heavy price for their "Holiday" by receiving an automatic Summary Court Marshal that included a "bust" (demotion) in rank and thirty days in the brig and work detail. If they stayed longer than twenty-nine days, they would receive a General Court Marshal and might go to a federal prison for years.

To a civilian (feather merchant) the penalty might seem heavy. However, these men knew they would soon be overseas killing and being killed. Any money they earned by having a higher rank could not be spent in the jungles and on the islands of the Pacific.

If a demoted man was a leader, his senior leaders would quickly reinstate him before going into combat. Why should the demoted man worry about it? The Japanese killed the ranking men first. The brig and work detail were much easier on the mind and body than charging over the California hills in training. Most of these men could train the trainers.

A Los Angeles newspaper picked up on the Marine Corps' Problem and interpreted it to mean that the men in the 5th Division had lost their will to fight. Nothing could be further from the truth.

A more serious problem arose. A young Paratroop sergeant was five minutes late making roll call one morning. I knew this young sergeant when we were in the South Pacific, and he worked under me by supplying "E" company. He reported late while we were actively training in the field. He was placed in the brig to await Court Martial. I did not think much about this. After all, that was the Marine Corps, and he knew it.

Later I learned this young man had accumulated a small fortune by gambling in the islands and aboard-ship on our return trip to the States. He had accumulated somewhere between twenty-five and thirty thousand dollars cash on himself and in a bank back home. That amount of money would translate into more than $200,000 in today's world.

Although he knew he had only a short stay in the States before returning to combat, he had married his high school sweetheart. He brought her to California and set her up in the finest apartment available near the base.

This young sergeant just radiated intelligence and fit perfectly into the Marine Corps. His father was a long-time Marine Warrant Officer. The sergeant was a good man in my mind. His job was obtaining food and other food-related things for the company. He made sure our company received better food than the other companies.

To better understand these veteran combat men, let me explain. When they were not in combat, they found the best jobs and stayed out of the hard work and dirty field problems. This young sergeant worked his way into the job of procuring food for our company. Others like him worked at the Officers Club and did other jobs of that nature. They would do these until a few weeks before combat. By that time they know what unit they want to join and do their best to get in that unit and train for combat.

It surprised me that he would get caught breaking a rule. I learned that trouble between him and his wife began when the Marine Corps forced us to train on the base for ten days at a time. He left his new wife alone in town. For a newly married man who had just returned from combat, and would be going back soon, this was too much for him to take. He took a chance and was caught.

After checking the trucks that brought supplies almost daily, he found that some trucks arrived in camp before roll call. Other trucks left camp after duty time in the evening. A truck driver allowed him to ride into town without a pass. His ride back was five minutes late the next morning. Veterans like himself knew and expected a "bust" in rank and thirty days in the brig.

Things got worse for the young sergeant. Our training was intense. It was hard for a Court-Martial court to convene. He was made prisoner-at-large and confined to the base. Thirty days elapsed before a court could meet. The court gave him thirty days in the brig and did not take in consideration that he had served thirty days as a prisoner-at-large.

Before a week went by, the sergeants that wrote up the Court Martial found a mistake and the court had to reconvene. Some officers that sat on the Court Martial were already overseas. The Marine Corps Rules and Regulations, as interpreted by someone in the battalion, made the sergeant prisoner-at-large again.

This represented sixty days with additional days counting. These many days of confinement were for leaving the base without permission for over-night and reporting back five minutes late the next morning. I do not blame anyone if they do not believe this. I did not believe it myself. Word came to me that his wife, with money and a luxury apartment, was entertaining off-duty sailors and marines.

As the weeks went by and we were getting closer to our ship-out date, he remained confined to the base. His wife was going through his money as if it were water. He came and asked me for help.

I told him that if the high command did nothing in another week, I would sure do something. I emphasized my remark with a few curse words. This man had served almost ninety days for a thirty-day sentence. The sergeant was recently in combat in the South Pacific, and he came to the States with us only a few months ago. He would be leaving soon for combat again, so why should he be treated this way?

When the additional thirty days rolled around, making it ninety days in all, I had the Easy Company on a live ammunition problem. The field problem was a nightmare, and the prisoner was furthest from my mind. Remember, I was barely twenty-two years old and a second lieutenant.

Our company field problem grew when I learned that the grass on the problem-range was powder dry and would almost explode when hit by tracer ammunition. Tracer ammunition had a small burning fire on the back of the projectile. The light of the fire would tell us where the shell was going and act as a spotter. We would no sooner begin a problem than a fire would start. The whole camp was in danger if the wind increased. Other rifle companies refused to fire with tracer ammunition or refused to fire at all.

The fire danger was so serious that our leaders did not allow cigarette smoking. At first, the many fires forced us to stop firing our weapons, take off our jackets, and fight the fire. In desperation, I allowed the company to finish the problem without stopping. Suddenly, fires were everywhere, but we soon put them out with our dungaree jackets.

I am telling this to explain the mental state I was in when I returned to find the battalion camp almost deserted. We were getting ready to ship overseas and everyone with any rank, or who could manage it, had left camp early. This included our company commander.

When I turned the company over to the sergeant for dismissal, there stood the sergeant with the P.A.L. (prisoner at large) on his sleeve. I soon found out that the senior officers and sergeants were also gone on liberty-early. They wanted to see their wives and precious girlfriends before they left to go over seas. I noticed that they thought it was important for themselves. Mad! I was so angry I could have cursed the Commandant. That is not true; but I was furious.

There stood the sergeant, the poor son-of-a-bitch. He had spent ninety days away from his new wife and nobody gave him a thought.

They did not have to give him a thought. That is "Regulations by the Book." My jacket was black with smoke and burnt grass. My face and hands were black, and I stunk. "Follow me," I told him and we went to see the colonel.

The colonel would have a hard time recognizing me. When we arrived at the Colonel's tent, we found that he was gone on early liberty. This fact got to me. He was an Annapolis man, but a fighting Marine. I did not expect him to do that.

I was fighting mad now. In the colonel's place was a young Second Lieutenant, "Officer of the Day." The Sergeant begged for just one night of liberty. I knew about his family ties to the Marine Corps. The young Sergeant had a good record until this incident happened. Against all regulations, I told the young lieutenant to give the sergeant an over-night pass. The lieutenant should not have issued that pass, but he did. The sergeant said he would be back before roll call the next morning. He was not back at roll call, and I was in deep trouble.

A week went by and the sergeant had not returned. Several company and platoon men went on liberty and searched for him. I did not ask them to do this for me, but I did appreciate the effort.

For a time it looked as if I might be Court Martialed or repri-manded in some way. Colonel Johnson told me that for my unautho-rized action someone in Washington asked for a letter of explanation. I wrote a letter not only degrading the officers immediately above me, but the Marine Corps also. I wrote: "We are not talking about disciplin-ing criminals. We are talking about handling first-class fighting men."

The colonel exploded. He had me report to his tent and tore up my letter in front of me. He ordered the sergeant who wrote the legal papers for the battalion to write a letter for me. Then without allowing me to read the letter, he had me sign it. His letter must have satisfied Washington. I never received a single day of restriction.

**As a foot note: Washington never asked for a letter and the colonel never sent one. I found this out in 1992. I have my records. It is interesting to read just what he did do. For the first time, he did not recommend me for regular commission on my fitness report.

We later learned that upon returning fifty four-days later, the Sergeant received a Summary Court Martial. This light a sentence, for this many days, was never heard of before in the Marine Corps. Any A.W.O.L. over twenty-nine days was an automatic General Court Martial. Later I got a letter from the young man, but I did not answer it. The letter was a long-winded, apologizing thing. I threw it aside; we had hard training and combat ahead of us.

Our training grew more intense as the days went by. An attempt

100

was made to make our training realistic and thorough. The smartest thing we did was form three-men fire teams. Whoever thought of this was a genius. Some of the "old Corps" had a hard time seeing it, but the young and new Marines caught on fast.

One Browning automatic rifleman (B.A.R.) and two regular riflemen formed a fire team. One of the two riflemen was the fire team leader and usually held the rank of Corporal. Three fire teams working as a unit would form a squad. Each fire team could also act as a separate unit or, in battle, join any unit. All three men were taught how to use the automatic weapon. At all cost the automatic rifle must stay in action.

The importance of this small unit and its ability to join and work with other like units makes it an important tool in battle. It proved to be extremely important on Iwo Jima, because we could not always function as platoons and squads.

We trained with live ammunition and reviewed experiences the Marine Corps had with the enemy. When talking with other organizations and sometimes with my own, it became clear that most inexperienced military and non-military people think that a determined enemy can be destroyed with artillery, rockets, bombs, and missiles; but, of course, they cannot.

To further explain my thinking, if a person is under siege by artillery, rockets, bombs, and missiles, he can lay down in a slight depression and save himself from ninety-nine percent, and if he moves slightly under-ground, he can expect ninety-nine and nine-tenths percent protection from the firepower. Sky burst, because shrapnel comes down like hail, can damage ground personnel. It can also be effective, if the troops are out in the open, on level ground and with no shrubbery or trees where the enemy does not need to worry about exposing themselves.

Generals who try to win wars with this aerial weaponry against a determined foe are doomed to fail. They may win a battle, but they lose the war. No matter how good this aerial weaponry may appear at the beginning, they can pin-down, demoralize, and catch a few by surprise - that is all. Infantry must take the objective, destroy the defenses, and move on.

Marines were familiar with the Japanese defenses. We knew they would be well dug-in, and they could re-man their firing positions fast. They had practiced this to a precise degree in past battles. Experienced Japanese would remain in a protected place until the Marines' firepower lifted to allow our troops to advance. They would quickly re-man their weapons, and if they could, they would catch the Marines out in the open. The last Marines leaving their positions would surely be caught.

While they were killing Marines, they exposed their weapons and positions. The Marines would soon overrun them. These Japanese were trapped underground and became easy targets for our flamethrowers and demolition teams.

I thought it might be worthwhile to mention that the Japanese were first to use the flamethrower, and they used it throughout Asia. Japanese armies had not changed their tactics, and we could depend on it. A few Marine Corps "By the Book" officers had not changed either, and the Japanese could depend on that.

The Marine High Command thought we must practice moving in on the Japanese at the time our heaviest weapons were shelling. This was dangerous, and there would be casualties in training. They believed that the result was worth the risk.

At first, we exercised without ammunition (dry-runs) to acquaint ourselves with the fire-team method. It also taught us how to take care of our weapons and other equipment. Next, we used blank ammunition with coordinated movement of demolition men and flamethrowers.

I only remember one tragedy at this time. Someone killed (murdered) a sergeant with a live round of ammunition. Our platoon was near by when it happened. High Command ordered us back to our tents for rifle inspection. Shooting live ammunition leaves the bore of the rifle shiny. Shooting blanks leaves the rifle bore coated with spent black-powder residue. There was an investigation, but we never knew who killed the sergeant. Later a dying man on Iwo Jima confessed. The killer was from the dead man's own platoon. Thank God, we had very little of this. Normally, an extra mean sergeant could focus the men's attention onto the enemy and off himself.

Next, we trained with live ammunition for all personnel to use. We also learned to use the bazooka. This weapon would shoot a rocket-like projectile resembling a small bomb in appearance. It had a soft aluminum nose. The soft nose would collapse and hold to the target it hit until a shaped charge inside it would explode and penetrate a concrete door, tank armor, or other enemy protection. Due to the cone shape of the explosive, the power would concentrate its energy into a straight line and penetrate almost anything.

Private First Class James Michels of the Third Platoon had the uncanny ability to fire this weapon. It would not fire accurately, but Michels fired it accurately. This was a natural ability, a gift from his ancestors. Why did they not give him the same ability to keep up with his shells and other equipment? People forget that heroes are human.

102

I liked this young man. I went to his funeral after the war. He was in the picture of the First Flag Raising on Iwo Jima.

Our Marines practiced moving one or more men up under heavy fire, until bullets were passing only inches above their heads. They would place a demolition package or push it in place with a rifle. The fire team would retreat enough for their safety before the explosion-then quickly move in on the target.

We had several accidents at this time. One accident killed one of my lieutenant friends. He was showing his men how to place the charge when one of his men, firing an automatic weapon, allowed it to fire too low and put several bullets into the lieutenant's back. I doubt that he was murdered, though that was possible. We thought the officer was well liked by all.

I remember that this lieutenant was a little wild and careless like the rest of us. When we were in the paratroops, this lieutenant's claim to fame was that he dove from the high board at the Hollywood Beverly Hills Hotels swimming pool in full uniform. I like to remember him that way and not the other.

Another officer told me I should be more careful because I always worked with or in front of the men. I told him that if anyone tried to kill me, he would need to do a good job because I would surely kill him or them if they failed. I meant what I said. This type thinking may not be understood by military men that are unfamiliar with close-in island warfare with an enemy like the Japanese.

In August, after I had served for several months as Company Executive Officer, Harold Schrier, a combat senior First Lieutenant from the Raiders, joined our company and became our company Executive Officer. Captain Severance put me in charge of the 3rd Rifle Platoon.

I will not forget that day, and I found out after the war that the platoon did not forget either. My mind was made up. Our training in the platoon would concentrate on and perfect our attack.

My introduction to the platoon was dramatic although I did not mean for it to be. I brought them to attention and told them, <u>Just give me fifty men not afraid to die, and I can take any position.</u> We could go through a great amount of speech, "blah, blah, blah," but it would all add up to the above statement. I did not want there to be a question in anybody's mind what our platoon objective would be. Richard Wheeler, a corporal in the Third Platoon, wrote about this in his book <u>The Bloody Battle for Suribachi.</u>

Soon after Schrier joined the company, he brought a sergeant who was formerly under him in the Raider Battalion and wanted him

Top: Cpl. Harold P. Keller, Pfc. Clarence H. Garrett, Cpl. Edward J. Romero, Jr., Cpl. Wayne C. Hathaway.
Bottom: Pfc. Manuel Panizo, Pfc. John H. Eller, Pfc. Phillip E. Christman. Part of 3rd Platoon.

in my platoon. His name was Howard M. Snyder. That is a name to remember.

Training escalated from small units to large-scale maneuvers. Just off the coast of California the regiment did a full-scale practice invasion on San Clemente Island. The island was a Naval firing range, and wild goats lived there. Sailors many years ago released goats there as a source of fresh food when they were in the area.

People who are strangers to amphibious warfare (transferring men and equipment from a troopship to a strange shore) would never believe what the Marines were subjected to. The simple processes of loading a troop landing craft at sea and then moving in unison with other landing craft to make a landing on a nearby island could be extremely dangerous, even without an enemy. On this day the sea waves were high, and the undertow was powerful.

Troopships loaded with training Marines were brought to San Clemente Island. At sea, they expected us to transfer men and equipment from a large ship over to many small landing crafts. We would do a realistic practice landing. Our Navy was firing live ammunition at the island and continued firing over our heads.

A net made from a one and one-half inch rope with a one to two foot open web spread fifteen to twenty feet wide was secured on deck. The net was then thrown over the guard rail to the waiting open-top

104

landing craft in the water below. Attached to both boat and ship, the net functioned as a wide rope ladder between the two.

An early morning haze clung to the ship like a blanket. Although a stiff breeze blew, the large ship lay in the water almost parallel to the on-coming waves and land swells. The ship wallowed one way and then another, almost crushing the small landing-craft as the ship rocked toward the small boat. A sinister atmosphere gave us the feeling that made us wish we were somewhere else.

To the men already in the small boat, hanging on for dear life, the ship looked like a building crashing down on them. They could not get away; the rope net held the two together. As the two vessels came together, a geyser of water rose between them.

The sound of the flat-bottom landing craft coming down and popping the sea-swells and the feel of power of the surging water was enough to give any man goose bumps. A terrible suction noise as the two crafts pulled apart would cause shivers to run up and down my spine. The power of the ocean waves as they lifted and moved the multi-ton ship about would make us wonder if there were not a better way.

Marines, fully combat loaded to a point we could hardly see each other, would attempt to work their way over the side of the ship and down the net. They would be hitting each other, stepping on each other, and cursing so loud even God could hear.

At times the landing craft would rise six or eight feet and sometimes more. The landing craft would smash into the troop ship, and if some poor Marine descending the rope-like ladder ended-up between the two, only God could help him. If something or someone knocked a Marine off the net into the water, not even God could save him. Thank the good Lord not many went this way, but some did.

Our senior officers made sure that every means of transportation-ship, boat, tank and man—that traveled in the direction of the enemy was loaded to absolute capacity. When the men were killed or wounded and the landing craft disabled on landing, they at least did their duty as pack horses bringing in supplies for others to use.

Platoon Sergeant Thomas and I went over the boat-loading procedure with each other and the men. We wanted to time ourselves with the roll of the ship so that we could step into the landing craft just as it reached the peak in its rise. The waves were not perfect; however, we managed to get in the landing craft safely.

We loaded the landing craft, but the Navy crew was unable to free us from the ship. The coxswain of the small boat was frantically trying to hold the boat away from the big ship to prevent us from being crushed. His helper was trying to unhook the small boat from the webbing that attached us to the ship. Our small boat was in danger of being hit by another landing craft trying to move into position to take our place in the loading zone. With help from the loaded Marines, we freed ourselves.

The next objective was to find the rendezvous area, a pre-selected spot off the beach. The rendezvous area should be out of range of small weapons. Once there, the small crafts formed a prescribed circle, and we stayed in that circle, going around and around, until our group's turn came to form a line facing the beach.

Small, flat-bottomed landing crafts, bobbing around like corks, make perfect seasick machines, and most of the platoon became seasick. At least one quarter to one half a mile of open water lay between us and the beach.

Finally, boats moved toward the beach as the heavy shelling of the island lifted. The circles of boats in front of us began forming lines and moving toward shore. We could see the island clearly when large waves lifted us. However, we could not see the beach itself or the activities taking place there.

What we saw as we drew near the landing zone was enough to make our blood run cold. Inexperienced boat handlers stalled their boats several yards from the safe beach. Apparently, they were thinking only of staying in line with the other boats, and not timing themselves to go in with the big waves. They were swept sideways by the under-tow, or riptide, as the water rushed back toward the on-coming waves.

Turned sideways, the landing crafts were at the mercy of the on-coming big waves that would flip the small boats over. Some boats would almost flip over and dump men and their equipment. A few men jumped into the water. We learned later that they were afraid that the boat would come down on them and trap them underneath.

On our right flank a landing craft flipped upside down just as it reached the shore. All personnel were pinned underneath. The boat landed with about one-third of it in the water. There was a mad rush to try to lift the boat, but it was too heavy. One Marine in his frantic state to help grabbed a loose rope and began to pull, not knowing that the other end was around a Marine's neck under the boat.

Men dumped into the water offshore remained trapped in an outgoing riptide. It would suck the men with their life jackets and equipment underwater. Their equipment would be lost, and the men would surface some distance out.

The purpose of the life jacket was to save the men, but here it was almost a sure death warrant. No matter how much the men tried to

106

swim out to sea to get away from the clutches of the onrushing waves, the wind would catch them and their jackets. The wind and the high waves would force the men toward the beach. Before anyone could reach them, the grip and suction of the undertow pulled on their life jackets and clothes. They disappeared under water again only to repeat the process.

A few Marines already safe on the beach rushed out to save their struggling buddies. The riptide sucked them under also, and they suffered the same fate. No one could resist the great suction of the out-going water. They had nothing to grip or hold. Some of us stripped down to bare skin to lessen the grip of the undertow and locked hand-to-wrist forming a human chain and saved a few men. I was never in the water deep enough for it to get a grip on me.

On shore, the Marines were trying every means to release the men under the flipped boat. I think they dug the Marines out and saved all but the one with a rope around his neck. I was too busy working with the undertow to notice.

One Marine fell through an open hatch while unloading equipment from the supply ship. The fall killed him. To the best of my knowledge, the Marine Corps lost eight men dead that day. After some time of reorganizing, we returned to the ship and got the hell out of there.

Remember, this day's problems and deaths happened without the enemy firing a shot. We did not like thinking about this type of landing. Easily, we could have the same conditions on the day we had to attack the Japanese, and that could just be the start of bad times. I will say one thing: this experience caused us all to do some deep thinking. I thought that only with the confidence of the men in their leaders can we keep tight control when conditions are much worse than this.

The normal thing to do after hitting the beach was to see that all the men and equipment were assembled at a given point. The only way I could do my part was to highly concentrate on one step at a time, and I hoped I could grasp the big picture while doing it. We could not do it without the finest non-commissioned officers and men, and we had that.

We were not like sheep being led to slaughter as some might think. The sergeants and I discussed at great lengths our chances of doing all that we must do, and our chances of coming out alive and in one piece. Everyone knew the odds were against this.

In camp, one of our routines as an officer in the Marine Corps was to serve as O.D., "Officer of the Day," of the unit. All officers except the senior officer have this obligation. He usually picks one from the junior officers. When the senior officer leaves the base, an "Officer of the Day" is designated, and he remains in charge of the unit until relieved. This is usually an overnight designation.

The designated officer should be awake the full time he is in charge. This job can be a real headache when the military police bring in Marines by the truck loads who are drunk, fighting, and God knows what else.

The Shore Patrol and Military Patrol brought in many A.W.O.L. Marines. The nearer over-seas ship-out-time came, the worse the situation got.

Once when I was "O.D." I reported to Colonel Johnson after a hard all-night vigil. I had left my field scarf (neck-tie) at the wash trough, where I had shaved before reporting; so, I reported out of uniform.

Lieutenant Colonel Chandler W. Johnson was Battalion Commander of the 2nd Battalion, 28th Marines. He was above our company commanders. My affection for this man has grown every day since the first day I met him, even in death, if that is possible. He was a rugged, heavy-set man, with firm features and at times a temper that showed. The morning I reported out of uniform he reprimanded me (chewed me out) in front of the Battalion Headquarters' personnel.

I had worked my rear-end off all night. This field scarf business was a little minor for me to have to take this reprimand in the presence of the Battalion Headquarters enlisted personnel. A senior officer reprimands a junior officer in private—maybe in front of other officers—but not in front of enlisted men.

Because he was treating me as he would an enlisted man, I came to a stiff attention and acted in every way an enlisted man would act. When he had finished, I asked, "IS THAT ALL, SIR." He blinked his eyes and said, "Yes." I quickly did a snappy salute and held it until he returned it. Then I did an about face and walked away. I knew I did wrong, and he knew that he did also.

Colonel Johnson was a visible man, and not just in his size. He showed himself everywhere when watching us train. This was not spying. He gave us the feeling that he was definitely interested in his officers and men and what they were doing.

The day came when the commander confined all officers and men to the base, and his orders allowed no civilians on the base. The evidence was clear. We were shipping out. High command approached me. They wanted my girlfriend, the exotic dancer, to entertain at the Officers' Club. She had entertained there several times before. She was good.

108

Hollywood Canteen; the dancing girl

I told high command that she had no gas stamps and that she was not sure she could obtain a seat on a train or bus. She did not tell me this. I wanted a good closed vehicle and the right to leave base and bring her back. They let me have what I wanted, along with a driver. She entertained us at the Club. When we carried her off the base that night, I stayed. When the driver and I returned the next morning, the Colonel had me report to him. The driver and I were the only men that stayed off the base that night. For punishment the colonel made me "Officer of the Day" on ship-out day.

We loaded all personnel early the next morning and headed for the docks. No one would know the hour we were leaving, or so we thought. Wives, kids and friends lined the road, almost waving their arms off as we passed. That scene is still a touching thing inside me. Many of these women and children were seeing their loved ones for the last time.

At San Diego, California, on 19 September, 1944, we went aboard the USAT Sea Corporal, a troopship so old I worried about us leaving the dock. We learned that this ship was caught in a storm off the Philippines some time later, and it broke in half and sank. Sergeant Hansen, Sergeant of the Guard, and I stayed on deck until after dark. We looked at the night lights of San Diego and talked.

High Command passed the official word to me to allow the officers to leave the ship on their own recognizance. They were told the hour to be back. You can guess how that went over with the men—and me.

Sergeant Hansen and I went below deck and made no effort to stop anyone from going ashore. The men could not use the gang-plank. We had guards posted there with orders to let no one but officers pass. We did not take the responsibility for the time to be back aboard. About midnight the ship hoisted the anchor and moved out into the harbor and demagnetized our ship, an action meant to protect us from the enemies' floating, explosive mines.

Two of the enlisted men from our company, L. B. Holly from Texas and G.E."Red" Graan from Chicago slipped ashore, and the ship was gone when they returned. We later learned that D. A. Carson from "D" company was with them.

Chapter 8

HAWAII ISLAND
Hawaii Islands, Territory of Hawaii
On the 24 September 1944 we landed at Hilo, Hawaii,
Territory of Hawaii.

Hilo was the leading town on the largest island of the Hawaiian group. Also, the town had a small, beautiful harbor with lovely tropical gardens around the buildings and homes. I say "was," because a tidal wave washed the town away some years back. I am not sure how they rebuilt it. When we trained on the island in 1944, most of the offices and retail buildings sat on the island side of the street. The buildings faced a large park with a beach and harbor. A tabernacle sat on the harbor side. Public speaking and other civic activities were held under the tabernacle. When the city's social and political business was over, families sat in its shade talking while they watched people shopping and their children playing. Beyond the clean park and harbor lay the ocean. Hilo was a lovely place.

The prime source of income for this Hawaii Island was sugar cane and cattle. The government rationed sugar in the States along with many other products. Here in Hawaii sugar was plentiful. Soft drinks, which included Coca-Cola, contained sugar, and we thought the taste was better than it was at home.

We disembarked from the ship and walked a short distance to a train. In front of us and between the ship and train was a small portable sandwich stand. Inside the stand stood three finely dressed middle-aged women wearing Red Cross arm bands. The women were local volunteers. We could tell that they were there to serve us. The look in their eyes gave them away. Instead of serving, they stood back in awe and let us help ourselves to sandwiches, Coca-Cola, and donuts. The local atmosphere helped; however, I believe the food and drink were the best. On-board ship, the Sea Corporal's cooks were "hash throwers," which made us enjoy this island handout even more.

Some men carried cases of "Coke" between them as they went to the train. I think the women were afraid to interfere. They knew this was a small price to pay for what they were getting in the way of protection from the enemy. The Japanese bombed Pearl Harbor, and that was close to their home. Many local Japanese on the island had hate in their eyes and were not friendly toward Marines. What would happen to these women, if we lost the war, was evident.

111

The cold Cokes made me think of home. Summers were hot and there were no air conditioners, but we had a freezer in our general country store. My father allowed me to help myself to things in the store. To combat the heat I soon learned to store bottles of Coco- Cola in the freezer and time them. Before the bottle burst from the expanding ice I would open it and drink the delicious Coke slush. These Hawaii cokes were good, but the home Cokes were hard to beat.

The children and teenagers liked the Marines. The local newspaper was full of news of young Japanese changing their first name to *John, Frank, Alice,* and other Anglicized names. Later, I had a Japanese girlfriend who taught me to speak some Japanese language. Her name was Alice Kataoka. Her mother taught sewing to other Japanese girls in town.

Alice Kataoka on my right.
Her mother and two student behind us.

Many adult Japanese in Hawaii opposed the United States. They had pure hatred in their eyes. Marines stationed at the unloading docks in Hilo and not attached to us said that Marines in the 2nd Division had fired into the crowd and killed some local Japanese. They did this soon after the 2nd Marines Division fought the battle for the island of Tarawa. When the veterans of the battle unloaded here to rest and reorganize, some local Japanese cheered—not for the Marines, but

112

cheered because the returning Marines were in poor condition and the enemy Japanese had inflicted so many casualties. The Marine Corps named Camp Tarawa for these gallant men. We were going there to train.

We walked to the miniature train that was built to haul sugar cane; it sat on nearby tracks. When I saw the train, I knew we were in for a pleasure ride. I think what made it special was that most of us recognized the fact and enjoyed the ride to the fullest. The rail cars had no tops or sides, just small, flat beds. We sat on the wooden beds. Some men hung their feet off and over the side. This was against orders. These combat-experienced men ignored petty orders.

We rode through a part of the town's living quarters. Spots along the track had low roadway bridges passing over the train. Native children, most of Japanese ancestry, lined the bridges. They stood or jumped up and down smiling, throwing fruit, waving, and holding up the "V" for victory signs with their little fingers. One Marine told us that he was hit in the head with a coconut. That child's father must have hated Marines, or it could have been an accident.

We skirted hillsides, and then we passed through sugar cane fields dotted with large warehouses. Scattered here and there in the fields were small living quarters. Small shacks stood with windows open and with no window panes. Native children climbed in and out of the windows and waved to the passing train. These window openings did not add to filth or untidiness. I do not remember ever seeing a fly or discarded trash on the Island.

At times we rode hundreds of feet high over gorges with waterfalls off to one side and water-chutes coming from above the falls. The wooden water chutes (flumes) looked like miniature bridges suspended high in the air. Some passed over and some passed under us. Diverted water ran down these chutes, possibly for irrigation. I think mostly these were used to transport sugar cane and fresh water to processing plants near sea level. On the other side of the train, down and far away, was the ocean as far as the eye could see.

Our destination was the Parker ranch and Camp Tarawa. In the open desert, tents marked the spot, about sixty miles from Hilo.

The only thing pleasing about Camp Tarawa was the distant scenery. Towering volcanic mountain cones, Mouna Kea, Mouna Loa, and the not-so-high Haleakala stood looking majestic against the deep blue sky. On the windward side of the mountains rain fell almost daily, and the beauty was unbelievable to a West Texan's eyes. It never rained on the Camp Tarawa side of the mountains, and it was as dry as any desert land. What is commonly thought of as desert sand did not exist

113

here. Instead, there were miles upon miles of finely powdered volcanic dust that lay several inches thick on everything.

Wooden chutes (flumes) carried water from rainy side of the island to the dry side.

The Parker Ranch was a cattle ranch second only in size to the King Ranch in South Texas. We were told that the owners of the ranch leased the ranch to the Navy for one dollar a year. The only thing there that reminded me of a cattle ranch in Texas was the prickly pear cactus.

Before we could get settled in camp, my tent overflowed with letters. Writing was in full swing, and some of these young Romeos (lovers) wrote volumes. It was the responsibility of the lieutenant platoon leaders to censor the platoon mail. Regulations specified that it had to be an officer. I hated this worse than fighting the Japanese.

The orders stated that we would take scissors, razor blades, or the like and cut out anything about the military, including the location of our camp. This was the most ridiculous thing I ever had forced upon me.

Both times I left the States I cut off all relationships except with home, and then I wrote only a short note to my family once a month to say everything was all right. In my way of thinking, I short-changed the Marines under me if I thought too much about home.

Regularly, Tokyo Rose reported from Tokyo, Japan. She was an English-speaking woman who used the radio for Japanese propa-

114

ganda. Tokyo Rose informed the entire Pacific Theater on the position of all American troops and named their officers. As far as I know, she was never wrong. Japanese the world over kept Japan well informed on the distribution of American troops.

Censoring mail had become a game with some Marines. *He-lo Howar ya, pineapple, grass skirts, and ukulele* were the most obvious. The men were crafty and inventive with words and phrases. A few officers enjoyed the cat and mouse game. Some enjoyed the detective work in exposing the clever writers and then physically cutting out the word or phrases from the letters.

I hated reading other people's mail, and in no time, I was in serious trouble. Mail several days old remained piled and stacked in the corner of my tent. The First Sergeant, John Daskalakis, called me in and let me know it was a court-martial offense if I did not get the letters out quickly. He was taking care of me, and I knew it.

I came up with an idea that worked like a charm. Every time I found a letter that needed censoring, I called the man in and gave him back his letter and told him to cut it out or rewrite it. In no time at all the game ended. That is not quite true. I think it was Pfc. Phil Christman who used letterheads. He and his family wrote on paper with Bible scriptures printed for letterheads. The Bible scriptures were not bad. They were all different and could be assigned different meanings. I stopped Christman from using his. After that, I just spot checked the usually guilty ones.

After the excitement of the ship ride and the settling in of the new camp wore off, we entered combat training on a grand scale. For the first time we could train with live ammunition on regiment and division level. This is where we used the big guns, large artillery, tanks, and planes in a full-scale ground operation.

With all this weaponry, we expected to kill more men accidentally in practice than we did. A spent piece of shrapnel almost knocked me down one day when we trained with live ammunition. I was standing almost straight so that I could see. The shrapnel buried into my breast pocket where I had some Japanese language cards. It hit my pocket flat and did not bury deep, but I was dumb exposing myself that much; I knew better.

When the military exercises made an unscheduled stop, the men knew someone was hurt. We hoped the injury was not serious, but we killed some and hurt many. Later Chopin's "Funeral March" playing slowly and softly could be heard through the thin walls of the tents. It reminded us that the weapons we used were deadly and the game we played was death.

115

Our doctors reported that on post-mortem, these men killed in practice had an accumulation of fine volcanic dust in their lungs. Volcanic powdered dust covered everything, and if we wanted to live, we had to breathe it and, occasionally, eat it.

There were times in the training area when the military traffic of both men and vehicles filled the air with dust. The cooks would bring the food to the field in containers with the tops covered. When they took the lids off to serve, the fine dust would soon cover the food. I refused to eat it. I began carrying three or four bottles of beer and no water. Beer was not my favorite drink, but it did take care of my food and water problem. Strenuous exercises eliminated any effect from the alcohol. I did not make a practice of this.

At noontime when we had problems in the field, the lieutenant platoon leaders lined up behind their men and ate last; at least I did. When they brought water, I saw to it that the men drank and filled their canteens before I drank.

I cannot explain it, but hunger and thirst were never my problems. My problem was standing around with nothing to do while the men ate and drank. Sergeant Snyder and others studied Japanese language and geography with me. We spent the waiting time studying.

The field maneuvers required that we form small landing craft groups and do practice runs on an imaginary beach laid out by panels on the ground. These exercises always had a small volcanic mountain on our left flank. When we would hit the make-believe enemy beach, we made a left turn. After advancing to the base of the small mountain, a designated platoon would scale the small mountain with live ammunition exploding just above the men's heads. When the artillery raised their shelling, the platoon would advance up the mountain to the area just shelled.

I dreaded the live ammunition part because we always caught some short-rounds and somebody could get hurt. Someone failed to put enough powder in the shell and it would fall short and explode among the Marines. I know this sounds like a tall tale. It isn't. We would laughingly say that the short rounds came from the wives of the men, because some Marines' wives worked in the factories making ammunition.

On one of these practice runs an old dog took up with me. He looked like he was part, if not all, pit bulldog. I did not encourage him. We had no idea where he came from. When I looked around, he was always there following close to my heels. He gave the impression that he did not give a damn whether the sun rose or set, and that feeling reflected my sentiments most of the time. The old dog did not seem to

116

mind the shells bursting just over our heads. If he ever looked up at me, I do not remember it. I am sure I never petted him. I guess he took up with me because he thought I was the dog leader of this pack.

One day as we made the turn to face the small mountain, the captain chose our platoon to scale it. We moved up each time the heavy shelling lifted, in plain sight of the General, Colonels, and all. Suddenly, in the middle of one of our advances the men came to a halt and there was a mad scramble. We were in the middle of a dewberry patch. The berries were almost as big as ping pong balls. The war took a back seat to this encounter. My platoon and I were gathering berries like grade school children gathering Easter eggs.

Right in the middle of the berry-picking party, my friend "the dog" came to life and pounced on a huge cock pheasant. He held the bird down until I got there. I killed the pheasant, tore his breast out and stuck it in my pack. I gave the remains of the bird to the dog. This is what he seemed to expect.

Leonard Mooney, our platoon radio man, came up and handed me the radio receiver. He had Colonel Johnson on the radio, and the colonel was watching us with field glasses. He wanted to know "What in the hell is going on?" Colonel Johnson did not hold it against us, and the daylight part of this problem was soon over.

To make matters worse, the field problem continued through the night, and the judges allowed no fires or lights after dark. To have a small mountain on our flank, we had moved to a part of the island that had some moisture. The weather turned cool, and there was mist. Nobody moved from his tent. I pitched my shelter-half against a Jeep trailer for more protection. My shelter-half made a lean-to (a one-sided tent). Normally, I slept by myself. Tonight, I saw the dog curl up near my feet.

When all was quiet, we slipped down into a creek bed. My dog companion went with me. I did not talk to him. He seemed to know what we were doing. For emergencies, I carried a wax candle with me on overnight problems. With melted wax, I could stick the candle to my helmet and study the Japanese language cards. Tonight, I used it with a cigarette lighter, some loose paper, and squaw-wood to build a small fire. I was cooking our pheasant's breast when I heard a noise. On the creek bank stood Colonel Johnson. He pretended to be angry, but he looked away and walked off.

Another incident happened about the same time, and everyone involved seems to remember it. We had finished a training exercise, and the battalion was taking a break. A cowboy on the Parker Ranch was riding through on a small island horse. Evidently, someone asked to

117

ride his horse. The cowboy told them the horse was a one-man-horse and that the horse would not allow anyone else to ride him.

Some Marines brought the horse over for me to ride. After all, had I not talked about my horseback riding as a boy and the horse cavalry riding at Texas A&M College. The men, expecting a big laugh, neglected to tell me about the horse's peculiarities.

Hawaiian cowboys are stout-built men with short stubby legs. They ride bare-footed and their stirrup straps are adjusted short to fit their legs. I was thinking about adjusting the stirrup straps when I noticed that the stirrups were small rings instead of normal foot stirrups. The Hawaiian cowboy stuck his big toes through the rings. This was new to me. I did not adjust the straps. They hung loose.

The horse was small, so I gathered up the reins in one hand and put that hand on the horse's neck. I caught the front of the saddle with the other hand and swung myself upon the horse's back. The short stirrup straps, with the dangling rings, hung loose. Before I settled to a good seat, the horse squatted and began pitching. He had me all over his back. Sometimes I landed in front of the saddle, and some times I landed behind. Every now and then, I came down in the saddle. The straps, with the rings, began flapping, and the rings beat up and down my body.

The yelling Marines never knew how badly the rings beat me. The men laughed and yelled, and the Hawaiian cowboy stood back and watched the show. Thank God, that horse never threw me. As a Texan and with all my horse cavalry training, I would never have lived that down.

I told the men that if we ever fought where there were horses, we would go mounted. I was anxious to fight on the Mongolian ponies found in Manchuria and other places the Japanese occupied. Just for the hell of it, I gave most of my orders to the Third Platoon in horse cavalry language. They used this cowboy and cavalry language in making the movie <u>Sands of Iwo Jima</u>. First Lieutenant Harold Schrier helped with the picture. He told them about it. I did not see First Lieutenant Schrier after the war, but we corresponded at Christmas until his death.

Maybe I should not tell this story. It is another story that does not look good. I like to blame it on deadly combat in the foreseeable future. Schrier was a hell raiser also, and when we had time off, things just seemed to happen. When the troops were getting ready for Christmas, 1944 just before our campaign on Iwo, the Sergeants of the 27th Marines gave a big party. They invited only a few officers from the 5th Division; Schrier and I were the only two officers invited from the 28th Marines. This was quite an honor or at least I thought so. We had beer, good food,

118

and entertainment. We continued to drink beer after we ate, and our hunger grew after we left the party.

On the way back to our tent area, we passed the 2nd battalion mess hall. I could see and smell turkeys cooking. The battalion cooks were preparing these turkeys for the enlisted personnel. I told Schrier we could steal a turkey. He doubted it but stood outside the door to catch the turkey if I could throw one out the open door.

I had held the job of Company Executive Officer for much of the training period in the States, and that position included the job of Mess Officer. Private First Class Ott and others from our company mess hall now held the same job with the battalion mess.

After entering the side door and working my way to the turkeys, I talked loud and acted more intoxicated than I was. With my eye, I judged the distance to the open door where Schrier stood in the darkness. The men working in the mess hall were ignoring me as best they could. I quickly picked up a turkey and threw it at the door. It missed the door and hit the sheet metal wall. The deafening noise caused the cooks and helpers to jump. They wheeled around and looked at me. I immediately came down on the table with my fist and did my best to make the same noise.

They had tolerated me to this point because I had friends there. Out of the corner of my eye I saw the nod and head movement that ordered one of my friends to get me out of there. I knew then that they did not suspect what I did. He directed me, and I made my way in the dark around to the door where Schrier stood. He had made no effort to retrieve the turkey.

At mess (meal) time, the men would form a line and move through this doorway and up to a counter. Servers dished out the food and the men moved through a side door. The serving counter blocked the view from the kitchen. It was this counter that the turkey slid back and under. It was out of sight of the cooks.

I crawled in on my belly, cradled the turkey in my arms, and backed out the same way. Once on the outside, I ran my fist up that turkeys rear-end and held him up like a popsicle. Schrier tore off a leg, and I grabbed a hand full of breast, and we went to our tent area eating turkey.

Our first stop was Colonel Johnson's tent, and I stumbled in and fished around in the dark until I found and turned on his light. Before he could get fully awake I almost hit him in the face with the turkey. When we left his tent, he was sitting on his cot eating turkey. Evidently that food was all I needed to put me into a deep sleep because I do not remember anything after that.

119

When I awoke the next morning, I was lying on my back. The rear end of the turkey skeleton was hanging down in my face, suspended from the top of my tent by a safety pin and string. I knew I was in trouble again and held my breath for two or three days. Not one word was ever said.

About twenty years after the war, I was telling this story when one man from the Third Platoon said; "You know why you got away with that, don't you, lieutenant? The Third Platoon had guard duty around the mess-hall that night, and I watched you. No one called the Sergeant-of-the-Guard."

Highly trained combat men going on liberty into the civilized world can sometimes be a disaster. The Marine Corps did not allow Marine officers to drive jeeps or any other type of Marine vehicle. They required the officers to have a driver. On this day Lieutenant Delbert O. Greenlee, from Sioux Falls, S.D., and I checked out a Jeep and driver for a liberty run into Hilo. When I saw the Jeep driver, I knew this was not going to be a normal liberty. I was with this driver once before, and that time was almost a disaster.

During the previous liberty, this driver told the other officer and me that he had a girlfriend named Rose in a part of town not normally visited by officers. He wondered if we might be interested in going with him to scout out (check for women) the area.

Usually Alice Kataoka and I went to the movies, had soft drinks, and talked with each other under the watchful eye of her mother, but nothing more. The young girl taught me Japanese language and that was good, but I was ready for a change of scenery. We agreed to go to Rose's house with the driver.

Rose, along with her father and mother, invited the three of us into the house. Rose's parents' house was clean and livable but plain. We had created curiosity in the neighborhood. Children were climbing in and out of the windows and looking through the front door. Rose had a cute little sister in her late teens, and she looked on with interest. Someone brought a good-looking Chinese woman for the other officer. I was wondering whom they would get for me.

Everyone was being extra polite, when out of the corner of my eye I saw the young girl, Rose's little sister, strike a match and light a cigar. She had a water glass full of island whiskey in her hand. She made her way quickly to me and sat in my lap. The young girl took a big drink of the whiskey and handed the glass to me. I looked at her father and mother, and they were laughing and seemed pleased. I downed a goodly portion of the whiskey, and she stuck the cigar in my mouth. The father and mother left, and the party got under way.

120

The music was loud, and who knows what else. Either someone turned us in, or the Military Police came by on a routine check. When the M.P.s stopped in front of the house, someone sounded the warning. Everyone ran for the back door. Why they were running, I did not know; however, I found myself in the lead. A bathroom commode was on the back porch in a small room with no door. I knew the way.

At least one M.P. had circled the house and had everyone trapped on the back porch. Just before he arrived, I stepped inside the bathroom and reeled it out as if I were taking a leak. I did not need to take one because I had visited the bathroom a few minutes before this happened. I stood there for what seemed like minutes just holding myself while they questioned everyone. After getting my friends' names and ranks, they told the driver and the other officer that this was a restricted area and the driver and officer must leave.

After a long wait, I thought they had missed me when suddenly an M.P. turned a bright light on me. There I stood for all to see. There was nothing I could do but give it a couple of shakes as if I had just finished and put it away. The M.P. took my name and rank and stayed with us until we left.

Now, here I was on another liberty trip into Hilo with the same driver. You notice I try to blame the bad happenings on the driver. As officers, we could buy and take with us our own booze. Lieutenant Greenlee and I had a few drinks on the way into town, and I saw our driver take one. He must have sneaked more than that. We entered town and found a political rally in progress. The speaker was of Japanese extraction. It seemed to me that the Japanese were the leading political force in Hawaii.

I told our driver that I wanted to go to the rally. He immediately

121

cut through traffic, scattering men, women, and children. The speaker's platform was under the large open-air pavilion on the beach. Our driver drove into and scattered the crowd as if we were dignitaries.

Lieutenant Greenlee and I dismounted to "fight on foot," and as we turned to walk away from the Jeep, I heard the driver order the children away from the Jeep. Our driver must have had more drinks. After I heckled the speaker for a short time, in my medium-to-poor Japanese, I turned to look for the Jeep and driver; they were gone.

At first, no one would tell me anything about the driver and Jeep. Finally, a young Hawaiian boy told me the city police left with both. I rushed out into the street, flagged down an Army Jeep, and had the driver carry me to the police station. There sat our Jeep; we had come to the right place. The police informed me, and not to my surprise, they had locked up our driver.

After a few minutes of straight talk, I demanded my driver. My determination paid off. After some discussion, they decided I could take the Jeep and driver under one condition: I must do the driving. That was their mistake. They did not know the Marine Corps regulations. Officers do not drive; they have drivers. In my anxiety to quickly get away from there, I forgot that the gear shift on Jeeps was backwards to regular vehicles. In reverse instead of low gear the Jeep went backwards through the prettiest flower garden that island could produce and maintain. Together the Jeep driver and I finally stopped the Jeep in the middle of the flowers. With him helping me, we shifted into low gear and spun out of there, throwing mud and flowers in all directions.

There was yelling, whistle blowing, and policemen running out of the doorway. They showed every indication of being more than just angry. I do not think I would have stopped even under direct gunfire.

Quickly, I drove down to the unloading docks, and the Marines stationed there washed the mud and flowers from the Jeep and hid it under a tarpaulin. They slipped me into the back door of the Noni Loa Hotel, where a Marine put me up for the rest of my liberty. We needed time. The local officers were too angry to deal with.

The Marine who put me up at the hotel was a private. He was much older than I. The local Marines told me he spent money freely. He wore expensive, tailor-made Marine Privates uniforms. They also told me that he joined the Marine Corps to stay out of prison. In civilian life he was in the rackets (illegal operations). We had never met, but he knew me or knew of me, and he insisted that I take the bed. He wrapped himself up in blankets and slept on the floor. I guess we were "kindred hearts"—dodging the law.

I will not swear to this, but I was led to believe that if a first-time criminal joined the Marine Corps before the police or government men caught him, he was safe in the Marine Corps. Would-be criminals were free men unless the Marine Corps gave them a dishonorable discharge. Also, the type of crime they committed may have dictated or had an influence on the government's decision. Some young criminals or would-be criminals changed their lives after training in the Marine Corps and fighting for their country.

You may wonder why I went to this trouble of hiding myself and the Jeep. The police had all the information on me. There was no way I could get away with this. I speculated that I would be better off disciplined by the Marine Corps. The chief of police was Japanese, and the officers were native Hawaiian. The Marines did not have a good record with the local police. Hawaii was not a state. I thought that if I could get the Jeep back to the base without being caught by the local police, we would have a better chance.

Upon returning to base, Lt. Greenlee and I had orders to report to the Regimental Commander's office. That is how I met Colonel Harry (Harry the Horse) Liversedge. Colonel Liversedge was over fifty years old. We had heard nothing but good things about this man.

Our Fifth Marine Division commander, General Rockey, a Navy Cross winner in World War I, told the young officers in the division that he demanded that all his regimental and battalion commanders be forty years old or younger. He then made one exception. Colonel Harry Liversedge was to command the 28th Marines, despite the Colonel being over fifty years old. Some of our Marines were with Colonel Liversedge on Tarawa. They had nothing but high praise for him. It was easy to see why General Rocky chose Colonel Liversedge, regardless of age.

I knew Colonel Liversedge on sight, and I knew that he knew me. Once he observed us on a live ammunition problem, where he expressed approval of my way of handling it. I received this praise through Colonel Johnson. Most of all, I think he knew me because of my girlfriend in the States, the exotic dancer. She danced at our Camp Pendleton Officers Club several times.

That is how things were when Colonel Johnson's office sent word for Lieutenant Delbert O. Greenlee and Lieutenant John K. Wells to report to Regimental Headquarters. As Lieutenant Greenlee and I walked toward the Regimental Commander's tent, every muscle of my body wanted to go in another direction. There could be no excuse. I was guilty.

Now, when a lowly second lieutenant is forced to report, past his

123

Captain, past his Colonel, past the low-ranking officers at regiment, to the Regimental Commander himself—that is bad. The Regimental Commander is not God, but he is as close to it as we can get here on earth. We were, or at least I was, "tickling the fickle finger of fate."

As we approached the Colonel's tent, Captain Joe F. Cason, the Colonel's Aid or Adjutant, returned our salute and escorted us in. We entered and stood at stiff attention.

When we reported our names, Colonel Liversedge directed his attention to me. He did not say much, just that he never expected to see me on charges again. He did not restrict me in any way; just the fact that I had to appear before him was enough. I was later to find that he was a friend of mine. This incident never entered my record book.

Thank God, he was a combat officer and not one of those by-the-book officers. He knew what he was doing. If after dismissing us, he had called us back and said, "We are marching on Hell tomorrow," I would have said, "Sign me up, Colonel."

You might wonder if I had discipline problems with the high ranking officers. What about Dave Severance, the company commander? Dave and I were as different as two Marine officers could be. Thank God, I was enough right each time there was a conflict between the two of us that there could be no disciplinary action.

Everyone knew, by my big mouth and actions, that I never planned to attend any military school that was not directly associated with physical combat, but that I would gladly attend any combat school. The combat schools included Parachute Training, Scout and Sniper, Tank, Rubber Boat, and schools of this nature. The Captain knew this.

Maybe this was my mind working, but because of the timing, I suspected the Captain was disciplining me the way he knew it would hurt most. He ordered me to go to Combat Loading School, where I would learn to load equipment onto or into transporting vehicles. The loaded equipment must be the supply needed, and it must come out of or off the transportation in the order needed for combat. If it was a ship to be loaded, we hoped the loaded equipment would come off correctly. Also, the loaded material must act as a ballast to keep the ship upright in rough weather. I tried everything I knew to get out of the assignment, but the Captain said I must go.

When it looked as if there was no way out, I received a call to report to the Regimental Commander's office. Thinking about all my past sins, I was apprehensive about returning to the Old Lion's Den. To my surprise, the Regimental Adjutant ordered me to take the regiment's liberty party to Hilo, Hawaii, for liberty. This group of men consisted of

124

enlisted personnel from regimental headquarters. It was hard for me to believe that the regimental office would entrust me with this job.

I informed the regimental office that Captain Severance ordered me to attend the Combat Loading School. The adjutant told me to disregard Captain Severance's orders. He said that my present orders came from the highest, even above Colonel Johnson. As I have said before, in the Marine Corps that is high.

Our regimental headquarters enlisted men were no problem on liberty. I conducted myself as a Marine officer should and brought the liberty-party back safely. When I returned, Captain Severance would not speak to me. I tried to explain but he would not listen. Dave Severance and I were together a long time; he should have known I would not disobey an order.

He made me walk behind him as he marched me to Colonel Johnson's tent. He left me standing outside while he conversed with the Colonel. When he returned, he ordered me to go inside the Colonel's tent. I quickly told Colonel Johnson that my orders came directly from Colonel Liversedge's office and that I was told to disregard Captain Severance's orders.

He asked why I did not tell Captain Severance where my orders came from. I told Colonel Johnson that I tried to, but Captain Severance would not listen. Colonel Johnson was angry, and he told me to send Captain Severance back in. My hell-raising may have caused some problems, but I also knew that I had friends in high places. I never had to go to that school or a school that was not directly related to physical combat, and that was the end of that.

The 5th Division had trained in Hawaii for a month or maybe a little more, when one day three men walked into camp fresh from the States. They had their civilian clothes with them. If you think that did not get attention, you are wrong. I mentioned these three men before. When they jumped ship as we were leaving San Diego, California, they were left behind.

Government men (F.B.I. and the like), appeared as if by magic. The government men were trying to find out how these three young men could stay in the U.S.A., work at defense plants, stowaway on a ship, and report to their own companies overseas without being detected. This happened when the United States was on a super secret hush-hush campaign.

L.B. Holly was one of the three that slipped off the ship at San Diego. He told me that when they returned, the ship was gone. They did not know that it was still in the harbor. The ship hoisted anchor and pulled out and away from the dock to de-magnetize the ship. We were

125

told that this process was designed to repel the enemy's magnetic mines.

Holly and his friends thought the ship left without them. He said the three of them went to Los Angeles and worked in a defense plant. They stayed in contact with friends who were in the rear echelon of the Fifth Division at Camp Pendleton.

These three made the decision to stow-away (sneak aboard), if they could, on the same ship with the rear echelon to Hawaii. Their clothes and equipment left with the first ship, so they were not in regular uniform.

When the Fifth Division rear echelon was loading to join us over seas, these three, L. B. Holly, George E.(Red) Graan, from Easy Company, and D. A. Carson from Dog Company mixed with the Second Battalion's rear echelon men. In the confusion of loading the battalion's equipment, all three joined a working party and carried something aboard the troop ship and then stayed.

The AWOL (absent without leave) men made beds out of life jackets, and D.A. Carson worked in the galley (kitchen) aboard ship and fed all three. All three went straight to the brig in Hawaii, and that is another story. Easy Company men in our company reported to me that Holly and Graan were great fighters on Iwo Jima.

Holly and Carson were wounded in the battle. D. A. Carson won the Navy Cross. "Red" Graan made a special effort to visit me on Iwo Jima. A short time later the Japanese killed him.

"Red" Graan, also known as Chicago Red, always called me Tex if no one else was around, and he would come up and talk. Our backgrounds were as different as you could imagine, but I liked that man. L. B. Holly received a petroleum engineering degree after the war, and D. A. Carson was doing well selling insurance. We stay in touch, and we see each other every two years.

The war was almost over, and killing Japanese was the only outside entertainment the Marine Corps had overseas. The Marine Corps became sophisticated and imported Bob Crosby, Bing Crosby's little brother, to help in getting us some entertainment.

While we were training in California, Bob Crosby was a civilian in Hollywood. The reason I know this is that Nate Libscomb and I were on liberty in Hollywood on a week day. We went into a cocktail lounge that was decorated like the jungle. It was early afternoon, and there were no other customers. Only the owner, Bob Crosby, was there. He let us know quickly that he liked Marines, and when he found out that we were from the 5th Marine Division, the drinks were on the house. Bob told us that he was joining the 5th Marine Division as a lieutenant and

126

would work with the recreation unit.

He was welcome; we had nothing up to that time. Marines in the South Pacific had a song about the Army and all their U.S.O. shows. Men in Australia wrote the song, I think. The song went something like this:

Bless them all, bless them all

the long and the short and the tall

there will be no promotion

this side of the ocean

so cheer up, me lads, bless them all.

They sent for McArthur to come to Tulagi

but General McArthur said, no.

He gave for a reason it wasn't the season, and

besides, they had no U.S.O.

Bob Crosby was angry before we left his cocktail lounge. Nate and I degraded the Marine Corps and the 5th Division in particular. We were just being ornery. We would have fought anyone else making those same statements.

In Hawaii Bob Crosby did have a good orchestra, made up of men of the 5th Division and assisted by Sergeant "Tubby" Oliver. They could play the popular songs of the day, which is what we needed. We were getting ready to leave Hawaii for combat, and Bob Crosby and his group presented a U.S.O. show in an amphitheater behind the 28th Marines officer's tent section.

On the Sunday they presented the show, a group of us returned from Kona, a small fishing and resort town on the far side of the island. While there, we had nothing to do but drink and sight-see. There was plenty of rain and an abundance of fruit, vegetables, and tobacco. This was my first time to see tobacco growing. In peacetime this was a thriving resort and deep sea fishing town, especially for the island's inhabitants. The village was practically closed due to the war.

When it was time for us to go back to camp, we stopped at a pier to throw coins to small boys in the water. They were diving and catching the coins. The Hawaiians were having so much fun swimming in the bay and diving for coins, Lieutenant Pennell and I could stand it no longer. Off came our shoes, socks and shirt, and we went swimming. We had no bathing suits, so we went swimming in our pants and underwear. Lieutenant Pennell had swum on a college swim team. I was more of a diver than a swimmer.

We rode back to camp in an open Jeep with the windshield down. The fine volcanic dust fogged us and our wet pants that were tied to the back of the Jeep. What we looked like when we arrived at camp, I do not want to think about.

Bob Crosby and the group responsible for the 5th Division U.S.O. shows had a show going near my tent. No matter what I looked like, I had to sneak a peak at the show. One of my enlisted friends, Fred Browne from the 27th Marines, who was watching the show, waved for me to come over. He wanted to talk a minute. His older brother, Captain Bob Browne, was our battalion supply officer on Iwo Jima. I talked to Browne for a short time and decided to go on to my tent.

On the stage hula girls danced to the rhythm and chant of the musicians. Hardly a sound came from the Marines. I tried to get a cheering section started but without success. My tent sat behind the open stage, and I decided to get there as soon as I could. My day was over; the drinks, swim, and Jeep ride had taken its toll.

The hula girls decided to go to a dressing tent as I was going to my tent. I must have been a terrible sight because the girls looked back and saw me and began running. The men started cheering, and I began chasing the girls. That must have been the best show seen all afternoon because more people remembered it than anything else I did. *** I was in Japan in 1983, and the Japanese Generals and junior officers of the Japanese Defense force teased me more about that than anything else. The Japanese Officers had all read about this little episode in a Japanese version of Richard Wheeler's book Iwo.

We were near the end of our training, and all the units that would support us in combat were joining with us in our last training periods. We had trained for a year to fight the same enemy. Our platoon, the Third Platoon, thought they were the best Marine platoon ever. It was only natural that they think that. They also thought they were the toughest platoon. Soon, they would have trouble living up to that.

First Sergeant John Daskalakis informed the company that the day had come for overseas medical shots, which included typhus, cholera, and plague. Our doctors, J.L. Wittmeier and J.H. Graham, set up a gauntlet line with a corpsman on each side. The Marines, stripped to the waist, would walk between the two, while the doctors looked on.

A corpsman on one side would jab us with a needle that looked as big as an ice pick. When we tried to dodge or lean the other way to absorb the shock, the corpsman on the other side would hit us with what looked like a bigger needle. This gauntlet was something to compare to some ancient medieval ritual. Thank God, they held this ceremony in daylight. The pure delight in the corpsman's eyes and "A dark and dreary night" would have set the stage for a Bela Lugosi (scary) movie.

Each platoon officer would take his shots and then step back and observe his platoon going through. I took my shots and moved back beside the corpsman giving the shots. Platoon Sergeant Thomas stepped up, took his shots, and fainted. Our next six men took their shots and fainted also. This was more than a little hard for this tough platoon to live down.

There was no question that we were leaving soon. Our senior officers received the information of our destination, and the colonels received maps of the target island. They decided the basic principles of the attack. Battalion Headquarters stored all these super-secret documents in the commander's office tent, and circled the tent with barbed wire. They even posted a guard.

They allowed the junior officers to see the outline of the landing area on the enemy beach. We had seen it laid out on the ground before when we did our practice runs. The officers in the Battalion Headquarters group and the officers in Regimental Headquarters treated this information as super knowledge and walked around with an air of great importance. The people who are going to fight the brutal war are the last to know.

Soon after all this super secret, guarded day and night, information arrived at our camp, we were awakened one Sunday morning by the yell of the newspaper boy. A Japanese boy from the nearby town of Kamuwela—yelled, "Buy a paper and see where you are going." On the front page, the Honolulu newspaper had a picture of Iwo Jima. We did not have to worry after that; we knew where we were going. The beach outline in the newspaper fit our working outline to the letter.

None of us had ever heard of Iwo Jima. We knew it was closer to Japan than the other islands we had taken, and that was all we knew. Our leaders told us that Iwo Jima had been under Japanese control for almost one hundred years and was part of their homeland defense system. This was enough to let us know that we had a hard fight ahead.

The men were in high spirits despite the fact we had been training as a group for almost a year and going over the same training often. Pfc. Donald Ruhl was the only one in the Third Platoon to show any signs of open rebellion. We all felt it, but he was the only one to

129

outwardly show it.

On one of our problems, not too far from camp, he showed indifference to the problem we were working. We had run this problem a hundred times and everyone was sick of it. We were flat on the ground working our way to a make-believe Japanese bunker when Ruhl jumped up and said he was sick and tired of this make believe and he was ready to fight.

"Send him back to his tent in camp and tell him to stay there," I told Sergeant Thomas. Ruhl could lie on his sack(bed) for the rest of the work day while we trained. He left, and we continued with the problem.

He was a good man, and we knew it. If we disciplined him too much on the spot, some men would defend him, in mind, if not openly. I know that I defended him in my heart if not my mind. We needed to get him and his attitude away from the men until we finished the problem. The solitude and his not feeling a part of the group worked because that was the end of Ruhl's rebellion.

Morale was not a real problem until Father (Padre) Paul Bradley, a Catholic chaplin, went against orders. He told the men at services one Sunday that they could expect as much as fifty percent casualties in the coming battle. Can you imagine what that did to morale? When Father Bradley announced the fifty percent possibility, the atmosphere changed abruptly. The highly competitive spirit dropped. Two-thirds of the Marines became sober, thoughtful, and at times even melancholy. The men spoke more of home and did not seem to have the same fighting spirit as before. I must admit, at the time this happened, I held this against the Padre.

The lieutenant platoon leaders had heard this prediction the week before. We knew we were goners-killed or wounded. Records of past battles showed that if the casualty rate was as much as twenty-five percent, the enemy would kill or wound all lieutenant platoon leaders.

Most of the young officers had already conditioned themselves to the inevitable. I do not know why we thought the men could not take this news. Bad news came from home daily. Girls and some wives back home had decided to break off relationships and wrote these "Dear John Letters."

Corporal Wayne Hathaway, ex-Raider with many war experiences and one of the best noncommissioned officers in the platoon, received a "Dear John Letter." He was a good man, he was dependable, and I thought the world of him. Someone told me, and it disturbed me when he did not show up for mess call.

When I looked in his tent, I saw Hathaway sitting on his cot just staring into space. I did not know what to say, so I sat on another cot.

Finally, I said "Hathaway, there are young girls becoming eighteen years old every day that are just as pretty, just as sweet, and just as good as that one." I should have kept my mouth shut, but I did not know any better. He did not say anything, and I soon left.

Some "genius" put his "Dear John Letter" on the company bulletin board for all to see and read. This became a news item, and after mail call the men would make a tour by the company bulletin board. It finally reached the point that the man receiving a "Dear John Letter" was a celebrity. Thank God, I did not write or want a letter. This was no time to think of home.

As we made ready to ship out from the island of Hawaii, there was an attempt to sabotage one of our troop ships. The local Japanese were getting in one of their last licks against us. I remembered the Japanese in California and their attempt to sabotage the West Coast. For good reason the U.S.A. made the decision they did by shipping the local U.S. Japanese off to concentration camps. It was a correct decision at the time for their protection as much as anything else. Some good Japanese got caught up in this, but there was no way of knowing. It was a matter of life or death, and this was no time to play politics.

If the American Japanese try to tell you they were one hundred percent American and for the America as we knew it, they are liars. The navy pilots had pictures showing how the Japanese farmers plowed arrows in their fields pointing toward industrial war factories and airfields. Many Japanese who were not active were sympathetic. Why not? Their blood brothers had destroyed the American fleet at Pearl Harbor. They had destroyed the American Pacific Armed Forces in the Philippines and seemed invincible.

Our American Japanese reaction was understandable. The American Japanese lived in a country that was dominated by another race. I was told that the white race looked down on the American Japanese and these American Japanese in turn helped their Japanese brothers in Japan.

Soon after the war started, some people spread the word that our American Japanese were not always treated well. In the Southern United States, where no Japanese lived, I heard people make statements like, "The Japanese will multiply like rabbits, and overrun this country the same way they did their own country." This talk came from people who had never seen a Japanese. These same people were accusing the American Japanese of doing the very thing that they themselves were doing. The only Japanese people I knew were the boys at Texas A&M College. We treated them the same way as we treated everyone else.

I studied Shinto, the Japanese religion, and other books on

Asiatic thinking, but I learned more from Lieutenant Schrier. He was in Shanghai when the Japanese overran that country. He drank at the same bar with many Japanese officers.

Lieutenant Harold G. Schrier, Easy Company Executive Officer, was next in command under Captain Severance. He and I were tent mates for several months, and I got to know him well. Schrier had a bad case of malaria. He came down with it periodically, and each time I thought he would die.

The only thing that our doctors had for malaria was atabrine tablets, which did little good. For extreme cases the doctors had some Quinine. The countries that produced Quinine were now in Japanese hands. Our medical personnel rationed Quinine.

Once when Schrier was sick and looked as if he were going to die any minute, I rushed to the medical tent and demanded Quinine fast. Doctor Graham was not the type to have someone else do his diagnosing. He let me know quickly that he would take care of Schrier when he could.

What the doctor was doing did not look like a life or death matter, and I insisted that he hurry. That did it. Doctor Graham said he was coming down to the tent, but the first thing he would do would be "whip my ass." Dr. Graham was a large, high-tempered man, and I knew I had my job cut out for me.

He came down soon, and as he neared our tent I took off my jacket and moved out in an open area. He went right by me and took care of Schrier. Thank God for that cooling off time. That man would have been hard to put down and keep down.

When Schrier would have one of these malaria attacks, he would be out of his head and talk about some bad experience he had in the South Pacific. Before coming to our Company, Schrier had a unique job. Our government would put him ashore on enemy-held islands. He would scout the islands. With the Navy's help, he did this before we committed the Marines. Sometimes he went by himself, and at other times he would take a small patrol. Our Air Forces would bomb the island and in the process land a sea plane. They dropped off the patrol while the Japs were taking cover. The Americans would bomb again a few days later and pick up the patrol.

If the patrol was small, it was easy to remain unnoticed. No one traveled off the jungle trail unless someone forced him. So, all Schrier had to do was remain off the trail and away from the occupied areas unless he was alone.

He and his patrol, if there was one, would work their way through the jungle and get close to the enemy's camp. Schrier would

132

count the enemy and make note of their disposition and equipment. He said that he always looked for the Japanese officers he met in Shanghai before the war, but he never saw one. He did not say what he intended to do if he saw one.

Once Schrier landed alone. He happened onto a small native boy. Schrier knew that he could not let the boy go, but he did not want to harm him. He gave the boy some fruit bars and candy. The boy spoke some Pigeon English and so did Schrier. Schrier let the boy wear his helmet and pack. This pleased the boy. The boy stayed with him, and they built a friendship.

On another scouting expedition he had a small patrol, and his top noncommissioned officer was Corporal Snyder. Schrier brought Snyder soon after joining our company and put him in my platoon. Unexpectedly, the patrol walked upon a sick Japanese. They guessed he was left behind when his buddies ran for cover to protect themselves from the bombing and strafing. The Jap knew and the Marines knew that they would be forced to kill him.

The Japanese Army had never suspected that they were being scouted, so this Japanese soldier must die and let his officers think that the natives did it. To keep the Marines' presence on the island a strict secret, Schrier and his patrol could not shoot him, because it would make too much noise and it would not be the natives' way. Schrier tested everyone's knives. They were all dull, but he chose one. Schrier had the rest of the patrol move on down the trail, but ordered Sergeant Snyder to remain as a witness. As the Jap lay in the trail with his helmet off, Schrier walked by him and clubbed the Jap with a rifle butt. The rifle handle broke off and flew into the underbrush, and, of course Snyder had to hunt for it. It could not be left behind. Schrier sawed with the dull knife until he cut the Jap's throat. He said the Jap's eyes almost popped out and then rolled back. At a rest stop in training, I asked Sergeant Snyder about the incident on the island, and he related the same story.

This imprint on Schrier's mind, I am sure, stayed with him until he died some years later. Every time he had a malaria attack, he relived this scene. We used this knife to open our beer. We gave one big jab down through the can and then we drank non-stop through the bottom.

Mental pressure constantly increased on each individual as the Marine combat strike force developed. The addition of large support weapons and technical personnel added reality to the forthcoming struggle. This included battleships, cruisers, and aircraft carriers.

The predicted battle casualties of fifty percent never left our minds. Recognizing and understanding this prediction revealed itself in the eyes and mannerisms of the individual Marines. The pre-battle jitters affected everyone.

Normally, men with more time and training in the Marine Corps readily accepted promotion to a higher rank and more responsibility; now, some refused to accept promotion. Higher rank that brought more money, prestige, and the things thought important in the past had lost their luster.

True leadership qualities began surfacing in others, some with lesser rank. The bond among the men grew tighter, and as a unit I knew we were growing stronger. What a good, deep-down feeling it was to witness and feel this transformation.

The Marines knew this was not a practice run. With pressure like this, most of the veneer that hides the true inner self is gone. Even with all the training, some Marines were at a loss while others made the transition easily. The married men seemed to suffer most. Those affected the greatest were unable to tear their minds from home.

There is nothing good about warfare. It is the absolute evil. However, with the veneer stripped off I could get a good look at myself and the others around me. Once a senior sergeant and I were talking about some high ranking officers whom we were observing. I said that I would bet that there was a thick veneer on some of them. This sergeant knowing the officers in question exceedingly well said, "Yes, and highly polished." The same veneer could be said about sergeants and enlisted men as well.

On 7 January, 1945, we went aboard the USS Missoula (APA-211) and sailed to Honolulu, Oahu T.H. From 13-17 January, we did a belated practice run on the Hawaiian island of Maui. I am not sure who benefitted from this run, but it was not the Marines. Some LCIs (Landing Craft Infantry) could not reach the shore. The practice run was called off when our Marines, in landing with full equipment, went under water and were forced to shed their equipment and swim.

We reported back to Pearl Harbor and observed one of the greatest, if not the greatest, armada ever assembled, congregated at and near Pearl Harbor—ships, ships, ships as far as the eye could see. When given the size of the small island we would attack, it was difficult for me to believe that thousands of Marines and the large armada that escorted them would join forces to take part in a furious battle on an island not much larger than a small city in Texas.

On the docks at Pearl Harbor, Hawaii, the Marine and Navy officers were landing in liberty boats. They quickly gathered in groups, mixing and mingling in an almost panic effort to catch rides to bars, Officer's Clubs, and private parties. This would be their last liberty before each would have a private role to play in a great outdoor stage show.

The Officer's Club overflowed, and space to pick up drinks at the bar hardly existed. A funeral-like atmosphere engulfed me as I walked in. Small groups talking in low tones seemed intent on making the last night of liberty, for many of them, a solemn affair.

We were all having drinks. I searched for anyone to talk warfare and possible problems ahead—anything to stay on a positive train of thought. After all, engaging the enemy in a full scale battle gave meaning to our training. This group had trained a full year for this event. When I could get no response, I paid the orchestra to play Chopin's "Funeral March" and left the mourners to their self-imposed misery.

In the States some of these same officers asked for special time off because they were married and possibly had children. The Japanese were not going to be lenient on them because they had wives, children, girlfriends, and mothers back home. The way I looked at this problem, nothing back home counted for anything. Everything that counted was all in front of us. Let's get on with the God Damn show. The die was cut; there was no turning or looking back. Truly, that is the way I felt.

Chapter 9

TRIP TO THE ISLAND OF IWO JIMA
27 January - 19 February 1945
At Sea Aboard the USS Missoula (APA-211)
LST # 481 (Landing Ship Tanks)

The Combat force sailed from Pearl Harbor, and on February 5, my twenty-third birthday, arrived at Aniwetok Atoll, Marshall Islands. Here we refueled, and six days later we dropped the ship's anchor near the islands of Saipan, Guam, and Tinian, Marshall Islands. We were about 700 miles and four days travel time to our target, Iwo Jima Island.

Here we switched ships. "E" Company, or at least our part, moved from the large troop-ship Missoula to a small, flat-bottom LST #481 (Landing Ship Tanks). The parked amphibious tanks were below the ship's deck. We did a full dress rehearsal for Iwo Jima, only we never hit the beach on Tinian Island.

Someone ordered this "make believe war," and it was almost as tragic as a real war because of the mental pressure that it put on men and officers alike. Small, open-topped amphibious tanks wallowed and bounced around like fishing corks on high-pitching waves. The wind, strong current, and rough coastline churned the waves off Tinian Island into a froth.

The waves drenched us with spray and engulfed us with water on every pitch, toss, and wallow of the slow-moving tank. Bilge pumps working at capacity could not keep up with the flow of water coming into the tank. With each heave and roll of the tank, all Marine combat equipment and the tank's loose equipment shifted and tumbled about. Water rose to almost knee level. If the training exercises off Tinian Island duplicated in any way our landing on Iwo, the Japanese would have an added weapon to their arsenal—seasickness.

Seasick! Even the word causes my stomach to jump. One-half or more of the men's heads hung low, and their eyes rolled back. Their eyes watered like those eyes of a sick calf back home. I could not observe the men long because my vomiting and retching emptied my stomach of everything including green bile and sapped all caring from my mind. If lying down in the water would have stopped all movement, I would gladly have done it. Philip Ward and one other teenager held my head above the water. We had four days yet to go before the landing at Iwo. The Japanese became my second enemy. The prospect of being seasick during landing on Iwo Jima would be my first.

136

Out on deck, aboard the LST, we studied a large plastic model made to scale of Iwo Jima with all the known fortifications. The number and type of fortifications were mind boggling. Navy frogmen sent revised maps to our boat. New near-water fortifications stamped in red ink boggled the mind. I did not bother studying the map after one glance. It was ridiculous to do more than take a glance. The floor after a New Year's Eve party would make more sense.

Closely protected by air and sea power, the 3rd, 4th, and 5th Marine Divisions and their support groups continued moving north into position to launch their attack. We were the Third Platoon of Easy Company, 28th Marines, 5th Marine Division, United States Marine Corps.

The tempo and pressure grew. A Marine on another boat committed suicide by jumping overboard. It was a dark night, and there could be no search. A five-stripe sergeant in Easy Company thought he had an attack of appendicitis. The appendicitis attack was not serious, and they brought the sergeant ashore some time after the landing.

Some Marines were writing letters and almost crying, some were singing songs, and some were staring at the bulkhead in an almost hypnotic trance. It was normal for the Marines to write letters.

The possibility that they might die caused some of them to write special letters, soul-searching letters, to family and friends. They wrote about wrongs they had committed in the past and wanted to make right. Things that dying men might say, they wrote. They left the letters with some of their other personal things on the ship. If the Marine lived, he would possibly destroy the letters. If the enemy killed him, the letters would go to his home. It would be the Marine's way of saying goodbye.

"We attack at dawn." Orders reached us, and clouds closed in as night approached. I walked out on deck, then moved over to the Third Platoon. Katy Midkiff, John Scheperle, Graydon Dyce, Clark Gaylord, and little Ralph Ignatowski sat in a close huddle with the rest of the platoon near by. Katy played the guitar, and they sang western songs, some they knew I liked. Sure, the songs made me think of home, but I came out on deck because I cared for these men, and I wanted them to know it. We all needed assurance.

Loose personal equipment, little comfort and pleasure things may have had value at home. They were valueless to us after tonight. Some musical instruments, games, game boards, and books were worth money, but money had no value where we were going. The men gave these things to the sailors or left them on the boat's deck. Combat is alien to all these distracting, home-loving things. They must be left behind and erased from the mind.

The remaining ties to a civilized world were useless. Most of the men kept at least one picture of a loved one. I refused to carry a picture or any other reminder of home. I did not want my mind occupied by anything except the problem that faced us. This may sound extreme; I can blame it on the predicted fifty percent casualties, which we were expecting.

A persistent thought that raced through my mind was that twenty-five percent estimated casualties eliminated the Lieutenant Platoon Leaders. The fifty percent casualties estimated here in this battle would eliminate all or most of the noncommissioned officers as well.

Platoon Sergeant Thomas, Platoon Guide Sergeant Hansen, and the sergeant squad leaders with their corporal assistants and most of the men joined our little get-together. I will not say these men were the best, but I will say that our Marine Corps or the nation could produce no better. I had confidence, and I hoped I radiated that feeling. I thanked God that I saw it in the eyes of each sergeant.

Easy Company's toilet bowl was the Pacific Ocean. The men chose misery outside rather than go below-deck. The company men camped out on deck with very little protection shielding them from the winter weather. They urinated over the side of the ship, and they hung their butts in a rack above the deck and out over the water. Anybody could watch from below. The watchers hoped there was no change in the wind direction.

Nervous eyes of the very young and some older men will haunt me for the rest of my life. Their eyes were looking, probing, and searching for encouragement. To me, the men were looking for confidence in the eyes of their leaders or searching for cracks in their leader's armor. I checked for nervous mannerisms and unsure eyes. In the very young, the teenagers, I saw what I believed closely related to homesickness. At least, they had the far-away gaze of a young men longing for the comforts of home and their high school friends.

Guitar music continued coming from Sergeant Midkiff's old throw-away guitar. The old guitar was cracked, warped, and wet from the ocean spray. Like many of these men, including Sergeant Midkiff, the guitar was not long for this world. One third (fifteen) of these forty-five men would be dead in a few days.

The cool weather turned to drizzling rain as the night closed in, adding to the misery of those exposed or partially exposed on deck. It's hard to describe the uncomfortable misery of the troops on the open deck except to say, "Rough, wet, and cold, dark iron and not one soft, dry, or warm spot."

138

I opened the Navy officer's quarters and allowed as many as could to work their way inside to sleep on the floor. It was dry and warm inside. The Navy officers said nothing against their coming inside. It was good they did not say anything. I inspected my equipment and hung it on the bulkhead shoulder high. With practice, I made sure I could slip it on in total darkness if an emergency arose.

Noise came from the officer's galley where a group of officers sat around a small two-way radio smoking and drinking coffee—too nervous to sleep. Different segments of the task force remained alert and talked constantly over the radio.

Something caused me to write three short letters to be mailed. They were to my younger cousins, and I told them I thought they should take foreign language in school and be ready for foreign trade after the war. After making a pillow out of my life jacket, I read one or two chapters in a Zane Grey book from the ship's library and went to sleep.

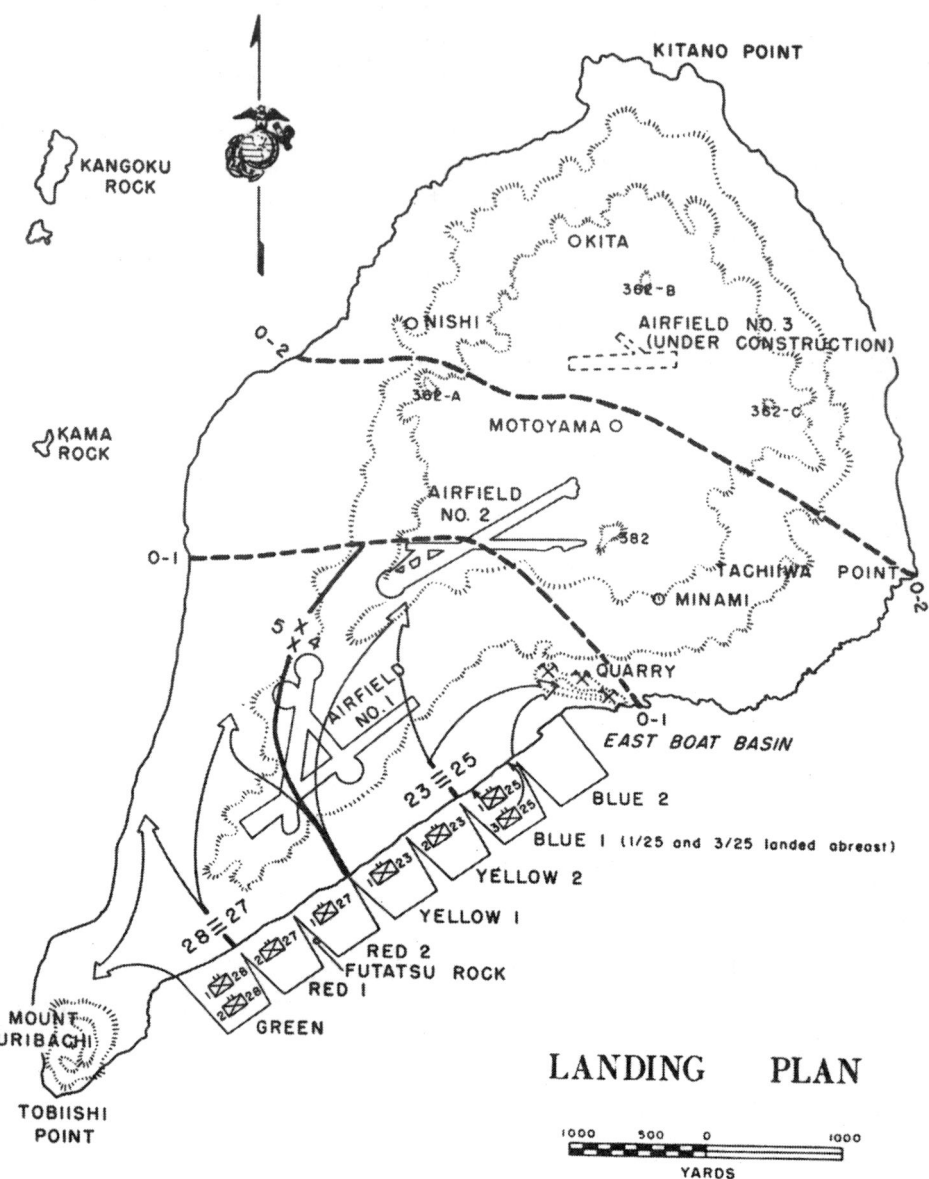

KITANO POINT

KANGOKU ROCK

OKITA

362-B

ONISHI

AIRFIELD NO. 3 (UNDER CONSTRUCTION)

O-2

362-A

MOTOYAMA O

362-C

KAMA ROCK

AIRFIELD NO. 2

382

TACHIIWA POINT

O-1

O MINAMI

O-2

5

AIRFIELD NO. I

QUARRY

O-1

EAST BOAT BASIN

23 ≡ 25

BLUE 2

BLUE I (1/25 and 3/25 landed abreast)

YELLOW 2

28 ≡ 27

YELLOW I

RED 2

FUTATSU ROCK

RED I

MOUNT SURIBACHI

GREEN

TOBIISHI POINT

LANDING PLAN

1000 500 0 1000

YARDS

140

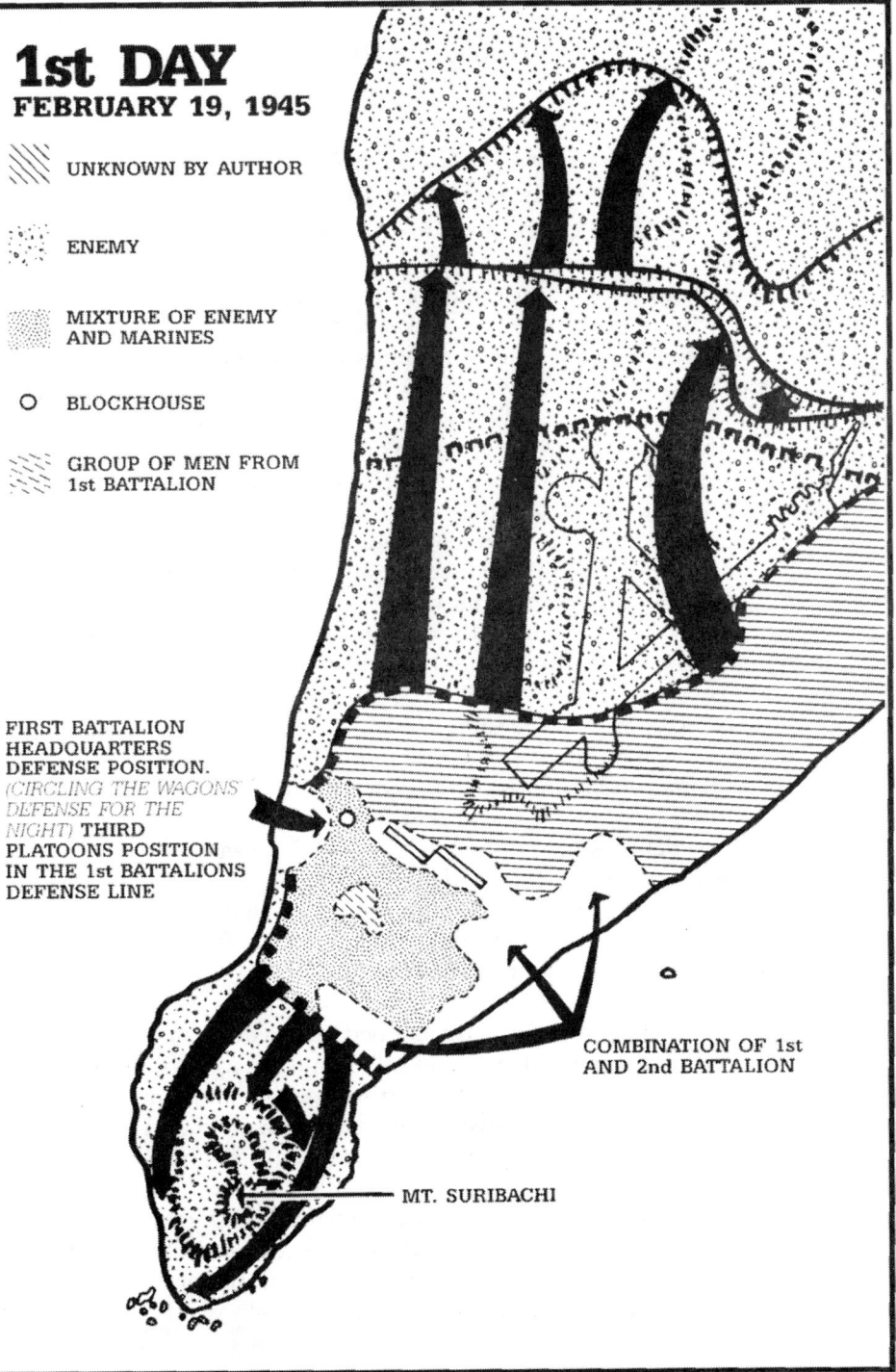

1st DAY
FEBRUARY 19, 1945

⬜ UNKNOWN BY AUTHOR

⬜ ENEMY

⬜ MIXTURE OF ENEMY AND MARINES

○ BLOCKHOUSE

⬜ GROUP OF MEN FROM 1st BATTALION

FIRST BATTALION HEADQUARTERS DEFENSE POSITION. *(CIRCLING THE WAGONS DEFENSE FOR THE NIGHT)* THIRD PLATOONS POSITION IN THE 1st BATTALIONS DEFENSE LINE

COMBINATION OF 1st AND 2nd BATTALION

MT. SURIBACHI

Chapter 10

D-DAY
IWO JIMA ISLAND
February 19, 1945
6:00 O'clock a.m. H-Hour 9:00 a.m.

Mumbling voices, the rattle of coffee cups, and the never-ending squawk of the ship's radio greeted me when I awoke from a short night's sleep. The fleet's intercom radios kept a continuous flow of conversation dealing with every phase as the task force poised for the morning attack.

If the Japanese stayed tuned to our frequency on their radios, they could stay abreast of the events leading up to the impending battle. Radio silence was not necessary for our attacking forces. Every Japanese in the world knew Iwo Jima was our target.

The Japanese were well aware that we were coming. "A Japanese plane is approaching from the north," a speaker on the boat's radio announced. It was possibly a forerunner of many planes, someone thought. The boat's radio continued broadcasting. It sounded the same as a radio broadcast of a baseball game back home.

I could hear over the same radio the orders that sent a young American pilot up to intercept the lone enemy plane. It was obvious the Japanese plane was an unarmed scout plane with cameras and that it would get the hell out of there soon. However, our attacking force could not take the chance, so our pilot flew up to meet the enemy plane.

The American pilot ordered to intercept the Jap plane must have been fresh out of the States and had the high-pitched voice of a very young man. When he received his orders, he said, "Well, here I go, gang." You would have thought he was substituting in a high school football game.

The sky lightened up, and I stepped out on deck. I froze there. In front of me sticking out of the water, silhouetted against the morning sky, stood a volcanic peak. It was so steep it would be almost impossible to climb with combat gear, especially if someone were shooting at us. We knew that climbing a steep mountain might be one of our platoon's jobs.

In Camp Tarawa, Hawaii, we had practiced shooting grappling hooks, with long ropes attached, into the air and over high cliffs. Marines fired the grappling hooks from the tubes of our mortars. Where the hooks landed we were never sure, and if the hooks would hold our

LST with LCT strapped on top -- with assault tanks below deck.

weight was the big question. It looked ridiculous, and several times the hook gave way and came tumbling down on the fallen man. The heavy hook could be deadly; we turned the project down. However, it did confirm that we had a steep mountain to climb, and it made our practice real.

After seeing the steep mountain peak, I worked my way through a crowd to the other side of the landing craft and received a greater shock. The first volcanic peak I saw was a small nondescript island in the Iwo Jima Island group. On this side of the boat the island of Iwo Jima almost jumped into the boat with us. Iwo Jima appeared so close I felt I could just reach out and touch it. Its mountain slopes looked more gentle, but Mount Suribachi looked monstrous in that flat ocean. Coming into sight through a curtain of smoke, dirt flying from exploding shells, and early morning haze, the island appeared like the body of a huge, vicious sea creature thrashing in the water.

Our Navy warships moved in close, bringing deadly accurate fire on the enemy's beach defenses. Our ships exposed and almost beached themselves to cover our pre-landing phase. They showed confidence in their firepower and a disregard for the Japanese weap-

Mt. Suribachi being pounded by shells by ships and planes.

onry. The ships began firing with every weapon. I saw pure arrogance in their self reliance.

While I was standing there, I saw large groups of men kneeling on the deck of our boat and praying. It was a custom, maybe a Navy regulation, that the men should have an opportunity to pray as a group before leaving the ship to go into combat. I was afraid that group praying could take the men's minds off the immediate task and undermine confidence in themselves and their leaders. I chose to let each man do his own praying.

"There are no atheists in a fox hole," Marines told us. Most of the men do their own praying. What would we say in a group prayer: "God-help us kill those sons-of-bitches" It was time to stop thinking about ourselves and quickly start thinking about killing the enemy.

Our enemy did not recognize any rules of warfare. They fought until they died. To win the war, we had to kill them. The old adage "Kill or be Killed" is a poor rule of conduct for combat. With these people Kill! Kill! Kill! is the thought to put permanently in each man's mind until the battle is over.

I was not an evil-minded man. I talked to my Maker continuously in early life, in Marine Corps training, and in combat. Always, I asked for help and for Him to show me the way. I constantly asked for His help in doing my job.

Destroy the enemy and the enemy's war-making ability as quickly as possible - no over-kill, just do the job and move on. I wanted never to think, much less stoop, to pick up a souvenir. The sergeants and I needed to think of the job to be done and the correct weapons to be used, and then think of the men themselves.

When not engaged in battle, the leaders will think of the men first in order to keep them together and under control. Sergeants Thomas, Hansen, Snyder, and Midkiff and Corporals Lane and Lindberg knew that way of thinking and always did it well in training.

At this time, sea sickness stayed on my mind more than the enemy. I managed it, and so I would put off going below-deck to the amphibian tanks until the last minute. This was a real concern of mine. It is hard for me to think straight at the time I am sea sick and soon after. The memory of my sea sickness four days earlier made me wait until all the men were below deck.

"An ideal day for an amphibious operation," a landing craft officer announced to the Marines in the assault waves. A light wind blew from the north and the boat faced into it. The boat was long enough to ride the ocean swells, so we had very little large-boat action. The officer was looking at the situation from his point of view. I was looking at the same picture but from a small, flat-bottomed, open-topped amphibious tank. Deep ocean swells would be monstrous to the small, heavily loaded tank making circles before churning toward the beach.

Thinking on that scale, the water movement grew more threatening by the minute. The bow of the large mother boat would open soon. The opening was like a large mouth that opened sideways. A ramp would extend, at a sharp angle, like a tongue sticking down into the water. Our small tanks could not turn back once they entered the threshold and their noses dipped down. They made me nervous when we went down the steep ramp and plunged into the water.

The tank would drop like a rock, nose first, into the ocean. There it would take on water and flounder. Bilge pumps may not handle that much water, and all or most of our combat gear would be awash in salt water. The Marine command expected us to fight with this equipment,

145

at least initially. Once outside and in the water, the tank would wallow around like a pig in a mud puddle.

Being too concerned about getting ashore with all the men and equipment in shape to fight caused my mind to over react. All I needed to worry about was myself because Sergeant Thomas and Sergeant Hansen would take care of those problems in their tank and Sergeant Midkiff with Corporal Lindberg would take care of it in our tank.

The situation reminded me of a cowboy preparing to ride a bronc horse at a country rodeo using makeshift equipment. The cowboy worried more about mounting the horse without being smashed against the chute. He was concerned that the excited horse might get down in the chute with him before he was ready to ride; also, he was worried about the many other distracting things that were not related to riding a horse. Once he is ready, the cowboy is anxious for the chute to be opened. He is impatient to get in the clear. There, he will put his mind and body to work so that he can do what he came to do.

The top brass and their group of intellectuals tried to think of everything. Someone read that the island had a deadly insect. Yes, I said, "Insect." We are talking about a tick that carried a dreaded disease, Scrub Typhus. It lived on the island. All our clothes, especially our pants, underwear, and socks received a soaking in sulphur water to repel the ticks.

To give us another wonderful thought, they told us that drinking water and a food supply did not naturally exist on the island. We would have only what we carried ashore with us. The weapons and ammunition we carried ashore might be all we would have for a few days. To ease the pain, they passed the word that the battle would last about four days.

"Women on the Island" was the next great secret. Now, women were another matter. In my youth, we were taught to respect women. They gave birth and raised our children. It did not matter what country they came from. However, the women thought to be on the island were not local inhabitants but prostitutes imported with the men, and there were very few women. There were not enough women for all the Marines to have one. I will not write what I told them to do with the women. It was a cruel joke. I told the platoon that if they did not come from hiding, without a weapon and their clothes off, do not hesitate to kill them.

To counteract all the negative thinking, I told the men to forget the Scrub Typhus tick and think about the Japanese; they were far more deadly. If the Japanese could live with the ticks, we could live with the ticks. As for the food and water shortage, I told the men I did not intend

146

to eat or drink for two or three days anyway.

While in training in Hawaii, high command informed us that in past battles there were more casualties from dysentery than from wounds. They designated our group to act as experimental animals. We took sulfa tablets a day or two before combat, and they expected us to continue. You can guess how far that went.

I thought that eating took away from my mental sharpness. Also, I thought that if I did not eat, I would not get dysentery. They taught us in college that drinking water made animals hungry. My best bet was not to eat or drink the first two days. Right or wrong, I came to that conclusion after studying animal nutrition at Texas A&M College and observing my drowsiness after eating. Thinking and talking were over now, and we must get down to the bare facts of killing. With the tank motors running in that enclosed place, the exhaust fumes were overwhelming. I remember thinking that these problems would be welcome if the people running this show would open the bow and let us have some fresh air. Then, they needed to get the hell out of the way and let us do our job.

We waited impatiently, and finally the front doors of the boat opened. Everyone checked quickly to make sure that nothing was buckled on tight. With the shoulder straps attached to the belt and it unbuckled, we could jettison the gear and swim if our tanks were shot out from under us. A fresh breath of air blew through the opening. The ramp lowered and the tanks lumbered down and splashed into the sea. As we cleared the ship, I looked up and saw sailors leaning over the guard rail drinking coffee as if they were in the harbor at San Diego. We soon formed a circle with a group of tanks. Our tanks would stay in the circle until we formed a line and headed for the beach.

Orders from above divided the 3rd Platoon and put us into two tanks. Sergeant Midkiff, Corporal Hagstrom, and Corporal Leader checked the men and equipment of the third squad, and Corporal Lindberg checked the assault squad in our tank. They did this after we cleared the ship. Sergeant Thomas and Sergeant Hansen would do the same with the first and second squads in their tank. We encountered no opposition at this time, so everything went according to plan.

Our great armada of eight battleships, five cruisers, and nine LCI rocket ships with all its power was performing much like some great stage show. The pre-battle picture was the most spectacular scene a man could ever hope to witness. The deafening noise caused a shiver to run down my spine. For two or three hours, every gun in the fleet pounded every inch of the island. Especially the two airfields, the landing beach, and lower slopes of Mount Suribachi caught the brunt of this shelling.

Our ships instantly shut down their firepower. Total silence gripped us. After seconds, U. S. planes struck with rockets, bombs and napalm, a deadly burning oil. Our planes of every description put on a fantastic air show. They finished their strike and moved on. Deadly silence that followed this part of the bombardment sent more chills down my back. Not one opposing weapon fired. Our Navy ships began firing again with all their power.

Despite their size, all ships wanted to get in on the show. Guns, every size and shape, began to fire. Rocket ships released salvo after salvo. Light colored streaks made by the rockets caused the sky to appear half full of flying rockets. Exploding rockets made a sound when they landed that reminded me of a string of firecrackers exploding on the 4th of July, only louder. With the dirt, debris, and smoke rising into the air from exploding shells, Iwo Jima appeared alive. As I mentioned before, it looked like some large animal rising out of the water. The intensity, the loudness of the noise, and the closeness made the experience almost unbelievable.

Then the assault began. A circle of tanks nearest the island

pulled out into a line parallel to and facing the beach. Immediately, a large speed boat pulled into the center of the line. The tanks' motors roared as they guided on the speed boat and the line slowly moved toward the beach. Another line straightened out every five minutes, guiding on a speed boat, and following the preceding line toward shore.

Large American flags, larger than any I had ever seen, fluttered on the fantail of the speed boats. They hung tilted backwards and the lower tip almost touched the water. It left no doubt in anyone's mind who was coming aboard this God-forsaken island. When I was a boy, I remembered seeing pictures of young men carrying flags in the forefront of battle. The reason was now clear; the boat with the flag deeply impressed me.

Heavy Navy shelling on the beach and near shore lifted just above the beach to allow the first waves to land. The minute the first Marine wave landed, they fired a green flair into the air. The battle was on.

Tanks began hitting the beach in waves and discharging Marines. After unloading, the empty tanks would turn and pass back through the advancing lines. They signaled to our tank drivers with their hands and fingers the number of tanks lost in their wave. The first

Tanks moving toward shore.

149

five waves, in our area, landed without a loss on the beach. Their drivers signaled with a closed fist and a wave of their hand. Everything looked great.

With the First Battalion landing first, the Naval firepower and plane activity shifted further in front to allow troops to move forward. When our Navy lifted their firepower, the flanks of the advancing Marines became exposed. Japanese gunners took advantage of the situation.

The heavily fortified base of Mount Suribachi and the mountain itself bristled with a chain of pillboxes, blockhouses, and a beehive of caves. Our First Battalion and part of the Second Battalion's left flank became exposed to this fortified mountain. From each cave spewed automatic weapon's fire.

The exposed right flank of the assault waves came under fire from large Japanese weapons on the north end of the island. Also, heavy weapons on the high ground near the two Japanese airfields began firing into the attacking Marines' right flank.

Our tanks bobbing in the open water were hard to hit. The large enemy weapons reduced their firing at them. Tanks of Marines hitting the shore and stopping became sitting ducks, loaded with ducklings. Enemy weapons increased their firing at the loaded tanks when they stopped and discharged men and equipment.

Tank wave six lost one tank. In what seemed like seconds the beach turned into a junk yard of destroyed tanks. We could not keep count of our tank losses after the sixth wave. This show of destruction took place in front of our eyes. A wave of tanks landed about every five minutes. We were in the twelfth wave and only a few yards from shore.

Mount Suribachi lit up like a Christmas tree with blinking lights. I did not know that when I looked down the barrel of a weapon as it fired at me, I would see a blink of light each time it fired. These blinking lights showed in the daytime. Bullets from Mount Suribachi splattered the water around our tank like hail falling from the sky.

Disbelief showed on the faces of some men as they realized the enemy was trying to kill them with small weapon's fire from that distance. Until this happened, we sat on any elevated spot and some jockeyed for the best standing room to watch this great performance. When the enemy's bullets showered the water, the rain-like splatter reminded us that we were not there for a holiday.

I remember the old saying "ducks on the pond." The ducks were easy to kill on the water; they were not that easy in the air. We looked like ducks on the pond to me. I kept my B.A.R. belt unbuckled so that I could dump my gear fast. The water was cold; I felt it when our tank

Small arms fire from Mr. Suribachi.

dropped into the ocean from the LST. Thinking of having our tank shot out from under us while we were still out in open water was not pleasant. We must get the men on the beach and unloaded safely. That was my primary thought.

We remained exposed, but I began to feel better. I noticed that most of the tanks were still going toward the beach. One tank near by took a direct hit from a larger weapon and disappeared. Other tanks moved over and picked up the men bobbing in the water.

F4U Corsairs used by Marines to support attack.

151

The Japanese had easier and better targets than we were. The beach overflowed with men and equipment. If the Japanese missed hitting the stalled troop-tanks on shore, they still hit targets. I stood there almost hypnotized, knowing we would travel through the exploding mess on the beach.

Our small platoon would land on the extreme left flank of the entire landing force, directly under the high ground surrounding Mount Suribachi. Japanese in their caves and gun positions looked down on us from the mountain. After the shower of enemy bullets around our tank, I had no problem finding room to observe the conditions at our landing area.

Ocean waves offshore remained quiet with no land swells, but I knew the surf could be treacherous. This underwater chain of mountains running from Tokyo Bay south for over 700 miles was nothing but volcanic peaks sticking out of the ocean. We knew this from studying the island's location on maps and the large model on the deck of the ship.

Wreckage on the beach and water's edge forced the tanks to land farther south than originally planed. At our new landing point, the beach turned east and faced the north wind. Nothing slowed the ocean water. The water was deep and the islands were only mountain peaks. Without land swells, the ocean moved with power when it hit the beach.

A lull in the Navy bombardment brought on aircraft strafing, bombing, rockets, and napalm spreading from our aircraft. A Japanese anti-aircraft gun, not far from the beach, began firing at low-level planes, and the Marine Corsair planes attacked it. Three Corsairs dived, one following the other, strafing the enemy's gun position. When the last Marine plane finished strafing and pulled-up, the Japanese quickly manned their weapon and shot him down.

The young Marine pilot tried to gain altitude, possibly to ditch at sea, but apparently he could not. We could see him in the cockpit, and he was trying everything. He was almost in the water and heading straight toward the approaching tanks filled with Marines. At the last second, the pilot turned the plane over on its back and dived it into the water between two waves of tanks. Water exploded into the air, and the pilot and plane were gone, forever. The pilot was probably some young kid fresh from the States. Boys were making great men decisions.

Our Navy ships lifted their shelling again to allow the troops to move further across the island. The volcanic dust began settling near the beach, and the Japanese firepower opened up in full force. In a matter of minutes the water's edge became choked even worse than before with disabled and burning tanks. Equipment of every descrip-

152

tion, parts of equipment, parts of humans, live, dead, and dying lay scattered and in small piles.

Amphibious tractor tanks armed with seventy-five millimeter pack howitzers and machine guns preceded the landing Marines. Most of the heavily armed tractor tanks were unable to climb the steep sand terrace in front of us. They became part of the congestion at the water's edge and on the beach. Because the terrace wall stood in front of them, the tanks lost part of their effective fire power. They did their best under these conditions. They chose positions and supported the close beach assault.

One heavily armored tank sat on our left flank firing into the machine gun nests that fired at us. The nests were built into the large land mass staring down at us near the base of Mount Suribachi. Another armored tank reached the summit in front of us. A large Jap shell disabled it, and the tank remained there burning. A man with a camera crawled to the tank. With the tank for protection, he lay beside the tank taking pictures of the activities on the beach.

At this point over seventy percent, possibly eighty percent, of the landed Marines remained on or near the beach. The battle itself raged only a few yards from shore. Marine-loaded tanks found it hard to land without running over men and equipment. The wounded Marines lying flat on the ground and away from the unloading area remained reasonably safe from incoming tanks and the fire power of the Japanese. Nothing could be done for these seriously wounded Marines. They just died.

Some Marines thought their wounded friends would be evacuated quicker if they carried them to the water's edge. Despite the wounded Marine's condition, the tanks took no Marines off the island the first day. They brought men from the ships to the beach. Sometimes the troop-carrying tanks ran over the dead and a few wounded Marines that were unable to move. They had no choice. It would take too much care and time to evacuate the wounded. We had to have enough Marines and equipment ashore the first day to resist being overrun that night. If we failed, the battle was lost.

Our tank was moving slowly; I guessed we were picking a spot to land. Mount Suribachi, dominating our left front, became more alive with activity, and the farther we moved in that direction the larger the mountain appeared. The enemy activity popped out of, and around, the mountain like pop corn. Above the roaring motor of our tank, we heard screaming shells and loud explosions. In front of us and to our right, puffs of dirt carrying dark splotches flew into the air, and each breath of air was filled with the odor of burning powder and oil.

As we neared the shore, my mind continued to arrange my priorities. The first law of combat is to have the men and equipment ready when called upon to do a job. Our first step upon reaching the beach would be to move the men and equipment out and away from the tanks as quickly as possible. Our second step was to take advantage of any cover but to keep control of the men at all cost. We had to move the platoon as quickly as possible to our rendezvous area.

The Second Battalion had already selected Easy Company to be in reserve. Easy Company selected the Third Platoon to be in reserve of the company. We had to be ready to join the assault if needed. Only in an emergency would our Third Platoon be committed the first day.

The main part of Easy Company was scheduled to land farther down the beach near their rendezvous area. The Third Platoon must land on the extreme left flank of the Marine attacking force. We gave room for the active assault force to move on across the island.

After the assault force moved out, it would leave room for us to make our way north and away from the base of Mount Suribachi. We would move down the beach two hundred yards and then inland a short distance to our rendezvous area. Running that gauntlet looked almost impossible with the Japanese firing at the beach area and the congested inferno building there.

Bent over and working my way through the men, I could still see over the edge of the tank. I moved to the front of the tank so that I could observe the landing area. All eyes followed me.

There was no use speaking because the noise was so great no one could hear. I remember working my way around Sergeant Midkiff, Corporal Lindberg, and Corporal Leader. They received hand signals from me, so they watched closely.

On our left flank and some distance down the beach, the other half of our platoon hit the beach. They were under Sergeant Thomas. I saw their tank pull high up on the beach. Their tank made a safe landing—"high and dry." Our tank hit the beach and stopped. The tank diver refused to run over any dead or wounded and refused to go any further up on the beach. The rear end of our tank remained close to or at the edge of the water. He knew and I knew that if the tank exposed itself much more and stayed on that spot very long, the tank would be knocked out.

As I said before, I had very little or no thought for the wounded; we must keep our maximum strength in the peak of battle. To do this, our dead and wounded must be left unattended. We gave the Third Platoon orders to leave any wounded men alone. If a man went down with wounds, we must let the Corpsman handle it. This included me.

One wounded man will take several men out of action if they try to take care of him. There are times we can carry our wounded with us if we are not fighting. Leaving the dead and wounded sounds cold and callous, but continuing the battle full strength provides added protection to the corpsman and stretcher bearers.

The tractor tank would go no further. That became clear to me. With a hand signal I ordered the squad leaders to get the men and equipment over the side of the tank. I jumped over and crawled clear. Rolls of telephone wire, pack-boards of ammunition, water, and food sailed over the side. As the men jumped over, a large wave engulfed them.

As the big wave swept out to sea, men and equipment went with it. I was never so angry in my life, not at the Japanese but at that damned Marine tank driver. This is what we did not want, and the driver deserved to be shot. Our equipment was lost. The men saved themselves and each other from the ocean, but not from the Japs.

On the beach the men stood, stooped, or lay exhausted, cursing every breath. Weeks on the troopship without proper exercise left them out of shape and added to their frustration. The off-beach sand that we were forced to travel through was made from volcanic ash. Walking in it was much the same as walking in a barrel of marbles or oozing mud. We would sink almost to our knees with each step. The holes left by our feet when we lifted them free of the sand would almost close behind us.

We watched men trying to dig holes in the sand and ash mixture. With each shovel or helmet full they threw out, almost as much mixture would slide back in. It was the same if a man dug a trench and laid down in it. If he then moved around, he would soon be back on top of the ground. I never dug one spoonful for protection while I was on the island. I swore I would not, and I did not!

A young replacement that I did not know was puffing and out of breath. He had traveled a short distance with a pack-board full of ammunition on his back. He looked up at me and said, "Lieutenant, can I leave this here?" With his eyes, he indicated the pack-board. He gasped for breath and thought he could go no further. I told him to go to the point he was designated to go, no matter how long it took; we would need that ammunition. Curse words that he could hear above the roar of exploding shells emphasized what I said.

The very ground the men were cursing became a blessing and life saver to many. The sand and ash material absorbed large shell concussion and shrapnel almost perfectly. Men scattered and in the open had a better chance against the large shells. It was suicide to stay on the beach. The water-packed sand would let the enemy's shells have full effect.

A flat beach area lay to our immediate front as we faced the island. Behind this area, the sandy terrain was like a huge stair-step

Destroyed Japanese ship in our landing area (Green Beach) with Japanese snipers aboard.

coming up from the narrow beach. This step rose sharply fifteen or twenty feet high. On top of the stair step, the ground was flat and had very few depressions. Japanese machine guns had a perfect field of fire shooting down the full length of the large stair-step.

Some First and Second Battalion Marines were slow to move across the enemy's machine gun fire-lane. This situation forced us to travel through a maze of men and equipment on the over-crowded beach. There remained the dead, the dying, piles of unrelated equipment, and landing craft wreckage. The situation was getting worse by the minute. Easy Company had a rendezvous area up the beach. I thought that the quicker the platoon made its way there, the better off we would be.

Some tanks, loaded with Marines, were working their way near and along the beach. They were trying to find a place but were unable to land because of the carnage.

Our Naval ship's heavy shelling shifted and raised to allow the First Battalion (we were the Second Battalion) to finish their dash across the island. The distance was less than one thousand yards. Their objective for the first day was to cut the island in two at its narrow part.

We moved up the beach away from Mount Suribachi, and we caught random firing from all quarters, including the water side. A wrecked enemy ship lay near the beach. I think it was Japanese. The Japanese placed observers and snipers in the ship, and they fired at us. Bert Freedman, a teenager, the youngest in our group, caught a rifle bullet in the foot or lower leg. Clifford Langley, one of our corpsmen, dressed the wound.

The only big problem the Japanese had at this time was choosing targets. John Scheperle became the second sniper target of our platoon. They shot his Browning Automatic Rifle from his hands. Scheperle looked discouraged but was not hurt. He worked his way up to me and brought the non-functioning weapon with him. He had a puzzled look on his face. The weapon could not be fixed.

We could neglect almost anything in the Marine Corps and get a few days in the brig, but neglecting or damaging a weapon deserved almost capital punishment. The Marine Corps treats their weapons like the horse cavalryman treats his horse. A cavalryman takes better care of his horse than he does his wife and children. A horse cavalryman on foot is in bad shape when his patrol rides off. A Marine caught mistreating or without a weapon is equally in bad shape.

Scheperle was a top-flight Marine, and he felt dedicated to take his weapon with him. I told him to throw that rifle down and get another B.A.R from a dead Marine. There were many dead Marines around us. Because of the Marine indoctrination, he evidently wanted to make sure he could throw the weapon away.

Dead Marines were already common sights. This did not bother me as much as a man's leg laying beside me oozing blood into the sand. The foot had a Marine Corps shoe on it. This feeling for slaughtered human beings did not last long. It would surprise most people to know how fast the human race can degenerate to the basic primitive state.

As our Navy shelling lifted, the Japanese resistance increased, and our platoon quickly lost another man; John Fredotovich in the first squad was seriously wounded, and he was one of our B.A.R. men. Snyder was Fredotovich's squad leader, and he ordered Richard Wheeler, the squad's second in command, to see that someone took the automatic weapon. He asked Wheeler to also take Fredotovich's personal watch.

Corporal Wheeler placed the weapon with Louie Adrian, a fine Indian boy and even finer Marine. Wheeler refused to take Fredotovich's watch. High command ordered us not to take personal gear from dead or wounded Marines. This order came from the top command. Wheeler was going to obey that order.

The trouble with that order was that the top command was not fighting the God damn Japanese — we were; the Marine Corps did not furnish watches. They expected us to attack on time and do other things on time. In fact, Sergeant Snyder was wearing one of my watches at that very minute. When he was killed, my watch went to his wife.

It had been almost impossible to buy a watch in the States. None could be bought on either coast of the United States where men were congregated to ship-out. When I went home on leave, I bought two watches alike so that I would have extra parts after one broke. I hoped it was not the same part that broke on the second watch. I did not need to worry about finding a jeweler. In World War II, we had men in the service from every walk of life, and many of them could do or fix almost anything.

In training I told the platoon's sergeants to take watches from the dead and wounded until we had enough. That is the reason Snyder suggested it. Usually the high command's order is a good order. It prevents robbing the dead. Before the battle was over, San Miguel, a young Mexican boy in company headquarters, gathered enough

Traveling through deep sand was difficult.

158

Japanese watches to furnish us all with two apiece.

Even with all the confusion I knew where the rendezvous area was, and I intended to keep complete control of the men until we got there. We continued moving down the beach, but now I had something else to be concerned about. I had sealed my Tommy-gun in a plastic bag to protect it in the landing. It should have been left that way. Firing it through the plastic would be easy.

Active fighting was going on just a few yards from the beach, and I got carried-away and tore off the plastic. From that time forward, I cleaned that weapon almost every time I hit the sand. At times, I cradled it like a baby and landed on my back to keep the weapon clean.

My Thompson Submachine Gun and pack held out of the sand while I'm scouting the situation at the top of the sand stair step.

My tooth brush came in handy as a cleaning tool. It wore out later, and the men brought me Japanese tooth brushes. Maybe I did not have to clean it so often, but I wanted to make sure it would work if I needed it.

159

Our hand grenades came to us in small pasteboard tubes. The adhesive tape that held the cap on the tube was extremely sticky. It was a practice to use this tape to attach grenades to pack straps and other easy-to-reach places. The tape was too sticky for me, and the hand grenades were hard to get ready for use in a hurry. I learned the first few hours to tie a handkerchief around my head to keep the sweat out of my eyes. My ammunition clips and hand grenades I carried in my helmet. I used the strap like a handle on a bucket. This may not look macho (tough), but it worked for me. It kept my clips clean and hand-grenades ready to use.

Marine with flamethrower treading deep sand.

Explosions raked the water's edge with direct hits. Live Marines struggled to get away from the concentrated enemy fire. They moved as quickly as they could, but in only a few minutes they looked exhausted. They carried their heavy equipment in sand more than ankle deep. Their faces had the look of defiance as they trudged standing almost straight up. First, they carried out their mission, and then they searched for protection from the heavy enemy shelling.

We moved along the embankment in leap-frog fashion, following very close to the rhythm of the enemy shells and working our way through the crowded beach. Second Battalion men were piling up behind remnants of the First Battalion. Some First Battalion men had not made the charge across the enemy's machine gun fire lane at the top of the stair step ridge. The enemy had a crowded beach to fire into.

I wish I could name every man in the First Battalion 28th Marines. I believe these Marines were the Marine Corps' finest. Their job was to cut the Island in two in the first few hours of battle, and they did the job.

It was easy to understand why the First and Second Battalion were piling up in front. Besides the fire lane, each ridge had an enemy machine gun trained down its reverse side. The enemy firepower came down the back side of the ridges from an elevated height on the mountain.

We continued traveling along the embankment. Weaving our way through the quagmire of men and equipment, we came to the point where we must climb the embankment and cross the flanking field of fire ourselves.

I propped my Tommy gun up to stay out of the sand and crawled to the top of the steep terrace. I stood on my knees high enough to see everything I needed to see in front of us. We were the reserve and needed to take no chances. If there was a safer place to cross, I wanted to know where it was.

While watching others cross, I noticed that the men had a better chance of avoiding being hit if they staggered themselves and crossed only a few at a time. They needed to cross at an angle away from the enemy's fire. In the loose ash and the angle of enemy's fire, there was little or no ricochet of bullets. We could cross at an angle away from the guns.

I learned this information watching a radioman from another group cross by himself. Our two-way radios with their heavy batteries, flame-throwers with their heavy liquid, and machine guns with their ammunition and water were almost too heavy to work in this sand. The men's feet buried deep in the sand with each step.

As I watched, the large enemy shells landing around us ceased for a minute. I quickly looked down the Japanese firing lane hoping to find a good place for the platoon to across. At this time I saw the radioman rise. His legs started churning up and down as he tried to get moving in the sand.

Quickly the Japanese saw him and began firing. They were raking the ground only a few feet from him, trying to catch him with ricocheting bullets. This is a trick we used when firing on hard ground. We held our breath and thanked God the radioman never stopped or fell. The enemy machine gun or guns gave the radioman the hotfoot all the way across the fire lane, but he made it. Marines who waited and watched along the edge cheered.

Several Japanese big weapons began firing again, and it was hard for me to think of anything except the safety of the men. Loud explosions around us sent geysers of sand into the air. Men were blown into the air. One Marine near us looked like a lifeless rag doll as he momentarily floated in the air. Everyone's nerves were as taut as bow strings; I could see the tension in their eyes.

A loud noise on the beach behind the Third Platoon followed by still another big explosion brought my attention to two large U.S. Navy cargo landing crafts (LSMs). They had rammed ashore on the beach just behind us and quickly unloaded their cargo; yet, they seemed unable to back off the beach.

Enemy shells exploded on and around the unloaded crafts. Our stranded cargo boats lay exposed and perfect targets for the enemy weapons. The enemy exposed their positions but seemed determined to keep firing.

U.S. Navy or Coast Guard crews on the stranded ships were darting out to repair damage, save something from going overboard, or pull some buddy to safety. They quickly darted back trying to protect themselves from the enemy shells. With all their efforts, they seemed unable to dislodge their ships.

These equipment-carrying vessels would normally drop their anchor as far out to sea as they could, let out anchor line, and then ram the shore. The ship's crew would lower the ships bow, and the lowered bow would form a bridge. This would aid the crew in discharging the craft's cargo. The craft would lighten after unloading. Then the ship's crew would, theoretically at least, use the anchor cable as a winch line to aid the vessel's engines in backing off the beach. I am sure this worked at the training base back in California, but it did not work well here. I guess the anchor would be almost under the ship.

These islands were only volcanic mountain peaks sticking out of the water. I suspect the water was too deep for the anchor to attach itself to the ocean floor. The ship's crew could not use the anchor line as a winch line. Heavy ocean swells continued hitting the fantail and driving the crippled ships beach-ward.

Other ships attempting to rescue these stranded crafts became easy targets themselves. The cargo crafts, one after the other, continued to land. Their crews knew they may not have the power to back off the beach; it was the ship's mission and crew's obligation to get the fighting men and equipment ashore.

I tried to keep my mind on our situation and away from the distracting sights and noises that were happening behind us. I knew there was no enemy back there. A much louder explosion with a tearing noise came from a stranded ship. It caused me to take a quick look to the rear again.

A large piece of metal was flying toward me from the explosion aboard the beached boat. I remember quickly judging its speed. Its large size made it appear to travel slowly. The distraction took my attention away from the important things happening in front of us. Enemy shelling had increased in the exact area we must cross, and I thought I could take one quick look before ducking away from the flying piece of metal.

Just in time, Corporal Harold P. Keller jerked me violently down the slope to avoid my being cut in half by that large piece of flying metal. He saved me from sure death. I returned to the beach to retrieve my Tommy gun and let the sergeants know we were moving out and how we would do it.

Forty-nine years later my wife and I met a man who claimed he was on a landing craft that discharged land-tanks on D-Day. Underwater obstacles forced them to land on the east edge of Green Beach. He said that heavy enemy artillery give them "Holy Hell." I laughed and give him a minute by minute description of what took place on his and other crafts unloading there. He stood in amazement. He said that I was the first man he had met that knew what happened. He said that the large explosion was caused by a large barrel tumbling through the air and the explosion from it sent a large piece of metal flying. The man's name was Robert Korczoski from Blue Eyes, Montana.

For protection in front of us, I could see flat no-man's land, and it was pock-marked with bomb craters. The Army and Navy Air Forces bombed and shelled this island heavily for two or three months.

As nearly as I could tell, the bombers accomplished a few things. They denuded the island of almost all vegetation, exposing the enemy's large fortifications and some smaller ones. Shelling done by our planes and ships, also enemy shells, exposed many of the enemy's land mines on the beach but destroyed very few. A direct hit would do it, but that was almost impossible.

New large bombshell craters were excellent temporary cover. I

163

suspected the old craters were traps and that the enemy's mortars and artillery were zeroed in on their coordinates. The Japanese could put one or many shells into the old bomb craters without wasting shells. This they did with regularity and caused many casualties.

Early in the attack, the beach was becoming congested to a point that there was very little movement, and the troop-carrying tanks were finding it difficult to land. All incoming equipment and supplies had, in effect, stopped. The vessels that did make it ashore quickly piled the equipment wherever they could, usually near the waters edge. The men who brought in the equipment would jump in their vehicles and get the hell out of there if they could. This added to the confusion and added

Most bodies were covered with ponchos

further to the mass on the beach.

There was no place else to go with the wounded and dying. The wounded were constantly being led, carried, or aided in some manner to the beach. Psychologically, to leave them lying unattended while they died was not in the basic makeup of the American people. The Japanese knew this, and later I was to learn that they used the trick, time and again, to lure the wounded Marines' friends out of protected areas to try to save the wounded friend.

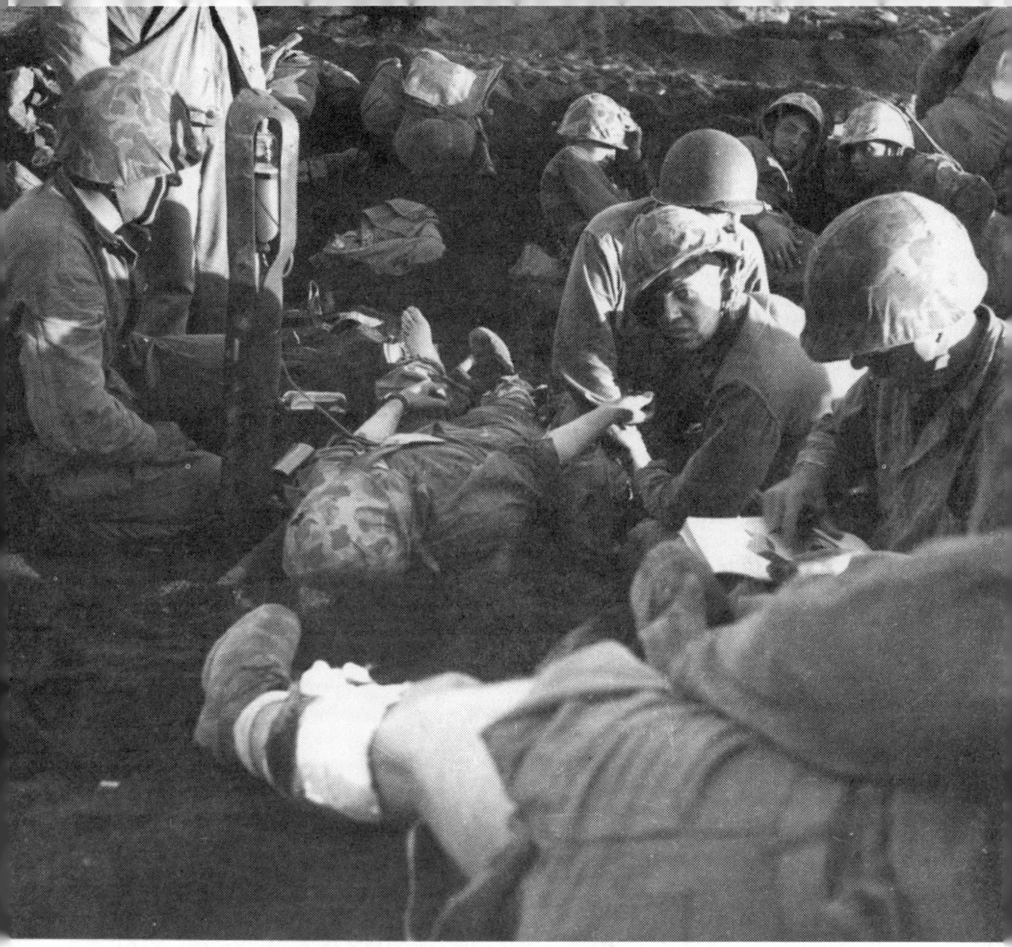

Most of the dead on the beach were lying on the ground where they fell or were stacked like corded wood, and a precious few were covered with ponchos.

Being on the beach was more of a disadvantage than an advantage.

Troop-carrying open top tanks would work their way through the carnage and wreckage to discharge their troops. With the beach congested, I looked for the beach crews. Where were the Sea-Bees, a spe-

cial Naval construction battalion?

The Navy Sea-Bees were a special group. They could build anything: airplane runways, roads. You name it , they could build it. Some of them were old enough to have boys in the Marine Corps. The Sea-Bees took care of the Marines as if the Marines were their little brothers or sons, and the affection went both ways.

The Sea-Bees found no protection on the beach, and they were never able to function. The Marines could not protect themselves, much less the Sea-Bees. On the beach, nothing moved fast.

We soon left our semi-protected area. We crossed the Japanese fire lane at an angle with a few men at a time and crossed without a casualty. A network of Japanese trenches appeared in front of me, and I headed for them on the run. We had studied these on the aerial photographs of the island. I picked these trenches to be one of our signposts on the way to the rendezvous area.

The first trench I jumped into had a live Japanese dressed in a new U.S. Army uniform—not Marine---but Army. He grinned and started talking in perfect English and convinced me quickly that he was one of us. He was an interpreter on loan from the Army. While we waited for everybody to catch up, Corpsman Langley and others spent more time talking to him. The Army Japanese was lucky to live.

Soon we passed a large shell hole, and in it was a group of men huddled in the center. Among them was a Navy Chaplain. The Navy furnished the Marine Corps with doctors, corpsmen and chaplains. I am sincere in saying that there were no better men than these three groups. However, this chaplain was as white as a sheet and appeared to be scared half out of his wits. The only Marines which I saw this white in color were dead and drained of all their blood.

I remembered this chaplain back in training camp. He was big and rough. I saw him manhandle young Marines when he was rough-housing with them. He looked as if he enjoyed it more than normal. It was not good for the younger men to see a scared chaplain cowering in the bottom of a hole. We had too many wounded and dying needing care for this chaplain to be holed up somewhere scared. He should be doing his job, I thought. I am sure he did later because I know that scared people can work.

We did not try to enter the hole. We passed the chaplain and continued to higher ground and the company rendezvous area. Our company headquarters had landed near this area, and our company commander, Captain Dave Severance, First Sergeant John Daskalakis, our "Music" Frank Crowe, our armory sergeants Frank Brown and Jack First, our company clerk Donald Brengartner, possibly San Miguel the runner, and the rest of the Company Headquarters were already there.

Thomas and Hansen soon had the platoon together; also a quick check revealed that we had only lost two wounded, Bert Freedman and John Fredotovitch. John Scheperle, who had his B.A.R. shot from his hands and damaged beyond repair, had found another one in good working condition. The Third Platoon was combat ready.

The Japanese were mostly underground with their concealed small and large machine guns, small and large mortars, artillery, and coastal guns. Most, if not all, of their weapons had mobility. The Japanese could move their weapons out and away from caves and other protected areas. They could open and close large slits in their bunkers. We were briefed that the large weapons were on small train-like tracks. They would fire for a specified length of time and then move back into the protected underground area. The Japanese had all the advantages.

From this observation point we could see the Marines crowded on the beach area, along with those crossing the island. We were perfect targets, but the enemy was busy killing Marines near by. This spot was chosen well for the men in the reserve platoon to watch the action everywhere around them.

We watched as the First Battalion moved in small groups against one pill box and then another. After silencing the enemy's weapons and destroying the enemy inside, they moved on to attack another emplacement. From our vantage point we could see the enemy quickly re-manning their pillboxes and their guns being re-manned again. They were behind the First Battalions front lines. After that, the enemy could fire in any direction.

It was near mid-day, and a few of the men were trying to eat. Thomas, Hansen, and I were checking everything we could while we had the time. Although our company was the reserve of the battalion and our platoon was the reserve of the company, we were sure our platoon would soon be committed to action. There were too many casualties in the First and Second Battalions. We wanted to be ready.

The active Marines were in desperate need of tanks with armor-piercing shells and attached flame-throwers. They desperately needed, extra fuel for their man-carried flame throwers, demolitions, shaped charges, and thermite grenades. Some of these the Marines had carried ashore with them, but they quickly used these expendable weapons. We needed these large and effective weapons but were unable to get them because of the wrecked vehicles and piles of unrelated equipment that were jamming the beach.

We soon learned that we were fighting an enemy with a five-foot coat of concrete armor protecting them. Also, their armor protected

168

them from their own weapons that explode on top of the ground. The enemy's firepower rained down in a deadly curtain to pin down Marines who might be making headway in destroying some of the defenses. Marine steadfastness to the point of suicide made this encounter something the survivors will think about for years.

The Japanese had years to familiarize themselves with the small allotted ground that we were fighting on. They also had months of detailed preparation by their General Kuribayashi, a mastermind of detail.

The First Battalion, 28th Marines was almost racing across the island killing everything on top of the ground and knocking out active pillboxes one after another. From the high vantage point and only a few yards away, we could see the life and death struggle taking place. We watched Marine squads, fire teams, and great individual effort. What a sight to see!

We watched wave after wave of Marines bypass many inactive blockhouses and pillboxes only to see Japanese open up and mow-down new waves of Marines. Japanese replacement crews quickly re-manned the guns that the Marines had knocked out. The enemy replacements appeared to come from small caves or protected areas that joined the knocked-out enemy position. We watched this, but we had no way of warning the group going on by or the group following.

I was told beforehand that the Japanese did this, but it was hard to believe they could take so much punishment and be back in operation that fast. Some of us remained standing to see better, as we watched the brutal life and death struggle.

While we stood there, some Higgens boats landed on the beach. Near us, the bow of one boat went down onto the beach sand and Marines charged out on the beach. Their charge slowed to a walk as the deep sand took its toll of their energy. They sluggishly put one foot in front of the other and climbed the terrace. The thought crossed my mind that they looked like a family carrying the beach equipment to the car in California. They were not in danger. The Japanese had all the targets they could handle.

Quickly, I looked back at the First Battalion men crossing the island. Each consecutive wave repeated almost the same battle as the wave before. Knocked-out Japanese positions were re-manned. We watched as two new enemy positions began firing. The first waves of Marines had bypassed these positions because they were not active.

Because Marines were being shot in the back by bypassed well and wounded Japanese that were pretending to be dead, word was passed, and the dead Japanese on top of the ground were targeted time

169

and again as each new group passed over. We watched as each new group would shoot the same dead Japanese so many times that I thought that only their clothes held them together. Soon, a mixture of dead, wounded, and live Japanese and Marines lay scattered across the island. The situation was a hodgepodge of death, destruction, and confusion for those who followed.

Still in reserve, Easy Company had to continue to form and wait its turn. We would not be committed to the fight unless someone was in serious trouble or the Marines needed a counter attack. Because the Third Platoon landed farther away from the company area, headquarters expected us to be last to arrive at the rendezvous area. Instead we were first. The First and Second platoons were having a much harder time landing than we did. They were in the congested area.

Lieutenant Ed Pennell and Sergeant McGarvey of the Second Platoon and Lieutenant George Stoddard and Sergeant Paljavcsick of the First Platoon were having trouble landing their platoons in the right spot, or for that matter, landing at all.*** Every minute of delay meant more congestion on and near the beach. For the present nothing moved in any direction.

To make matters worse, a large part of the First Battalion made it across the island. They left patches of Marines fighting their own small battles with by-passed enemy. The large group of First Battalion Marines that made it across the Island were cut off from the rest of the Marines on the island. They radioed back that they had wounded and they had no corpsmen.

Captain Severance sent for me, and I took Sergeant Thomas with me. He ordered the Third Platoon to cross the island to join up with and support the First Battalion. It seemed unusual that the higher command would order a lone platoon from another battalion to do such a thing, but that was the order. I suspected the company was ordered to do the job and that only the Third Platoon was ready. This was a tall order considering the Third Platoon would be acting alone. I do not know what orders were given to Captain Severance, but that was the order he gave the Third Platoon, so we moved out.

We would be fighting every inch of the way, I thought. Earlier, I had told Sergeant Thomas to have the platoon drop all gear except weapons and ammunition. It had become clear to me that there would be plenty of everything lying on the ground on the island. Any extra weight would be tiring and in the way. We could take the essentials from the dead and seriously wounded men. This was a life and death struggle, and comfort was not given a thought.

I passed the word to "Mount Up." We would not give these

170

Cowboy and Horse Cavalry orders long, because the noise was getting too great. The Third Platoon moved out running in what I called a column of bunches with me in the lead. We did not go far before I saw a loose canteen lying on the ground. I scooped it up, unscrewed the top, and tried to take a drink but remembered that I did not intend to take one. I threw it to the next man, and he passed it on. It was mentioned before, natural fresh water did not exist on this island. That one swallow of water, if I got it, would be the only drink of water I intended to take in the first three days.

Running and exposing ourselves, in a chain of four squads, we drew a hail of lead, sand, and some ricocheting bullets that buzzed around us. We were now in an area of cropped vegetation, and the bullets would ricochet more than they would in the pure volcanic ash and sand. We hit the deck, and I saw quickly that correct decisions must be made fast. This was not the time to send out scouts. To accomplish this impossible mission, I knew I must go first and make decisions on the spot.

We could hear the exchange of gun fire, and the machine gun stopped firing at us; someone helped us by attacking it. I gave the hand signal to move out. The platoon moved to one side and let stretcher-bearers pass. A large man lay on the stretcher. The wounded man yelled, "Hey! Wells, what do you want me to tell your dancing girl?" It was Captain Dwayne E. Mears. Some of us called him Bo Bo Mears. He and I had dated girl friends. Bo Bo thought he was on his way home.

Cracking of rifle fire, rattling of machine gun fire, and the sound of exploding artillery shells filled the air around us. Loud and earth-shaking explosions just to our rear caused me to turn and see what I already knew. Bo Bo and his stretcher bearers were blown to bits by one or more large shells. Bo Bo was a good man and a friend of mine, and now, he was gone. As I said before, the Japanese gun emplacements that the First Battalion thought were destroyed were not. We watched the enemy re-man them. The Japanese "dead" were not always dead, and they would quickly shoot Marines in the back after the Marines had passed.

We must kill, even re-kill, every Japanese to make sure. That is easy to say but hard to do at first. After watching the First Battalion, I knew that everything must be destroyed, because the enemy would not give an inch. Our sergeants saw it, and I hoped the men did. I thought, if it is not a Marine, kill it; and if there is enough cover to hold a Jap, destroy it.

We continued to move across the island. I crossed the open

171

ground alone and quickly. This gave me a slight advantage in crossing. When I ran across open areas, I never knew precisely what I was getting into, but the platoon was backing me. Finding a protected place from which to scout the area was a problem. Total concealment was impossible; Japanese were everywhere. The enemy on the high ground fired down the reverse side of ridges that looked as if they were places of protection. We had the feeling that we were exposed and always watched.

We found very few protected areas, and I was skeptical of the ones we did find. The platoon continued moving into a brush area when abruptly we found staggered Japanese antitank ditches running parallel to our line of movement. First Battalion men partially filled the ditches, some of them seriously wounded.

The anti-tank ditches were fifteen feet or more wide and three to six feet deep. In these ditches the protection was almost too good. We did not trust them. I thought the enemy was herding us like cattle into these traps. Enemy artillery pounding the earth only a few feet away, threw dirt over us as we moved. I expected any minute for the enemy artillery to zero in on the ditches.

The First Battalion Marines moved against the side of the ditches as we passed through. We had no choice but to move down the ditches stooped over and in single-file. The anti-tank ditches were staggered with a connecting crawl-through trench. When we reached the end, I entered the shallow connecting trench on hands and knees and crawled to the next anti-tank ditch. The platoon followed in squads—First, Second, Third, and Assault squad. Sergeant Hansen brought up the rear and saw that there were no stragglers.

Wounded Marines lay unattended in the ditch. Some asked the men for help as we passed. None of them spoke to me; they knew it would do them no good. The platoon left them lying; we had a job to do. We passed through the other ditch in the same manner. More wounded lay there, some in pitiful condition. Combat Marines can lose a war tending to the wounded, dying, and dead. We continued toward the other side of the island.

More than once I crossed a wide stretch of open ground where it was hard to communicate back to Sergeant Thomas. I swore then that if I were responsible for men in combat again, they would know a full sign language. My Horse Cavalry commands that I used in training would not work here. The cavalry commands were too long and could not be heard above the roar of combat. When crossing the open ground, I needed someone with me to send back with instructions.

"Let me work with you, Lieutenant," said Donald Ruhl, who came up from the Second Squad and volunteered to be our platoon runner. We needed a runner only occasionally, but at that time we needed one badly. Ruhl had been our problem man in training and the man who, two or three months before this battle, said he was tired of training and wanted to fight. Ruhl wanted action. He soon got it.

Machine gun fire sprayed us as we approached a heavily fortified area. The enemy machine gunner was trying to hit me. The enemy loved killing leaders. The sand and bullets were flying all around me. I quickly dived into a small hole and buried my right knee into the open stomach of a freshly killed Jap. If I could have crawled under him, I would have. There was just enough room for the two of us.

He had not had his early morning bowel movement, and that is where my right knee landed. The odor was almost more than I could stand. I stayed in there with the dead Japanese until the bullets and sand quit flying over me. Rapid bursts came from the enemy machine gun. Between bursts, I got a look and saw the enemy gunner firing from a partially destroyed pill box. on our deep left front. I knew we had to outflank the gun or run the gauntlet, and we would be running almost at him. At that minute, I did not know how we were going to do it. That decision did not have to be made.

Extra loud explosions were coming toward us, walking one shell after another approaching and crossing our right front. Japanese artillery or large mortar shells were doing their best to hamper the movement of two Marine Corps' tanks coming to our rescue.

The Marines soon learned that the Japs fired their big weapons at the tanks, and there was a mad rush for extra cover when the tanks appear. Marines, working near the tanks, were often hit by shells or from shrapnel ricocheting off our own tanks. Bags filled with sand covered the top of the tanks. This prevented the enemy shells from doing extra damage to the tank and absorbed some of the shrapnel.

Most of the Japanese defense remained partially underground, and the dirt on top and around the sides of their emplacements grew plants. This made the enemy hard to see. With limited visibility, the tank crews had a hard time finding the enemy. The Japanese knew that if they could keep outside Marines from pointing out targets or talking over the outside tank phone, the tanks would be almost blind.

Two tanks lumbered into view led by two Marines. The Marines quickly pointed out the machine gun nest in the partially destroyed pillbox. Both tanks acted quickly and destroyed the machine gun nest and continued pounding until little was left of the pillbox. I learned to love those tanks and the Marines brave enough to expose themselves to direct the tanks.

Small groups of First Battalion Marines were fighting all around us. Each group had its own small battle going. Dead, dying, and wounded lay everywhere. Most of the exposed Japanese were dead.

Thomas and the First Squad set up a protective line of fire, and I ran across open areas looking everywhere. I dived into the brush on the other side, scouted it out, and then signaled to the others to cross a few at a time. With Ruhl and me out in front, we moved rapidly across the island.

We arrived at an open area that was cleaned of all trash and anything else that might afford protection. In the center of the clearing loomed a shallow trench that crossed the deadly looking area. A tail section of a Japanese airplane lay in the trench. We had to cross the area here because, going around would take too much time. The airplane tail looked as if it would be perfect protection while crossing the open area. We could see where the Japanese were using it. One or more Jap trails led to the end facing us. It looked too perfect.

174

I decided not to use it, but instead to cross the area a few at a time. I would cross first, check it out, and on my signal, Thomas would send the men across a few at a time. I ran across the open area, expecting to be shot at any minute, and jumped into the trench at the far end of the airplane tail section. Only by the grace of God did I miss a trip wire on a mine that would have blown me to pieces. The tail section was a large booby trap.

Ruhl and the first two or three men came running when I gave the signal. I prevented them from setting off a booby trap explosive by bodily catching the men one after another in midair and throwing them to the other side of the trench. These men soon made a line to force the rest of the platoon to go around the booby trap area.

We did not like leaving that booby trap without being detonating, but we had too many things to do and too many things to think about. Sergeant Hansen flagged it with a piece of rag and left it.

We were on the other side of the clearing where the brush grew thicker and then became open again. In front of us we could see a large blockhouse three or four times larger than anything else we had seen so far. It was at least ten or twelve feet high and was camouflaged by soil and plant growth on the side facing us. There was open bare ground on the right side as we faced it. Someone had intentionally cleared it of plant growth.

We saw movement in the clearing next to the block house, and I recognized it as Marines. Thomas and Hansen scattered the Platoon and kept them out of sight. Ruhl and I began making our way over to the isolated Marines.

Awesome and *bone chilling* are the words that come to mind when I think of exposing Ruhl and myself to the presence and mercy of this monstrous Japanese blockhouse. In the open we began running stooped over; we quickly made our way to the Marines.

A huge, closed concrete door about four feet wide and five feet tall stood exposed on the side we were approaching. The brush was cleared away in front of the door and for some distance straight out and away from the door. I saw no trails or wheeled tracks leading to the door. It was puzzling.

Two wounded Marines lay on the ground in front of the closed blockhouse door. They had a young Second Lieutenant playing nursemaid. The blockhouse was inactive. I told the Marine lieutenant we would move his men and that our corpsmen would treat them. He said; "You will not move my men."

I looked at them quietly lying there. The two young men looked at me with a questioning look in their eyes but noncommittal. I remember thinking what fine-looking young men they were. They were both shot through the chest more than once. The Marines knew and we knew that they were dead men. My heart breaks now, thinking about them.

There was no way on God's green earth we could save them. Even if we thought we could save them, we had to move them. We must leave nothing standing. We observed what happened when the Marines bypassed the inactive blockhouses. None of these seriously wounded would have much chance of living. The time and effort to save them would make it impossible to fight a war. It is a hard decision at first, but it must be made.

I told the lieutenant we would move the men away from the door or we would blow them away. I ordered Rhul to tell our demolition man, Clarence R. Hipp, to prepare a charge to blow the door in and Robert Goode and Charles Lindberg to be ready with flame throwers.

The concrete door on the large block house was the only weak spot I could see. The Marine rifle platoons had two weapons that could breach these concrete doors. These weapons were shaped charges and bazookas; also possibly a third would work, a satchel charge if placed just right and reinforced with rock or dirt.

The young Second Lieutenant contacted Captain Wilkins, commander of Able Company, First Battalion, 28th Marines. I do not know what the lieutenant told Captain Wilkins, but he told me over the radio not to blow the blockhouse. Our platoon was not under Captain Wilkins, and I told him, clearly, we were going to blow the blockhouse.

We had already seen what could happen by by passing them. Surely he saw that too. Before Hipp could get his charge set, orders came over the radio from my captain, Dave Severance. Severance said in a very authoritative voice that Captain Wilkins thought it was some kind of storage place and for me to bypass it.

I was not trying to be a smart-ass, but I saw earlier that we could not run this war dug in some distance away. This war must be run on the spot. Many of these Japanese strong points stayed inactive until the Marines passed them.

To the Marines who were facing a newly opened emplacement, it was almost impossible to fire at it without hitting Marines who had just passed it.

How Captain Wilkins made that decision without ever looking at the block house, I do not know. Maybe he took the word of his lieutenant. The large door may have fooled everyone.

I do not know what the First Battalion lieutenant was doing besides baby-sitting the two dying men. We had a war to fight. Our platoon moved on.

We bypassed the block house, went through some brush, and were soon in the First Battalion Headquarters area. Lieutenant Wesley Bates was the first officer I saw. He was a friend of mine from Marine Parachute days. Bates had a bullet hole through his arm just above the wrist, and no one had dressed it. Clifford Langley, our corpsman, doctored and bandaged his arm.

There was a lull in the fighting. It was getting late in the day, and the First Battalion men who had made it across were preparing for the night's defense. They cleaned and tested their weapons by firing them out toward the sea. We thought this an excellent idea, and Thomas ordered the platoon to do the same. I cleaned my Tommy gun, fired a few rounds seaward, and reloaded with my large clip of ammunition.

Part of the First Battalion and the Third Platoon of Easy Company, Second Battalion were isolated from the rest of the Marines. We were also isolated from any support weapons that might be on the island or at sea. I mentioned that the Third Platoon was from the Second Battalion because it is unusual for a unit that small to be fighting with another Battalion. Our small platoon was the only one from the Second Battalion.

We formed a perimeter defense, a half circle with the ends at the beach. The Marines used this defense often in the South Pacific. In Officers School, we called this type of defense "circling the wagons."

Loud explosions sounded, and they had the rhythm of artillery. It came from the direction we had just passed through. A company runner approached with the message that they were unable to close the defense. There was an open section near the midway point.

"A large unknown type field gun is firing through the doors of a monstrous blockhouse," the breathless runner blurted out. It was firing at small groups of First Battalion Marines that were not able to reach the coast and were trying to set their own defense for the night. It was firing through a large door.

The runner said that one of their Marine lieutenants and a few men attacked the blockhouse soon after it opened a big door and began firing. The enemy evidently called their own artillery down on the blockhouse. Consequently, on top of the ground, everybody was a target, which included the lieutenant's platoon.

Large Japanese shells were exploding on and around the blockhouse with no harm to the Japs inside but a total hell to the Marines exposed and lying on top of the ground outside and around the blockhouse.

These Japanese artillery shells were coming from the north end of the island, and the artillery fire was precise. Not an inch of the area on top of or around the blockhouse was left untouched. The bone-chilling noise caused us to give it our respect.

Exploding shells filled the sky with dirt, brush, debris, and whistling shrapnel. Only being near an exploding volcano would strike more fear.

The officer in charge ordered me to report to him. I took Thomas with me and left Hansen with the platoon checking out their weapons. The Officer gave the Third Platoon orders to move into the area being shelled and close the defense gap. This enemy shelling had prevented the First Battalion from closing it. Now, they expected us to move directly into that deadly fire.

Enemy artillery shells fell with terrifying accuracy. We must move forty-three men and one officer directly into the heavy shelling and make contact with men that we may not know to complete the half circle defense already set in. Shallow drainage ditches faced us in an off-beach area of shredded scrub wood. We had very little daylight left.

Japanese were underground everywhere, and we guessed they would be coming out all night. They had us out numbered and out gunned. First Battalion defense, which included us, could not receive help from the rest of the Marine Corps, Navy, Air Forces, or anyone else. We were alone, without large weapons.

I knew only one thing to do and that was to move the platoon in the direction of the shelling and hope that an opportunity would present itself. The platoon quickly reached the area, and I saw a small drainage ditch leading into the space being pulverized by the enemy shells. This had to be the area they expected us to occupy.

In single-file, we dropped down and crawled up the ditch a short way with shells bursting on each side. I knew one thing. While the shelling was going on, there would be no Japanese moving around and coming through the defense line in that area.

With me leading, we continued to crawl, hoping there would be a change. As quickly as the siege started, it lifted and began to pound the First Battalion headquarters area near the beach, the area we had just left. In some primitive way I enjoyed the First Battalion command post taking that shelling. After all, they had ordered us into the area that had been receiving it.

Do not get me wrong. The officers and men of the First Battalion had suffered unbelievably. If I had been in the commanding officer's shoes and he in mine, I would have ordered him to do the same thing he ordered me to do. During the first day of battle, the First Battalion suffered more casualties than any other battalion in the 28th regiment, and, I suspect, any other Marine battalion on the island.

We quickly closed the gap in the perimeter defense, and our men dug-in. We tied ourselves into the half circle defense line facing the Marines and the side of the island we had landed on earlier. Our platoon was near the center of the defense circle and facing the large blockhouse that the First Battalion captain ordered me to bypass and talked my captain into backing him up. The huge block house we had wanted to destroy was now a death machine for the First Battalion men.

Now that the Japanese artillery shifted to the beach area, the Marine lieutenant, who was attacking the block house, began another attack. I am sure he is the one the runner talked about. I recognized the lieutenant. He and I were not good friends. We were more like cross-town rivals. I guessed he was a good man, but we cannot always tell from outward appearance or actions in training.

The big doors had evidently closed during the artillery bombardment, and now the attacking Marines swarmed toward the top of the blockhouse. They were on one side and away from the two doors. Apparently they saw something on top that I did not see before.

The lieutenant, in plain sight, was urging them on. I could not believe what I was seeing. The men were attacking the blockhouse with nothing but hand weapons. Abruptly their attack came to a halt. On top of the block house I saw what looked like an enemy machine gun firing into the Marines. I do not know how many Marines that Jap machine gun killed or wounded.

Thomas and Hansen took charge of setting up our platoon defense. The sides of the drainage ditch that we used to enter this area aided us. It left a ridge to lie behind while facing the blockhouse and the part of the island we had just crossed. On our far left, our First Squad crossed another drainage ditch before connecting with the First Battalion. Immediately in front of our lines and bordering the drainage ditch on our left flank was waist-high brush.

Earlier, on my command, we had left our food, entrenching tools, blankets, and some ponchos on the other side of the island. I thought it was excess weight. Now, cold evening air moved across the island. The platoon began working hard digging with their helmets and hands to make a spot for the night. Our job was to complete the defense line. The Japanese could attack any minute.

While our defense was setting up, Donald Ruhl and I scouted out the brush in front of our lines. We made our way over to the block house door that had opened earlier and given the Marines Holy Hell with the large weapon they had inside. This door opened on the opposite side from the door by which the wounded men lay earlier. I should have guessed, but I did not know this door existed.

If the door flew open again, Rhul and I would be in trouble unless we acted fast. We moved close to the door, so that if it opened we could step to one side and be out of the line of fire. The enemy machine gun on top either could not fire in our direction, or the crew had all they could take care of in front of them.

I felt confident with my freshly cleaned and test-fired Tommy gun with the large clip of ammunition. Being armed with a Garand rifle and a fixed bayonet made Ruhl and me look like David fighting Goliath as we approached the blockhouse.

Late evening light hung in the sky as we watched the blockhouse and everything around us. One man in the First Battalion platoon raced up the side of the blockhouse and placed a shaped-charge. This explosive concentrated the power into a straight line and could penetrate almost anything. The shaped charge went off with a loud explosion and shot a hole through the concrete blockhouse, but that was all. It was designed to shoot a hole through almost any type of armor. That included five or six feet of reinforced concrete. For a moment the attacking platoon seemed stunned, as if they expected more to happen. The shaped-charge did what it was designed to do, no more.

Again, the Japanese machine gun on top of the bunker began firing and mowing down everything on that side. They had to silence it. These poor men had fought hard all day, killing and being killed. They fought until the few survivors were totally exhausted.

Ruhl and I stood and watched this concentrated battle. We were only a few yards from the life and death struggle. We could do this and feel fairly safe while doing it. If the Japanese in that area and the brush on our left could help their heavily fortified friends, they did not show it. Ruhl and I wanted to help, but the First Battalion had the show. We could only watch and wait.

Rapid firing from the roof of the blockhouse swept Marines away like toy soldiers in front of a mother's broom. The Marines moved to the far-side flanking position and silenced the machine gun again. The blockhouse was still a hot potato, and everything had to be done over. This time the lieutenant in charge of the attacking platoon carried a thermite grenade to the top and in some way pushed it down and into the blockhouse. The Marine weapons personnel claimed that this grenade could burn through concrete.

Only seconds after the thermite grenade dropped in, things started happening. Ruhl and I were standing by the big concrete door when suddenly the door flew open and a billow of dense white smoke came out. At the bottom of the smoke I saw little Japanese feet. The

180

Japanese were bent over. Each man was holding onto a piece of equipment of the man in front of him. They were that close together, and as they turned to follow the smoke, I could see their loose hands. At least two or three were carrying hand grenades but no rifles or other weapons. At point-blank-range, I emptied the thirty-round clip from my Thompson submachine gun.

There were easily six or eight Japanese on the ground and only one trying to get up. The dense smoke from the hot grenade emptied the block house. My Thompson submachine gun had tremendous knock down and killing power. Its forty five caliber lead slugs would blow a hole in a man we could put our fist through. This action happened so fast I am not sure Ruhl got off a single round; he may have. Rhul ran over to bayonet the Japanese trying to get up.

From the brush on our left and some distance away, I saw an enemy hand grenade sailing through the air toward the two of us. It was getting dark, but I easily saw it as it arched in the air. It was coming down near where Rhul and I had been standing. It sailed a little more toward Rhul and in the direction of the downed Japanese. With only a few steps, I was out of its range. I yelled at Ruhl to watch out for the Japanese hand grenade and ran toward the place where the hand grenade came from. If I switched to the fresh clip of ammunition, I do not remember.

We knew the Jap did not have a rifle, or he would have shot us. It was getting darker by the second, and I was running low through the brush trying to skyline him. If he threw another grenade, it would direct me to him.

I moved one way and then another dodging brush and trying to keep my eye on the sky while I looked for him. I was kicking brush as I went through it, hoping I could excite him into throwing another hand grenade. To have had that much confidence in flushing this Jap out, I must have loaded my Tommy gun. Doing hand-to-hand combat was not my way unless I ran out of weapons. Killing the other Japs had fired me up, and I was intent on killing this man. He had dealt himself into this card game.

The platoon had a ringside seat to this two-man show. Ruhl bayoneted the cripple and inspected the others. The Jap or Japs that I was chasing never showed themselves or threw another hand grenade. If I passed near him, and I must have, he did not show himself.

It was almost too dark to see now. To me, coming back out of that brush was more dangerous than going in. Now, I had to look behind me, on both sides, in front, and in the air. I worked my way through the brush, but that Jap never let me know where he was.

181

Ruhl was in a hand-to-hand struggle with somebody when I made my way back to the blockhouse. It turned out to be another Marine. They were fighting over Ruhl's rifle with the bayonet on it. The man was out of his mind, and he wanted to mutilate the bodies on the ground. He said they had killed one of his buddies. When I walked up, he looked at me and let Ruhl have the rifle. Ruhl said the Japanese were dead, and he and I made our way back to the defense perimeter.

The Platoon watched this show as they dug in for the night. Sergeant Thomas and Sergeant Hansen had the night defenses set up and gave me the report. Sergeant Snyder and the First Squad would protect our left flank. Sergeant Midkiff would protect our right flank with the Third Squad. Corporal Lane and the Second Squad stayed in reserve with Corporal Lindberg and the Assault Squad. Navy Corpsmen John H. Bradley and Clifford R. Langley stayed near the middle of our small defense position. Except for Pfc. John J. Fredotovitch and Pfc. Bert M. Freedman, who were wounded on the beach, our platoon was still intact and in good shape for the night's defense.

OUR DEFENSE

1st Squad on left flank	3rd Squad on right flank
Sergeant Howard M. Snyder	Sergeant Kenneth D. Midkiff
Corporal Harold P. Keller	Corporal James C. Hagstrom
Corporal Edward J. Romero,Jr.	Corporal Robert A. Leader
Corporal Richard J. Wheeler	Pfc. Graydon W. Dyce
Pfc. Louie B. Adrian	Pfc. Leo J. Rozek
Pfc. Phillip E. Christman	Pvt. Kenneth S. Espenes
Pfc. Edward S. Kurelik	Pvt. Clarke L. Gaylord
Pfc. James A. Robeson	Pvt. Ralph A. Ignatowski
Pfc.Ramond A. Strahm	Pvt. John G. Scheperle
	Pvt. Charles E. Schott

Lieutenant John K. Wells
Platoon Leader
Platoon Sergeant Earnest I. Thomas
Runner Pfc. Donald J. Ruhl

ASSAULT SQUAD
Corporal Charls W. Lindberg
Pfc. John H. Eller
Pfc. Clarence H. Garrett
Pfc. Clarence R. Hipp

Pfc. William J. McNulty
Pfc. James R. Michels
Pfc. Richard S. White
Pvt. Robert D. Goode
Pvt. Edward Krisik
Pvt. Philip L. Ward

Sergeant Henry O. Hansen

SECOND SQUAD
(in reserve)
Corporal Robert M. Lane
Corporal Wayne C. Hathaway
Corporal Everett M. Lavelle
Pfc. Robert L. Blevens
Pfc. William S. Wayne
Pfc. Alvin E. Jefferson
Pvt. James D. Breitenstine
Pfc. Manual Panizo
Pvt. Ogle T. Lemon

Thomas had set up the platoon command post at the edge of the little drainage ditch through which we had entered the area. We were just a few feet behind the two front line squads. The squads on line were connected at each end with First Battalion men. The First Battalion had isolated pockets of men outside and in front of their defense line.

As Sergeant Thomas and I were inspecting the Third Platoon defense, a pocket of First Battalion men in front of us thought we were the enemy. We were close to the blockhouse, and I believe they were the ones fired upon by the large gun in the blockhouse. They were getting ready to fire on us when I waved and yelled at them in curse words that not one Jap could imitate.

We were so close together that I let Sergeant Hansen handle the reserve squad. Sergeant Hansen was not only dependable, he was also an excellent Marine, and he would fight a "circle saw." He was told to join us, and we would form our own circle of defense if the First Battalion lines gave way during the night. Our flamethrowers were full and ready; our weapons were all cleaned and test fired out toward the sea. With the Japanese in the blockhouse destroyed and our defense line set up, I believed we could hold our part.

Still, I did not eat or drink because I was sure the Japanese would launch a night attack. Our Navy was gone for the night. We had no large weapons. In my estimate, it was the enemy's only chance. If they overran us with their vastly superior numbers, there was nothing we could do but fight them hand-to-hand, on their own ground, and under the conditions they liked best.

The battle would be decided the first night, I thought. Even If we had large support weapons, what would they shoot at after dark? Shot-up Marines lay exhausted, disorganized, and scattered across the island. The Japanese had us out-manned and out-gunned for this night.

Our defense was set. I scooted up and down with my back to wear out a smooth place in the bank of the drainage ditch so that I could spend the night partially sitting up. I was that sure of an attack.

Not far behind us, the Japs were still shelling the First Battalion Headquarters on the coast. Partially lit by the bright flares of the Marines and the dull yellow flares of the Japs, the night was eerie. Some shells, both large and small, were exploding here and there. There were many night noises.

Thomas and Ruhl squatted on each side of me, and I knew they were just as exhausted as I. If I could get two hours' sleep before the big attack, I thought that would be enough. I told Thomas and Ruhl to let me have the two hours' sleep and they could have the rest of the night.

I had mentioned that before we embarked on this high adventure trip, we soaked our underwear, socks, and God knows what else, in a sulfur mixture. The high command said there were deadly Scrub Typhus ticks on the island. I never had time to give that a thought, so I scooted down and worked my helmet up and down to get a head rest. Something was crawling between me and my dungaree jacket and down my back. DEADLY TICKS? I said a few curse words and went to sleep.

Chapter 11

20 FEBRUARY 1945
SECOND DAY
RE-CROSSING ISLAND
BUILDING ATTACK LINE AT BASE OF
MOUNT SURIBACHI

I awoke about two hours later and found Thomas and Ruhl asleep. I knew this was dangerous and against my rules, but I did not say anything. The blockhouse remained quiet; it stood like a sentinel in front of us. On the other side of the blockhouse someone heard, saw, or smelled a Japanese and threw a hand grenade. The explosion was loud but muffled by distance.

We heard explosions and yells scattered over the center part of the island as each group of Marines thought the Japanese night attack had started. The Marines knew the dreaded night attack would be hand-to-hand combat, and they wanted to be ready. They had to be ready.

Night-flares made a loud pop in the air. Suspended by small parachutes that opened, they drifted slowly through the air on a light breeze. Japanese flares were off-white or yellow in color; and Marine and Navy flares were white. As they floated down, the flares flickered and reflected eerie moving shadows on the brush. I watched the ever-changing shadows and realized that a Marine with an overactive mind could visualize seeing anything.

The cool night air chilled us. At times, I wished I had allowed the men to bring their packs. I knew they were cold and possibly hungry. Yesterday's activity was enough to rob energy from everyone. I shivered every few minutes, but the freedom of movement was worth it. We did not want to get too cozy; all hell could break loose any minute.

"Studebaker!" The password blasted the night air loud and clear. "Why didn't he kill that God-damn Jap?" Instantly, I let out a string of curse words. In Snyder's squad, on our left flank, someone yelled the name of an American car. The quietness before this happened made the password ring like a loud bell. Darkness caused us to strain every sense to know what was happening. I knew a Marine would not be in front of our lines this early in the morning—so kill it.

A loud explosion followed the password, just what I expected to happen. After the loud explosion, we heard the rattle of rifle fire, and one or two hand grenades exploded. Then silence. The Japanese moved

185

away, or somebody killed him.

Sergeant Thomas reported to me that the Japanese hand grenade wounded two First Squad men. One of Snyder's B.A.R. men, Ed Kurelik, received serious wounds. Phil Christman got lesser wounds and stayed with the squad.

Sergeant Thomas also reported that one of our Corpsman, John Bradley, moved up near the squad with the two wounded. I heard Bradley yell at his nervous friends that he was coming to keep them from shooting him. He treated the wounded. From the time we landed on the Island Sergeant Snyder's first squad had suffered three casualties, and two were men with automatic weapons.

Sergeant Snyder, the wounded man's sergeant, saw to it that someone else took over the automatic weapon. Jim (Chick) Robeson did not surprise me the next morning when he showed up with the B.A.R. in his hand. He had the straps over his shoulders, and the heavy B.A.R. belt around his waist. The little boy, Chick Robeson, grew up fast.

Our morning wake-up call from Company Headquarters was for the Third Platoon to recross the island. Crossing the island the first day, I moved cautiously, making all the decisions and leading the way. We had no time or opportunity to do anything else. In going back across the island, I decided to let Thomas take the assault squad and lead. We would follow and return the same way we came by using the anti-tank ditches connected by trenches. With all the heavy equipment, the assault squad usually stayed in the rear until called forward to destroy something. By being in the lead, they could set the pace. I expected little or no action in crossing. We needed to rejoin Easy company and take part when they moved against Mount Suribachi's defense.

Before we left, Corporal Wheeler said, "Lieutenant, the Jap tried to say something to us before he threw the hand grenade." I said "Yeah, I guess he said a few Japanese curse words."

Every chance we got, Snyder, Wheeler's squad leader, and I studied Japanese language. I think Wheeler was teasing us with his dry humor.

Snyder said that before they left their defense area, the First Battalion found a large dead Japanese Marine non-commissioned Officer just to the left of our front. They thought they killed him during the night. One of Snyder's men brought the Sergeant's special chromed bayonet and gave it to me. This was the area I kicked around looking for the man that threw a hand grenade at Ruhl and me. They described him as a large special dressed Japanese. I wonder how that fight would have turned out if I had located him.

As we moved out, we passed the large blockhouse that created

186

all the excitement last evening. I knew that several Japanese had manned the blockhouse and the machine gun nest on top. Only three Japs lay where Ruhl and I shot down at least six or eight. Some may have played dead, but Ruhl bayonetted the wounded one and he was satisfied that they were dead. Ruhl said they were. When forty-five caliber slugs from my Tommy Gun hit them at point-blank-range, they went flying. They fell like sacks of potatoes pitched from a truck.

First Battalion men began yelling, and all attention went to the big blockhouse. The Marine "mad man" that tried to take Ruhl's rifle from him was attacking the blockhouse. Apparently he was doing most of the attacking, or his group was letting him have the big part. He squatted like a frog on top of the same blockhouse door that opened last night.

First Battalion men knew that one or more Japanese entered the blockhouse during the night because the door was closed. Experience told us that the Japanese hid their dead to prevent us from having an accurate count. I was sure there were not three or four healthy Japs in the blockhouse, but we did not know.

Someone dropped another thermite (heat) grenade into the top of the blockhouse. We waited only a few minutes when the door flew open and a lone Jap ran out. The angry Marine jumped on the Jap's back and knifed him to death while his fellow Marines cheered.

This was not my way to fight a war. The crazed Marine exposed himself to being killed or wounded, and it took too long to kill the Japanese. If there had been more than one Japanese in the block house, the knifing Marine could have been in the way. I did not allow myself the time or thought of revenge killing. Thank God our men did not do these things, and I think only a crazed Marine would.

We traveled along the anti-tank ditches while working our way back across the island. Many wounded men lay exposed to the enemy's artillery and mortar shelling. The concentrated enemy shelling kept almost everything on the island at a standstill.

When I looked behind me, I saw that the First Squad was carrying Ed Kurlick in a poncho. We were not actively engaged. There could be exceptions to my rule about leaving the wounded where they lay, but I was against our being responsible for Kurlick because battle condition could worsen at any minute. Someone passed the word to us that stretchers and transportation to a ship were available to a few that made it to the beach. This was scuttle-butt; it may or may or may not have been true.

The Japanese anti-tank ditches filled to overflow with dead, dying, wounded, and live Marines. Everyone who could crowd into the

anti-tank ditch for safety did. Enemy artillery, pounding the earth around us, herded us there like cattle.

Some tried to bury their dead friends but could not without exposing themselves to deadly enemy fire. To make room in the ditches, they stacked the dead and covered them with ponchos. If the dead or near-dead were out of the ditch and in the open, they laid there. With the heavy enemy shelling and the crowded ditches, our forty-three men moved slowly across the island. We wanted to move faster but could not.

Silent Japanese defenses would awaken periodically and wreak havoc among the Marines, but we had learned our lesson. When the enemy's large weapons shifted their concentration, the Marines, with tanks and demolition, began destroying all enemy blockhouses, pill boxes, and bunkers. They did this whether the enemy was active or not.

Large enemy shells burst only a few feet away from the edge of the anti-tank ditches and the shallow trenches that joined the ditches. Chills ran up and down my spine when the deafening explosions shook the ground around us, and dirt filled the air. The loud explosions did not hide the high-pitched rattle of the small Japanese machine guns or the louder but low rhythmic chatter of their larger machine guns. The air carried all the different odors of burning residue from the exploding shells. We could smell the strong odor of burning flesh as the flamethrowers moved in on the caves and gun emplacements. These weapons destroyed the enemy with fire.

I heard my name and turned to see Mr. Howard T. Olson, the Red Cross man. He surprised me. I did not expect to see him under these conditions. His large frame adjusted snugly into a notch scooped out of the wall in the ditch. He grinned and asked about my arm. I told him that the wound did not come from the enemy. On board the ship, I did something foolish, and the Corpsman bandaged my arm. Olson wished me well and handed me a package of Raleigh cigarettes that he pulled from a full ditty bag hanging around his neck.

As we neared the end of the big ditch, we approached a shallow trench that was one man wide and just deep enough that we had to crawl. The shallow trench lay perpendicular to and joined the two large anti-tank ditches. We had traveled down this ditch yesterday. We had no other choice. Now, the enemy's artillery shells fell like rain, and it was dangerous to expose any part of our bodies above the ditch level. I was impatient to move on across the island but not impatient enough to expose the platoon by moving it outside the ditch and trenches. We must crawl one after another down the connecting trench.

Thomas and the assault squad moved one behind the other crawling down the shallow trench. I kneeled down and began crawling behind the Assault squad. Without warning, the Assault squad turned in the trench and while bent over they rushed back, knocking me into the big ditch. I landed flat of my back, and the assault squad and Thomas physically ran over me. It was a shock and mystery to me.

Japanese artillery shells were bursting and throwing dust and dirt over us, but nothing was hitting in the large ditches or small trenches. It was a jolting mystery to me. I heard no shots, and the trench looked clear. Thomas quickly made his way over to me. He said, "The enemy has a machine gun trained down that ditch." I asked him how

189

he knew that and he said that someone from the other end of the small trench yelled to them.

We could not wait, and we could not move out of the large ditch to avoid the trench. Enemy artillery was so heavy outside these that nothing moved on top of the ground. I told Thomas to station B.A.R. men on each side of the trench for protection. He would send the men through the ditch scattered one, two, or three at a time.

Thomas and Hansen quickly stationed B.A.R. men on each side of the ditch, but there was a hesitation. Who would be the first to crawl down that shallow trench? We had no choice; we had to use the trench.

This hesitation made me so mad that I dropped down on my hands and knees and began crawling down that connecting trench. I expected to be shot any minute. Yes, I will admit I resented that no one offered to be first. It did give me the opportunity to show the men that I would not order them to do anything that I would not do. When I cleared the other end and looked back, others were coming, and we soon cleared the trench without incident. I kept the lead after that.

It was near the middle of the second day, and the battle was at its absolute peak. The island was shaking with the explosions of large shells and demolition. The noise was so great that it was like dead silence. We could hear nothing. The smell of burning flesh was overwhelming.

Dead and dying Marines along with bits and pieces of human flesh lay everywhere. Large flies, which lived on the island in great numbers, did not realize their lives were in danger while feasting on pieces of human flesh. All we could see were their butt ends as they covered a piece of flesh. The flies covered the flesh so thickly that they looked like fat, overgrown hair.

On the second day we were still playing the role of a reserve unit. A reserve unit is used in "Hot spots" and called on to relieve and support units in trouble. A feeling inside told me that the combat veterans were beginning to wonder why this war was raging on every side of us but we did not take an active part. It was hard as a leader to be like an old mother hen taking care of her brood of chickens.

True, we had crossed the island twice; true, we had two or three skirmishes; true, we had not been fully engaged in battle. Yet, we had played our part. We had lost only three men wounded and no dead, and we stayed fully equipped with clean weapons and ready to fight. Troops in reserve can be committed anywhere and at any time.

I realized that with all the distractions it was hard to stay firm with the men, and I had to keep reminding myself. Taking part in the action around us was tempting, but I knew we must keep the men healthy, with reliable and clean equipment, and keep the platoon in tight control until fully committed.

We rounded a bend in the ditch, and there sat a Marine in plain sight of the enemy. Congealed blood covered the upper part of his body, and I could hardly see his eyes peering through the blood. His eyes had the look of a man in shock. An enemy machine gun was still kicking dirt over him and us. Someone had attempted to treat him and left him sitting there in danger of being hit again. One from our platoon pulled him off the bank and leaned him against the dirt wall.

Ruhl asked permission to carry the wounded man a short distance to the beach. I said no. He knew my orders were to leave all wounded alone and let the corpsman and stretcher bearers take care of them. It made no difference who they were. There is an old saying in warfare, "Don't kill'em, wound'em." That way, it takes more men out of action, tending to their buddies.

Without my knowledge, Ruhl refused to obey orders. Two men went with him, Alva Jefferson and John Eller. Ruhl came back; the other two did not. I was mad. We were short five men and we had not been in a full scale battle yet. If the two were cowards, it was a good riddance. If not, we lost two more wounded men. I did nothing to Ruhl, who was already condemning himself.

We were about two-thirds across the island when a First Battalion Marine came striding down the ditch. He carried a rifle over his shoulder and walked as if he did not have a care in the world. He looked at us in an inquiring way and asked if we knew where the Jap Nambu was? He referred to the Jap machine gun that wounded the other Marine and was kicking dirt over us. Every few minutes, we could hear the sporadic high pitch rattle of the small bore weapon. The Japanese gunner alternately held and released the trigger or changed direction of the weapon.

"The brush is too thick," Sergeant Snyder told him. Snyder made this statement with a hang-dog expression as if he thought we should take care of the enemy machine gunner. Our Platoon had orders from me to leave it alone. Whether Snyder intended to or not, he was telling me he did not like this no-action part of the war. I knew his record. He loved combat and killing the Japanese. This was his fourth or fifth battle.

"I will find it," the young Marine said, and then, over the side of the ditch he went. We heard the exchange of gunfire, and back over the side of the ditch the young Marine came with a grin on his face. He was carrying the enemy machine gun.

We soon cleared the ditch, and in small two-and three-men fire teams, we crossed an open area. We found protection in a small ditch behind "E" Company's command post. Captain Severance ordered us to stay in reserve near a catch of food rations and water. The men began eating the rations. I continued to think of dysentery and slow thinking caused by food and water and refused both.

The platoon occupied an area near the spot where we dropped our packs yesterday. Company Headquarters had moved a short distance to the south of their original hole, and they dug deeper. They had the biggest shovel I ever saw. It looked larger than a grain scoop.

While we waited, I told Thomas and Hansen that I was going to the place where we dropped our packs before we crossed the island. I thought I needed my poncho. My pack was excess baggage in this type of warfare because my B.A.R. belt with large pocket served as my pack, and I filled the pockets with bare necessities.

As I trotted back, I noticed that large numbers of dead Marines lay scattered. They appeared to lie as they fell. I soon found my pack, and on my way back to the platoon area some enemy small-arms fire made me drop to one knee. Beside me, three or four dead Marines lay head to toe. At the top of this line of Marines, and nearest to me, a dead Marine lay without a helmet. His bloodless light complexion and red hair flying in the wind made his head look as if it were on fire.

On the other side of the red-head, a live Marine lay so flat that I thought he was dead. On his out-stretched hand, nearest the Red Head, two or three fingers dug or scraped small holes in the dirt. His actions looked ridiculous. At first, I thought something was wrong with him. I asked, "What in the hell or you doing?" Not moving, he rolled his eyes up toward me and said, "You just stay there, you son-of-a-bitch, and you'll find out." He had witnessed the other Marines killed in that same spot, I guess. With the others lying there, I knew what he meant. The small enemy weapons quit firing, so I moved on.

When I rejoined the platoon, Thomas and I watched the Marines attacking the base of Mount Suribachi. "E" Company had two platoons in line facing the mountain. The two platoons lost many of their men, the First Platoon especially. They were out in the open and more exposed.

With one exception, our platoon was the only reserve of the Second Battalion. A squad of men from the First Platoon remained unnoticed. Sergeant Gorden Still did not understand why his squad remained in the rear, uncommitted. I asked him to join us, but he refused.

Out in the open, near the center of the island and facing the mountain, was the First Platoon of Easy Company. Their Platoon

192

Commander was Lieutenant George Stoddard, and their Platoon Sergeant was Paul Paljavcsick. On Stoddard's left was the Second Platoon under Lieutenant Ed Pennell and Platoon Sergeant Joseph McGarvey. These men and the men under them were fine men, and there were no better Marines. "I" Company of the Third Battalion was on Stoddard's right. They were near the center of the island.

I studied the company's position on line facing the enemy. The Second Platoon's left flank dropped off into partially broken ground. The First Platoon lay out in the middle of the island facing the mountain with nothing between them and the enemy but sunlight.

Someone at the Company Command Post told me that Lieutenant Stoddard was wounded, and one of the Marine tanks moved over him for protection. They picked him up through a trap door in the bottom of the tank and evacuated him. They said Lieutenant Pennell had leg wounds. How they evacuated him, I do not know.

Captain Severance ordered the Third Platoon to replace the First platoon. From our position in reserve, the front line looked about two hundred yards away. I studied the open ground we would cross and the ground where we would set up our defense for the night. I saw little or nothing to shield us from the enemy's fire power. The men of the platoon would be open targets all the way.

There was nothing hidden from my sight. I knew about where the First Platoon, whose place we would be taking, joined "I" Company. The sun shone brightly in the mid-afternoon sky. We would move without military preparation or protection of any kind.

The roar of the worst thunderstorm could not match the noise as all weapons on both sides fired at their capacity. I thought that we could not move the platoon, as a group, across the open ground safely. We could move them scattered and a few at a time.

I decided to make a personal reconnaissance and then let Thomas send down small groups. Doing it this way, I would know where the Marine front line was and how to place the men. If anything happened to me, Thomas would know. I would be in plain sight of everyone on that end of the island and also the supporting ships. He was to give me about fifteen minutes to get there and get set. We were not attacking, so we had the time. As I saw it, we needed to use the best odds to save the men while crossing no-man's land and setting our defense when we got there.

The squad leaders checked the men's equipment and took a quick head count. With my poncho in one hand and my Tommy gun and helmet in the other, I took off running. It was all open ground. Every Marine, every Jap, and every ship at sea could see me. I was a moving target, and, unless I stopped, the enemy's small-arms fire would need to be lucky to hit me.

Any automatic weapon that fired at me would expose itself. If they knew I was an officer, they would not mind the exposure. Also, the Japanese would not hesitate to shoot at a lone runner if there were no better targets.

I trotted toward the mountain fortress in a zig-zag fashion, trying my best to understand the situation as I came closer to the enemy. Our attacking forces had advanced to less than one hundred yards of the enemy. Facing the attacking Marines was a chain of interlocking pillboxes and gun placements that ringed the base of the mountain. The Japanese worked, watched, and remained snug in their underground network. None of our ships' big weapons could get enough direct hits to reach the enemy inside the concrete emplacements.

Bursting shells, shrapnel, and bullets whistling and singing in the air around me made it almost impossible to avoid the enemy shells. All I could think of was, "I'm not hit yet, I'm not hit yet." I remember at this point laughing, not the laugh of a happy man, but the laugh of irony, fate, or at whatever put me in this situation. I was approaching the spot that I thought to be the front line. Enemy bullets came from every direction and seemed to concentrate their firepower into the scattered remnants of the First Platoon.

A large-caliber enemy machine gun began firing at me from some distance away. With thousands of weapons firing, I heard this unusually strange-sounding machine gun. Before it could close in on me, someone stopped it.

I did not travel far until a small machine gun began firing at me in earnest, and the sand flew around me. Near me was a shallow pot-hole. It was little more than that. A Marine from the First Platoon occupied the only safe end of the small shelter. Just his head and shoulders had protection. One very quick glance assured me the Marine was dead. He looked drained of all his blood. I was wrong.

When I landed in the far end of the shallow pit, the other man opened his eyes and gently shook his head. Quickly, I jumped and landed behind a small mound of dirt. I left my poncho in the depression. The Japanese machine gun ripped the poncho to shreds.

I knew then how the other Marine from our company received his death wounds. He saved my life before he died. I wish I could remember his name. This was a trap, and I hoped the others would see it.

As I looked back, I expected a few or possibly a squad of the Third Platoon heading my way. Instead here came the whole God-Damn platoon. They looked like wild animals. Sergeant Thomas was in the lead. Mad, I was never so mad in all my life; I get mad now thinking about it. We were not attacking. We were setting up a defense for the night, with a planned attack tomorrow. How could anyone be so stupid? We had all the time we needed. Thomas would not do that, I thought.

To me there was an impossibility in front, and impossibility coming up from behind; we had a hot Jap machine gunner on the loose.

The platoon came in a massive wedge shape following Thomas, who was running toward our area. I had a mental vision of the Japanese machine gunner waiting until the platoon stopped and gathered around me. He would have a field-day.

Thomas saw me and headed straight for the hole from which I had just jumped. Lying on my side, I was waving with all my might for him to stay away. The hole evidently looked like a good spot to him, and he looked at me with a questioning look and continued to run. I kept waving and shaking my head. The last second, he changed his mind and landed near my feet.

I waved to the men to get down, and they hit the deck. They were in groups along the line of defense but too close together. However, it looked as if we were going to get away with it. Luckily, we did not lose a man.

When the enemy machine gun began firing again, one of our machine guns found him. I could hear the familiar series of bursts from one side and then from the other. This lasted only a few seconds before the Japanese machine gun went silent.

"Why didn't you send only a few at a time, like I told you?" "Why didn't you carry out my orders?" Sergeant Thomas said the Captain had ordered them all down at once. I could not imagine a Marine officer making that decision. This was the second time in as many days it happened to our platoon. First, it was the blockhouse and now this. I said a few curse words and thought, "Why doesn't the Captain come down here where the God damn bullets are flying if he is going to run this platoon,"

Our rendezvous area was in the middle of "No Man's Land," directly under the eyes of the Japanese and in range of all their weapons. The men hit the ground un-oriented, but each squad leader was in full control.

Soon, two tanks lumbered up to nullify any immediate opposition while the two company platoons, second and third, prepared their positions for the night. We guessed that was the tanks' purpose; that is the way we used them.

As I said before, the tanks always drew heavy fire from the enemy, especially big weapons. Shells and pieces of shells ricocheting from the tanks were extremely dangerous to infantry.

The tanks moved around like blind elephants in an arena, first one direction and then another, looking for targets. We saw the Marines diving for cover when the tanks headed their way. In the second and third platoons, the men reacted much like schooling fish dodging sharks.

The Japanese produced the almost perfect camouflage by putting all their weapons underground years or months before this battle. Their entrances or slits that they fired their weapons through did not appear disturbed recently by man. Our weapons, both air and sea, pounded the island and exposed many of the enemy's defenses.

Quickly we learned that some enemy weapons could be brought out, fired, and then quickly moved back underground. We could see the small weapons do this and guessed that some large enemy weapons had that capability. The large weapons would fire at us from the north end of the island, but before our Navy could locate them, they would be gone.

The Japanese depended on interlocking fire (weapons cross firing) to cover their entire front. When we destroyed one part of the interlocking fire, it left a safe blank space for the Marines to take a breather. We would be safe regardless of how close we were to the enemy or the targeted area.

When the enemy did risk bringing their big weapons out of hiding and firing in the daytime to cover the blank areas, the Japs exposed themselves to fire-power from our Navy ships and all the air forces. Detecting the caves that the enemy fired their big guns from was a chore, and destroying them beyond a quick repair was almost impossible.

We still had time before dark to set up our defense for the night. This close to the enemy, we must be ready for anything at any time.

In our area, the tanks moved slowly forward firing their French seventy five millimeter cannons. It was mostly random firing. Moving along with the tanks, the Third Platoon's left flank attached itself to the destroyed enemy's anti-aircraft gun. The gun sat in the middle of a large circular pit. Thomas and I worked together to get two squads on line and spaced right for a night's defense. Then the line would be in position to attack the enemy the next day.

Why the Japanese allowed us to do this, I do not know. Their destroyed enemy anti-aircraft gun pit continued to bother me. It was in front of our left flank. The enemy could rush to the pit, throw flanking fire, and pin us down until their men could try to overrun us.

Suddenly we heard random firing on our right. A single Japanese began trotting. He was near the west side of the base of Mount Suribachi, and he was trotting toward the east side. The winding and undulating trail he was using was generally parallel to the Marine defense line. Marines began shooting at him almost at the time he came into view. By that time he reached a cave near the east side of the island, I think every Marine weapon on that end of the island was firing at him. No one hit him. This was a factual lesson on firing at a moving target or a lesson on being a moving target.

The lone Japanese casually trotted across the base of the mountain toward the entrance of a large cave that formerly protected a large coastal gun. He stopped and bent over to enter the cave. At that point I think every weapon hit him at once. He exploded. I am almost sure he intended it that way.

My theory of fighting the Japanese was to "Zig and zag and get in among them." This worked since the Japanese in the daylight hours stayed underground. A moving target is hard to hit, especially one that

Mt. Suribachi - Lone Japanese trotting toward cave with all Marines were firing at him.

is "zigging and zagging." Once we got on top of them, the Japanese lost most of their advantage.

While we stayed occupied with the shooting gallery, shells landed close to us from Japanese knee-mortars. These were small mortars and very portable. Military men do not fire mortars the same as they do other weapons. These rocket-like, earth-to-earth bombs jet into the air much the same as a rocket. They normally arch high in the air, slow-down, stop, and then fall back to earth. If we watched the air above, we could often tell where the shells came from and where they were going to land. We could tell, especially, if they are arching above us, and these were.

Although they called them "knee mortars," I suspect the Japs placed the butt plate on the ground and not the knee, as some thought the Japanese did. Someone said that a Marine tried it and broke his leg. I watched the mortar shells and spotted several Japs around one, maybe two, small mortar tubes. They were beyond our platoons effective range. The Japs were busy as bees working at firing the weapons. The shells were not accurate, but the Japs had explosions going off over the attack area.

If we could get a tank crew to see them, we could destroy the Japanese mortar crews. I looked for a tank. The two tanks working with us moved back to a protected area for the night, but I saw a tank nearby. Corporal Robert Lane and I ran to the tank.

Our tanks did have a telephone on a spring-retrievable line just back of the rotating turret. This telephone would put the Marine on the outside in direct contact with the Marines inside the tank. Often the tanks would be almost useless without Marines talking over the phone or standing in view in front of the tank and pointing at the target with their weapon. If the pointer was on one side of the tank, it was hard for the tank to judge the direction. The enemy knew this, so the question was, who would use the phone? Who would direct the tank's weapon?

We ran to the back of the tank to get the phone. I grabbed the telephone line, but there was no phone. From our company, two Marines lay dead at the back of the tank. One freshly killed Marine from the Second Platoon fell on top of the telephone he was using. The spring retrieve would not work. The tank had backed up and cut the phone line. I rolled the dead marine over, retrieved the phone and pitched it to the top of the tank. It landed among some sand bags, and I hope it stayed there until they could repair the line.

Time was precious. I did not want Lane and me to spend much time there with the tank. We could see the result of that action by looking at the two dead Marines lying there. The Japanese were zeroed-in on that spot. With the butt of my Tommy gun, I beat on the side of the tank until I got the attention of the Marines inside. I saw one look at me through the small window. I wanted the Marines in the tank to open the hatch, but they would not. They were trying to get me to use the phone, I think. The phone was "out of order."

It was good that he could not hear my cursing. I think I called him every name in the book. Here I was, standing outside pointing at the phone and shaking my head. He would not crack the hatch. Of course he had his orders, but there have to be exceptions. The only thing left to do was to stand in front of the tank and use the old method. I stepped toward the target and pointed at it with my weapon. To me it seemed as if it took forever before there was some response from the tank. Time was precious, precious, precious.

The French seventy five millimeter tank gun swung back and forth on the front of the tank; it looked like a snout on a walking elephant. Just as I was about to give up and get the hell out of there, the

big gun settled and began firing. That was the end of the enemy fire teams. A tank shell must have burst at the feet of the Jap operating one of the weapons, because his body ballooned high into the air.

We turned to move away from the tank and dead men. Bob was in front of me when a large mortar shell hit close behind me. Thank God the shell buried deep before it exploded. The power of the explosion lifted me off the ground and put me astraddle of Bob Lane's shoulders. My ears rang, and sand from the exploding shell blasted me, but that was all. Bob suffered the shock of being hit by a flying body. I think that if I had opened my legs I might have cleared him.

After a few minutes of getting back our senses, we rushed back to the defense line. Evening was drawing near, and the whole atmosphere of battle was changing from offense to defense. The tanks were moving back to a more protected area for the night. Our large ships were pulling out to rendezvous some distance at sea. The planes would be useless at night; they were returning to their mother ships.

The younger men began asking for food and to relieve themselves. I still had not eaten, drunk, or relieved myself since we hit the Island. Once, a Marine officer told me that I would never make a good officer, because I never got hungry, thirsty, or tired. He said I would not be considerate of the men. Eating would make me drowsy. I did not drink water or urinate. If I had it to do over, I would drink water. I did not realize I was so dehydrated. My mind was working clear as a bell-or I thought it was. I knew our main job was ahead. I was still deeply impressed with the strength of the Japanese weapons and positions.

All the power of our battleships, cruisers, destroyers, dive-bombers, and Marine Corps weaponry did not destroy even one blockhouse or pillbox facing us. I cannot exaggerate the effect that this powerful fortress, Mount Suribachi, had on us. I thought that after tomorrow most of us would need no food or water.

Being a military tactician (at least I thought I was), I knew the Japanese' last chance was this night. It would soon be dark, and we would lose our good observation. We would also lose our heavy Navy weapons, our multi-air forces bombing and shelling, our tanks with their firepower and flame throwing ability, and all other advantages that daylight gave us. At the end of the second day, the enemy still had us outnumbered, and the Japanese were famous for their night attacks. If the Marines could make this night, I thought, the Japanese were doomed.

Company Headquarters sent down a sound-powered telephone and a roll of telephone wire. The man bringing the equipment down got as near as he dared and threw the wire and telephone at me and ran. I should have said something to the Captain about this, but I thought, "What the hell." We did not have to expose ourselves going back to get it. Fear is contagious, and I thought that it was best that the runner did not come near our young men. The men considered me an old man. I had advanced to the ripe old age of twenty-three years just two weeks before we hit the island.

We received a call from Company Headquarters. They wanted someone from the platoon to come back and pick up barbed wire concertinas and trip flares. These concertinas looked similar to large wheels of barbed wire, but when pulled apart by handles on each side they would form a continuous roll of wire for some distance. They are portable barriers, and the enemy must consider them before attacking.

I noticed several things. Company headquarters did not bring our supplies to us when they brought the phone. They did not mention food, water, ammunition, or anything else. This was another time we got the feeling we were expendable and the Marine Corps was about to expend us. From Snyder's squad, in reserve, four men went back for the wire and trip flares. They were Jim Robeson, Phil Christman, Louie Adrian (all teenagers), and Corporal Richard Wheeler.

These men went back about one hundred yards or more to the company command post, picked up barbed wire, and trip flares, and returned without being fired upon. This gave me some hope.

If the Japanese decided to make a night attack, the wire would need stretching in front of us beyond Japanese hand-grenade range. We attached one end of the barbed wire concertina to and worked around the Japanese anti-aircraft gun emplacement. The large gun-pit was on our immediate left front. This was the large open-top Japanese gun emplacement, the one I spoke of before. It had two caves leading away from it.

This anti-aircraft gun was the one that knocked down the Marine Corsair when we landed. The enemy crews could stay protected in the caves until they wanted to fire the gun. They could rush out, fire the weapon, and rush back into the cave. If the Marines knocked one enemy crew out, then the other crew could man the gun.

Chuck Lindberg, Donald Ruhl, and maybe others had checked it. I knew there were some good souvenirs, and best of all there were some beautiful all-wool white Japanese Navy Blankets. We were cold. We found out later that Enemy Navy personnel manned this gun.

Company Headquarters ordered us to string the barbed wire with trip flares. I stalled as long as I could. Whoever strung the wire would be just a few yards from the enemy, and right in front of their face. They could kill the wire stringers as easy as shooting dogs in their own back yard. That God-damn wire was going to be strung, but under my conditions, if possible.

There was no way I would order the men to do this job while I sat back cozy. I picked Adrian, Robeson, and Christman. Thomas picked Bob Lane, Clarence Hipp and William McNulty, and we went out and strung that barbed wire.

I looked up and down the defense line, and I saw no one else stringing barbed wire. I could imagine the Japanese saying: "What in the hell is going on? What on earth are those dumb-ass clowns doing? We are not going to attack them tonight, and they have to cross that Kami-dame (God Dam) mess tomorrow." While we worked out in front of the Japanese, I never felt so naked in all my life, and the seconds went by like hours.

I do not know why they did not kill us. They could have easily. Others near us tried to string their rolls of wire, and the Japs fired at them. We raced back to our little protected spots just in time to hear a loud crash of artillery shells on our Platoon's left flank. A series of explosions followed the first. These explosions were walking up our defense line. Every explosion was getting nearer, and I had no place to go. I am not sure who it was, but there were two men in a shallow depression beside me, and I laid down next to their spot. I guess I wanted company.

With my face down, my helmet pushed back to help cover my head, I covered the rest of my neck with my arms. The shells continued walking up our line, exploding only a few feet away, and literally raising the earth into the air. We could hardly breathe, and I opened my mouth to help equalize the pressure. Someone told me it would prevent the bursting of our ear drums.

I was sick, sick, sick. To me it appeared that we had lost the battle before we began. Tomorrow they will expect us to attack that mighty fortress with only a handful of men. All the planning, the precautions, the mental and physical strain to see that the men would be present and properly equipped for the great battle ahead was for nothing. The explosions were coming directly up our line with no wasted shells. All I could think about was the great loss of men.

There is no way of expressing the horror of this experience. I believe this was the most nerve-racking experience I have ever endured. I just knew they were blowing the men all to pieces, and there was not one thing I could do about it. What made it even more horrifying, it stopped soon after passing through us and started back through. My muscles were so tight that I thought they would burst.

When the shelling quit, I was shaking like a leaf. Before this happened, nothing scared me. I did not have time for that luxury. The ear-bursting noise stopped instantly, and the silence seemed just as loud or louder. I got rid of the shakes; there were too many things to think about.

As it turned out, they hit Ogle T. Lemon from Amarillo, Texas, but his wounds were minor. We had the men scattered, and the absorbing power of the volcanic sand and ash gave us the odds.

In the deafening silence a booming voice yelled, "Hey! Lieutenant Wells, wonder what your dancing girl is doing tonight?" I recognized the man and yelled back, "I don't know, but, by God, she had better be thinking of me." There were others who yelled, just to break the tension.

The young man who yelled at me was an ex-Raider and close friend of Sergeant Snyder. He was a machine-gunner in "I" Company, and had his machine gun set up next to us, on our right flank.

This young man worked at the Officer's Club in Camp Pendleton, California. The officers placed the club back in a canyon to be away from the eyes of the enlisted men, because the officers did not always act like officers should. This young man had observed my girlfriend (the exotic dancer) dance there.

Some of our Easy Company machine gunners came by our line. Sergeant Lawrence Wayne was in charge. He was one of my best friends. God, how I liked those machine gunners; they had the fighting spirit. I was in charge of them for several months when we were back in the states. The Japanese always tried to kill them first.

Wayne had spent so much time in the Brig(prison) that he knew all the brig language, especially the Kangaroo Court. "In the hall, backs to the wall, I don't mean one, I don't mean two - I mean the prosecuting attorney and the whole damn crew. This old Kangaroo Court is now in secession." He could hold the whole court. He was a good combat man though. Yes, they killed him.

Our Marines brought heavy water-cooled machine guns with light machine gun tripods. Light tripods cut down on the weight. All of our machine gun fire-power fired directly at the enemy, and at close quarters. We did not need heavy tripods. Our machine gunners carried everything in their hands and on their backs.

Platoon Sergeant Joseph McGarvey guided them into position for our night's protection. McGarvey was thirty years old at the time, and I think he was the oldest man in the company. I believe he was in charge of the Second Platoon. McGarvey was not only a good Marine; he was a good man. It was a good feeling to have these two men and their fine dependable men near. McGarvey saw me and yelled, "Where are the Mongolian Ponies?" He never tired of teasing me about a statement I made to the Third Platoon when we were in training. If we ever go to Manchuria or wherever the natives have horses and the enemy is there, I told them, "We will go mounted into combat" (fighting on horseback).

Ruhl knew that I was worried about the large unoccupied Japanese gun emplacement in front of us. We must not neglect it. I thought it was in a vital spot on our left flank and crucial for our night's defense. Japanese in control of the gun-pit could put flanking fire into the Second and Third platoons. They could pin us down until their troops tried overrunning us. We must occupy the pit, I thought.

Ruhl volunteered to do this with very little help. He knew it needed to be done. His volunteering was nearly suicidal. He could not stop the attack, and he would possibly be killed. He could sound the alarm that the attack was underway. With this time gap we could move the reserve to help him or wherever the enemy attack looked the strongest.

Darkness was moving in on us. We got a call from Company Headquarters that there were shaped charges and two five gallon cans of water for our platoon, "Would somebody come back and get these?" I thought, "Why didn't somebody bring something?" I said a few curse words. I was so tired of hearing "COME BACK."

It would soon be that time of day when Marines kill anything that moves, friend or enemy. We were not sure if the enemy was the Japanese in front of us or the Marine Corps behind us. It was not total darkness yet. Everyone looked set in for the night, I decided to go back to Company Headquarters for the cans of water myself. Clarence Hipp, our demolition man, was near by, so I asked him to go with me to bring back the shaped charges. Hipp and I had not gone far when I heard my name called. I returned the raised-hand recognition to a corporal that I knew in "I" Company going back to the front lines with his load.

Hipp and I were following the sound-powered telephone wire to be sure we found Company Headquarters. By now, I was cursing so loudly Marines could hear me across the island. There was no doubt in anybody's mind that we were Marines. Marine cursing was the best password; no Japanese could mimic that. I was running the phone wire through my hand because it was getting that dark. Suddenly the wire disappeared into a hole smaller than my fist. I tugged on the wire and got some action.

The Command post was a converted Japanese bunker. They had five feet of concrete over them what a layout! For a minute, at least, I hated everyone in that bunker. We got the supplies that we came after, and quickly made our way cursing and talking loud until we reached our line. My "bunker" for the night would be a Japanese white wool blanket wrapped around me, and a can of water lying on its edge in front of me.

Sergeant Midkiff and the Third Squad had the defense of the left side of our line. Corporal Lane and the Second Squad had the defense of the right side, and Sergeant Hansen had the First Squad and the Assault Squad in reserve. Sergeant Thomas and I moved up on the front line. We agreed to help Ruhl if possible. However, if the Japanese pulled a "Bonsai," (a fanatical charge) we would lose Ruhl, but we believed we could hold the Japs.

A small amount of daylight remained in the western sky, and it back-lighted the east side of Mount Suribachi. Silhouettes of enemy figures showed them working intently. I called this enemy activity in by phone. I am sure there were others who called it in also. In no time a Destroyer moved in so close it almost beached itself. It turned its searchlights on the working Japanese and blew them to bits.

Darkness settled on the battlefield, and the cold night air moved in. The Japanese Navy white wool blankets brought from the enemy's anti-aircraft site by Ruhl were welcome. We soon received a phone call from Company Headquarters. They said that our white blankets showed up with every night flare. This was said in a know-it-all voice, like, "You dumb bastards, you should know better." It surprised me that they stuck their heads out of the concrete pill box to see how we were doing. Of course the Japanese could see us. They had been looking at us for two days. Headquarters left unsaid that it might be a good thing if we did away with the blankets. The Japanese could see us plainly. We were only yards from the Japanese, and we were that far or farther from company headquarters.

Of course the Japanese could see us with or without the blankets. All day, we withstood their machine guns, mortars, and artillery. Once yesterday and one time today, the enemy shot at me with a machine gun that I could not identify. At close range we walked in front of them, and now am I expected to be concerned about whether they can see us or not?

I am not saying what I wanted to tell Company Headquarters. If I did, they would not allow me to associate with civilized people again. I am sure I did not say it over the phone; nonetheless, I thought it. We would not give up our blankets to anybody, including the Japanese. Headquarters meant well, I am sure. I would bet good money that Battalion Headquarters was the instigator. Colonel Johnson always kept an eye on his men.

Earlier, the Japanese machine gunner had shredded my poncho and I was cold. The blanket was warm. We knew one thing for sure—none of the high command would come down and take the blankets away from us.

The glowing flares that gave an eerie atmosphere in the cold night air also exposed us in our white blankets. These flares went off almost continuously. Japanese yellow flares would at times change colors, and the enemy shelling would become more intense. I could hear the Third Platoon men talking. They were more alert and concerned about the heavy shelling on the beach and elsewhere than I was. If the shelling was not falling directly on us, Thomas, Hansen, and I had our minds on the Japanese directly in front of us.

After our battleships and cruisers left for their night's rendezvous some distance away, the Japanese had a rocket-powered bomb that they fired at dusk. A high screaming noise in the air told us the bomb was on the way. Somebody named it "Screaming Jesus." When it hit the beach area, there would be a noise so loud we might think the island was blowing up. Scrap metal would fly everywhere. One of these shells set off some ammunition stacked on the beach, and the firework's display was like something dreamed up by Hollywood movie producers.

Short glimpses of Mount Suribachi appeared when flashes of light from exploding shells reflected from prominent crags. The crags made a picture that looked like the nose and cheek bones of a five hundred foot cold and sinister monster staring down upon us.

I think the officer who predicted that I would fail as a good Marine officer was right, because some men had no food, and I was not going or sending for any. In the pockets of my B.A.R. belt was an emergency supply, so I gave them all the food I had. It would do no good for me to eat now.

The young men asking for food reminded me of children wanting water and other things after being put to bed early and told a scary story. No movie director could build a more scary horror scene than this one. This bedtime story had a "real, live Bogey man."

"Don't give a God damn inch" was my order for the night.

206

Chapter 12

21 FEBRUARY 1945
THIRD DAY
THE THIRD PLATOON ATTACKS
MOUNT SURIBACHI

I was awake. No sound came from the enemy in front of us. A faint glow of light in the eastern sky announced the coming dawn and the United States Marine Corps' third day attack. The chill of the morning air matched the cold that lay in the pit of my stomach. The coming frontal Marine Corps assault on the mountain fortress facing us had all the earmarks of the Marines making one of their famous suicidal attacks. The men called them "suicidal" because we had very little room to maneuver on the small islands the enemy occupied.

My mind worked razor-sharp, the way I suspect that of a cornered animal would. I searched for any means to attack and destroy the enemy that faced us. No one could pray harder than I prayed for God to show me the way to do my job. Many Third Platoon men would be wounded and killed in the next few hours. I knew it, and the men knew it.

While we waited for more light, I continued thinking about how best we could use the men. It looked hopeless. We had little or no protection from the enemy. I had a full five gallon water can in front of me and a white wool blanket wrapped around me. I wondered what in the hell we were going to do, and how were we going to do it. My weapons were already clean, but while I was thinking I cleaned them again.

The warlike professional sports—football, hockey, and other combat games—are pure child's play. Cheerleaders work themselves and the cheering crowd into a high-pitched frenzy in expectation of the coming conflict. Ball players feel the energy flowing from the playing band and yells from the orchestrated crowd. On Iwo Jima no crowds were cheering, no bands were playing, and no flags were waving. Death, the cold dark truth, stared us in the face.

The atmosphere was much like that in a cattle and hog butcher-house I knew as a boy. My father owned his own butcher house and meat market. I helped him kill almost every week. I noticed that when the door closed behind us and the cattle smelled the inside of the butcher house, the cattle knew instantly what was about to take place. After two days of fighting on Iwo Jima, every man in our platoon and every man on line facing the Japanese at the base of Mount Suribachi that morning knew that many men would die and the blood would flow that day.

Human electricity, vibrations, or whatever we call the substance that saturates the air surrounding the death struggle was so thick we could smell it and taste it. Here, death hung in the air like a gaseous shroud.

With shrubbery and camouflage blasted away from the base of Mount Suribachi by the three air forces and Naval weapons, we could see the ring of interlocking concrete pill boxes, blockhouses, and connecting trenches. They were strung like a string of beads around an old lady's wrinkled neck.

The area immediately in front of the platoon and between us and the enemy was almost flat. There were a few old death-trap bomb craters that the Japs had "zeroed in on" and three rolls of interlocking barbed wire. The enemy's defense from the top of the mountain, the potential cave openings around the sides, and the mighty power we could see around the base of Mount Suribachi was an awesome sight. We could not use our platoon's reserve to support our morning attack. They could not fire from our flanks because other Marines were there. They could not fire over our heads, and if they could, what would they fire at? The enemy remained underground.

A place of protection from the enemy fire did not exist. Our Third Platoon did not have a single weapon that was effective at this distance against the enemy bunkers. The reserve squad and assault squad would follow us in our mad charge when we attacked. The situation was comparable to a little boy attacking a cornered tiger with a toy pistol. We could not expect help from company level; at least, we could not depend on it.

Japanese infantry were not killing and wounding us now. We guessed they were tired. They had shot thousands of Marines the past two days, and today they would shoot thousands more.

Dim outlines began taking shape near the base of Mount Suribachi. I thought maybe I could see a weakness in the enemy lines if I were closer as daylight grew brighter. I threw the white wool Japanese Navy blanket off my shoulders. The captured warm blanket that Ruhl, our platoon runner, had literally risked his life for would be of no use in today's battle. It would be left behind.

Nothing, I mean absolutely nothing, had meaning-not home, not mother, not wife, not children, not girlfriend, not hometown, not cold, hot, or hungry—nothing mattered except today's forthcoming battle, and it would commence very soon.

Now, dawn was breaking, and the platoon must prepare for our morning attack. I laid my helmet full of hand grenades and ammunition and my Tommy gun on top of the blanket. This was a one-man scouting party; I did not need a weapon. I crawled to a higher spot some distance in front of our line, squatted, and studied the enemy's defense. I was looking for any weakness to improve our chances in the frontal attack that I knew we were about to make.

My eyes were continually searching for the enemy in the early morning light. Dark gray shadows and ghosts of the enemy appeared behind each mound of dirt. Suddenly, movement caught my eye and centered my attention on the trenches that joined the huge concrete blockhouses and other pillboxes.

The enemy was moving its men in a unique way. Ruhl and I had seen them do this two nights before but thought it was a matter of convenience. Each man held onto a piece of equipment that belonged to the man in front of him as the group moved in a single-file. They moved without losing men or having anyone lag behind.

Ten or twelve men would be bent over and moving train-like one way and then another in the shallow trenches. This could be an excellent way to move combat men while they were in close quarters. We could do very little about this because only direct gunfire down these trenches would greatly affect the enemy. The trenches were perpendicular to our direction of attack.

The morning light grew brighter, and the Japanese defense looked stronger. Suddenly, a form took shape in front of me. There, in a shadow, not more than fifty or sixty yards away, squatted a Japanese officer looking straight at me. He was studying our lines, the same as I was studying his. I had left my Tommy gun on the blanket behind me. I had the .45 caliber automatic pistol. It was no good at this distance, so I turned to the men and yelled, "Get that son-of-a-bitch." The Jap officer stood up and showed all the teeth he could with a big grin and quickly stepped behind a large bunker a short distance behind him. The bunker had a damaged roof. I made a special mental note of that. The officer's grin was, no-doubt, a grin of confidence. He must have thought he had us just where he wanted. I was not sure that he did not. If there was a weakness in their defense, I had not found it.

Our Army Air Force, Navy Air Force, Marine Air Force and the large shells from our cruisers and battleships had exposed but not destroyed a single huge concrete emplacement in front of us. How in the Hell did they expect us to destroy them? We knew that Marine Corps expected the absolute maximum from its officers and men, but even that seemed doomed to fail.

The side of the mountain was like a honeycomb of small and large caves. Naval gun fire temporarily sealed the mouth of most of the small caves, and many sniper and machine gun nests lay waiting inside. The enemy would peer through small, scooped-out holes, and when targets were plentiful, they pushed out enough dirt for their weapons and began firing. Most of the Japanese with the smaller machine guns stayed and died with their guns. Usually there were other guns and crews inside ready to dig out and take their places.

In the morning attack, instinctively, I expected the utmost in coordinated support from the array of weapons we used in practice. The U. S. Navy had dominance of the sea. Not one enemy weapon fired against our Navy's big gun ships. Our ships could move in close to the island and pulverize the side of the mountain that we faced. They could maintain the fire power. This type action would either prevent the many caves on our side of the mountain from opening or they could close them instantly.

I felt sure our tanks would lead us in the attack. They would flatten the rolls of barbed wire in front of us and silence any large enemy weapon they could see. The tanks would blow holes in the concrete defenses. Lindberg and Goode could then use their efficient flamethrowers.

The Marine Corps' large artillery could help with the larger caves and do their best, along with the Navy, to neutralize the enemy's artillery that shelled us last evening. The shelling came from the north end of the island.

The Marine Corps smaller artillery, like the 37 millimeter, were positioned just back of our left flank. They could be selective in knocking out newly opened small caves at close range. I must have been living in a dream world to expect this much help. Even if we did receive most of it, I could not see how we could run across the open ground, cross our barbed wire entanglement, and breach and destroy their defenses. We had watched the Japanese fight the last two days. There would be a great loss of life in the frontal assault.

The OLD MAN (God) had not given me a clue, and it was getting late. He always gave me a clue. I depended on it.

Time was drawing near to jump off, and I had received no information or help from Company Headquarters. I picked up the sound-powered phone and asked for help. Their reply was that the tanks were back in a semi-protected area refueling. Well, the tanks had been behind the line all night. I thought, "How long does it take to refuel the damn things? The tank-Marines needed to rearm, refuel, repair, eat, sleep, make plans, get orders, and have some reasonable protection while they are doing all this. We all knew that - but we had a war going on.

Company Headquarters went on to say that the only Marine artillery piece on the island was facing the other direction. They stated that there was no 80 millimeter mortar ammunition. The mortars were useless anyway because the Japanese were underground and our weapons could not reach them. Then, they informed us that the battleships, cruisers, destroyers, and other Navy ships had not returned from their night's rendezvous, which was some distance away.

The very thought that we were attacking without any help from anyone was sobering and a deep, deep concern of mine. If the battle is a continuation of the kind of fighting we saw in the first two days, I thought that our platoon and everyone on the front line would be slaughtered. At a time like this we hate the people who are ordering us to our death. Especially, when the only three times we saw them, we stood and looked down. They dug in deep and did not show themselves.

Over the phone, I asked Company Headquarters just what help could we expect, and they thought that they could get us an air strike. Dive bombers would come in at a low altitude to bomb and strafe. This sounds good, but this action would only distract the Japanese long enough for us to get out in the open, where they could massacre us.

211

We got the air strike. The noise and action from the air attack were startling and bone chilling. Our attacking planes swooped down like mad bees in waves and in perfect order. Underground and well protected, the Japanese waited.

To avoid hitting any of the Marines, who were on top of the ground and not dug in, the dive bombers made their strike too far up the mountain to help us even a small amount. When I raised my head above the water can to have a look, I saw what I expected. If we could kill Japanese or scare them to death with noise and ground vibrations, that air strike would have done the job. Our end of the island had shaken violently while dirt and debris flew in every direction. I am sure not one Jap received the Japanese equivalent of the Purple Heart for combat wounds from this raid.

Since the expected enemy night attack did not take place, the barbed wire night-protector that we had so boldly laid last evening had now switched sides in the battle. A barbed wire entanglement can be a real hazard to the attacking force. That was the reason we had strung it. There was no way we could destroy it without tanks or help from our big weapons. It had become part of the enemy's defense.

It was time to attack! Over the phone came the orders to attack that fortification directly in front of us. We had nothing to attack with but our hand weapons and nothing to protect us but the clothes on our backs. So help me God, our orders were to do just that: "ATTACK!"

I asked Company Headquarters if that were all the help we would get, and they replied, "You should have jumped off one minute ago." Our situation looked so hopeless that I could not order the platoon to follow me. I stood up, pointed my Tommy gun toward the enemy, and took off running straight toward that God-damn grinning Japanese officer's bunker. It was the pillbox with the hole in the top. I could think of nothing else to do. Only God could help us now.

Corporal Richard Wheeler's account is impressive: "As the last group of planes droned away from the target, Sergeant Snyder, beside me in the shell hole, stood up and looked toward the rear. 'Where's our tank support?' He asked with a frown. It turned out that the tanks had been delayed by refueling and rearming difficulties. Lieutenant Wells decided not to wait for them. A few minutes later he launched our platoon's attack. Climbing out of his crater, he signalled with a sweep of his Thompson sub-machine gun for us to follow him, and began to trot toward Mount Suribachi. By this time we had learned that Wells' courage was not just talk. As we forced ourselves to rise from our holes and imitate his example, I could feel the fear dragging at my jowls. We seemed to be heading for certain death." <u>American Heritage</u> June 1964,

Alone, My God, how alone! Never did I feel so alone in my life. I ran toward the barbed wire entanglement, the Japanese line, and the bunker the Japanese officer disappeared behind. Insanity! The attack was unreal, like something out of the movies. To me, I thought it was a great waste of life.

I thought I needed to see better, so I ran slightly bent over. The urge to look back to see if anybody was coming was strong, but I fought it off. What I would do when I got to the enemy, I had no idea except to attack something.

Out of the corner of my eye, I saw Sergeant Thomas pulling one roll of wire out of the way, and then I saw Hansen and our Platoon runner trotting close to me. The others were coming; I just knew it.

The machine gunner in "I" Company that yelled the night before, yelled again: "Lieutenant, I'm going with you." He left his company and brought his machine gun and ammunition bearer with him. A great surge went through my body! What a lift their presence made! We jumped the other roll of wire and continued to run straight toward the massive enemy military might. I expected them to begin firing with all their weapons at any minute; but they did not. The closer we got to their line, the blockhouses and pillboxes seemed to grow in front of us and became larger. We paused every few minutes to catch our breath, check on any change, and look for any help. I did not want to stop often because it was hard to get started running again. I could see no support coming.

Our platoon had very few weapons to attack the enemy with when we reached them. If they opened-up on us at this close range, they would slaughter us quickly. There was no protection. The feeling surged through me that we were being led into a trap. They will close the trap and mow down the late comers, I thought.

In front of our right flank that joined "I" Company stood the two largest enemy emplacements. We ran toward them. Parts of our Third Platoon were already in trouble. They were the furthest away and the last to leave our night's defense. I could hear and feel the earth-shaking explosions behind us as we ran. The Japanese were working the area with 90 millimeter mortars. They were loud and powerful and lacked the rhythm of artillery.

I looked up, and I could see the large enemy mortar shells arching high above our heads. The shells would slow, stop, and start back down. Since their shells were directly overhead, I could tell where they came from. By the arch I could predict the area in which they would explode. The enemy put shells into the old bomb craters without a miss.

213

They worked the craters like a fisherman works his nets. Several men from the First and Third Squads were caught in the Japanese pre-planned defense barrage.

The Japanese did everything by the numbers and carried that work plan to the finest detail. I did not know if they were letting us reach their line intentionally or if we were surprising them by attacking without help from the Marine Corps or anyone else. They would activate their defense, do their routine, even if they did it later than planned.

I heard extra loud explosions on our left. A quick look told me the enemy's artillery was beginning to fire from the north end of the island. An orange colored smoke rose to show their artillery spotter that they were on target. Smoke from the spotter shell drifted over us. It smelled something like a poisonous gas that we had sniffed in practice. Yellow liquid that came with the shell painted the spot where the shell landed. Also, the liquid painted the brush and men nearby.

We did not have time to worry about that. Small Japanese machine guns began firing. On our right flank I heard what I thought was the same unknown large machine gun that I heard yesterday. It soon stopped, as did the artillery. Someone helped us out.

Ruhl, Hansen, Thomas, and I were leading this wild attack. Immediately behind us was a sprinkling of four squads, including the young machine gunner and his helper from "I" Company.

The immediate area along the enemy's defense line remained clean of any possible protection for us. Our Navy and our many air forces had apparently tried everything. Shell and bomb craters marked the area. Black spots on the ground and shrubbery pointed out where they had dropped napalm, a burning oil that burns the enemy and uses up oxygen in caves and closed-in areas. Nothing worked, and the enemy remained snug underground.

We continued to run straight at the enemy. I could not believe they were not shooting at us. Close and in front of the two big concrete emplacements was a large bomb crater that we jumped into and ran out the back side. Ruhl and Hansen continued running.

I stopped on the far edge and quickly looked back across the open ground. "I" company was still in their defense position. The Third Platoon's right flank remained exposed. Shells were landing among the last to leave the defense positions, but when the dust cleared I could see some men stand up and continue running toward us and the enemy.

The enemy pillboxes and blockhouses had slits to fire through, but they remained closed; we ran on past the slits. We were not more than ten or fifteen feet from the large blockhouse on our right, and not much more than that from the large pillbox with the damaged roof. The Japanese officer watching our lines early this morning had disappeared behind the one with the damaged roof. The four of us were past the gun-ports of both.

Ruhl and Hansen charged on ahead to the trench joining the two concrete houses. This trench ran behind and connected many defensive positions circling the front of the Mountain. It was the same trench where we had observed the human chains of men moving about early this morning.

I turned around from watching our struggling platoon behind us just in time to see both Hansan and Ruhl drop to their hands and knees and look over the edge of the trench. They must have almost bumped heads with the Japanese because they jerked back fast.

Ruhl and Hansen had kneeled down side by side; now they lay that way. Immediately, over the side came an object much larger than the enemy's hand-grenade. The large explosive charge landed between the two men. Ruhl yelled at Hansen, "Look out Hank," and then he flopped down on the object.

We heard the muffled explosion. From the power and shock of the explosion I saw Ruhl's body rise into the air, then flop back. Hansen grabbed Ruhl by the pants-leg and began dragging him back towards me, but I yelled and waved for him to quit. One of Ruhl's shoulders fell back. It looked disconnected from his body, and I could see a great cavity that was once his chest.

Ruhl's body prevented a large amount of dirt and dust from flying. We could see Japaneses' backs as they traveled to our right down the trench. They were jabbering like crazy people. They were about ten or fifteen yards away from me. Thomas was on our right next to the large blockhouse and just behind me. I think that when Ruhl and Hansen almost bumped heads with the enemy was the first knowledge that this group of Japanese had that we were on top of them.

Corporal Robert Lane, Private First Class William Wayne, Corporal Everett "Pappy" Lavelle from the Second Squad and Private First Class Richard White from the Assault squad were just behind us in the large bomb crater.

The enemy trench that ran behind and connected the enemy's concrete defense line bulged with Japanese, but they moved just far enough away and possibly round a bend in the trench to be protected from us. Near the spot where Ruhl was killed was a place that commanded the trench and looked down the throat of the Japs that tried to use it.

When I looked back to see how many men got through the

concentration of mortar and artillery shelling, I noticed that our right flank was still unprotected. "I" Company had not begun their attack. I saw that Sergeant Snyder was near with part of his men. The machine gunner and his helper from "I" Company joined up with Snyder and his squad.

The noise of combat was so great that uttering a word was useless. With a motion of my hand to Snyder to get his attention, I pointed to a location that commanded (looked down) the Japanese trench. He did not hesitate. Snyder took Adrian and Robeson up close to the spot.

It was an ideal place to sweep the trench clean of Japanese. Sergeant Snyder and Corporal Keller started throwing hand grenades into the trench, and this gave Adrain and Robeson time to get in place to use their B.A.Rs. Both teenagers had inherited their B.A.R.s on the first day and night of battle. I have said this before, but he constantly amazed me-Snyder was a small man in size but a giant of a fighting man. He was a natural warrior.

Snyder was kneeling and unhurriedly throwing hand grenades. The timing was close enough to keep the Japanese off guard while Adrian and Robeson reloaded. After he had thrown several, I pitched my grenades up to him.

Adrian was firing directly down the trench. He was only arm's length from Snyder. Adrian looked intent on shooting the Japanese. He quickly rose to his feet as if he wanted a better shot. Adrian dropped to the ground in an unnatural way. I looked for a corpsman but did not see one. When I looked back, Snyder was gently turning Adrian over. He checked close, looked at me, and shook his head. His lip movement said, "Through the heart." I could never praise the Reservation Indian boys enough. Adrian was one fine American. His mother is in her nineties (1993). She lives by herself on a reservation in Washington State. Chick Robeson keeps us posted. Robeson's mother lives near her.

We were out of hand grenades and almost out of ammunition. Some men in our platoon were caught in the heavy mortar barrage, and the enemy trapped some by a flanking fire coming from our unprotected right flank. Only a few could work their way through to us.

Private Edward Krisik from the Assault Squad landed close and worked his way up to me. I looked back to the Company or Battalion for help of any kind but saw none. I told Krisik to leave his extra weight he was carrying and go back and get us some "God Damn" help. We needed ammunition, hand grenades, and shaped charges.

Our flame throwers were on their way. I could see them coming, but we could not use them until we could make a hole in the enemy's

216

concrete defenses. Krisik left in a hurry. I turned around in time to see Snyder wave the "I" Company machine gunner and his crewman up to take Adrian's place. Snyder pointed to the spot to place the machine gun. If there was ever a professional machine gun crew, this was it. They got the Japanese's attention, and I mean quickly.

With this gun crew's help, we cleaned out the trenches in our immediate front; however, we were catching hell from our right flank each time we moved out and away from the big blockhouse.

Thomas said he was going back to help "I" Company come up and join our right flank. I agreed. I hoped he could make it. I had sent Krisik back, and they evidently killed or wounded him. We could not afford any more men.

Behind us was a "no-man's land." I did not want Thomas to go, but we were running out of everything fast, including men. He knew "I" Company needed to be hooked into our line, and with their help, the enemy flanking fire would stop. The job needed to be done, and if anybody could do it, Thomas could.

Corporal Wayne Hathaway crawled up to me and said, "Lieutenant, I will get what we need and get it back to you." He had several battle experiences behind him when he was with the Raider Battalion. I thought that if anybody could do it, he could. God, I hated to risk the two men.

We were fighting in plain sight of everybody, and nobody helped. The little "I" Company machine gunner was firing his machine gun in short bursts when suddenly the full power of the Japanese on our right flank descended on him, and he was blown away from the gun. The machine gunner's ammunition bearer quickly took over the gun, and he was blown away also. Robeson was jerked away from the line of fire by Keller or they would have killed him also. Corporal Keller had now saved both Robeson and me. How Snyder missed this barrage, I do not know.

As the battle raged in every direction, we were getting a shower of hand grenades from the concrete bunker on our right. This blockhouse protected some of us from the enemy fire power from the right, and we were past the door that would expose us to enemy fire from within.

The Japanese could not reach us with their weapons. We were past the gun slits in the blockhouse. They would quickly throw hand grenades and then close the opening. These were concussion grenades; we did not worry about shrapnel. When the grenades fell near me and the others, which was almost every time, I could squat down on one leg and bend my body away until after the explosion. The power of the explosion was almost straight up, so if we could bend to one side, all we would catch would be a shower of dirt. The deafening noise and sand blast from the grenades kept us pinned down.

Because the Jap's timing was not regular, we could not catch him with the door open. The grenades were a real problem, but we had too many other things to think about. We needed to protect ourselves from weapons that were more deadly.

More men from our Assault Squad arrived. With them was Clarence Hipp, our demolition man. Hansen wanted to blow the door in with a satchel of C/2 composition (explosive). What became of our shaped charges I do not know. I did not think the composition would work, but that constant harassment with the hand grenades kept us in a state of dodging and adjusting ourselves. We started this wild morning party with two shape charges (explosives that might penetrate the closed aperture. The explosives did not make it this far.

Hansen was impatient with Hipp. When Hipp set the fuse, Hansen grabbed the satchel from Hipp and charged the bunker. Instead of placing it, he thought he was close enough and threw it. He missed by several feet, and now we were all hunting protection from a big explosion. The smoke and dirt had not cleared when the enemy grenades sailed again.

I continued to look back and to my right flank. Hathaway and Krisik, men that went back, disappeared; I heard no extra weapons firing. We were desperate. I did see Colonel Johnson watching us through binoculars. Almost halfway to us was a small, open top tank with some men and what looked like supplies.

How the Japanese hit the moving supply tank, I do not know, but they did. The tank along with the men went up in smoke, and that was the end of that bold effort.

Now the Japanese mortar men were bringing their shots from behind us and walking them in toward us. I could tell that by the sound. I looked up and saw the large mortar shells arch almost over head.

A single man, loaded with a telephone and telephone wire, was headed in our direction. I did not have to guess. I knew who it was, and I knew where he came from. No shape charges, no hand grenades, and no men, I let out a string of curse words so loud that God could hear. I could not imagine what was more important than getting more men and equipment to us.

As I worked my way back to the big shell hole, the Company Communication man dropped the roll of wire in the bottom of the hole and handed me the phone. He said, "The Captain wants to talk to you."

I took the phone and returned to the front edge of the crater lip,

218

*Lt. Col. Chandler W. Johnson
....finest Marine I ever knew.*

the lip nearest the Japs. With my head and shoulders out facing the enemy, I could watch the progress from there. I answered the phone.

Captain Severance at company headquarters wanted a "God damn" casualty report. We had dead, dying, and wounded men everywhere. We were out in front and in plain sight of everybody, and he wants a casualty report. Every few minutes the Platoon lost men killed and wounded. The last men to jump-off were caught in a mortar barrage. I thought that if he would get out of that concrete bunker and use his eyes, he could count them better than we could. I noticed that no one was coming down to help us, and no one was bringing us anything to fight with. I said, "God damn, Captain, leave us alone and let us fight!"

As I threw the phone down and turned to climb out of the crater, a large jap mortar shell hit the roll of phone wire near my feet and exploded. When I could catch my breath, I looked at Snyder through the volcanic ash flying. On his face I saw a deep frown as he looked in my direction.

The shock and blast of sound numbed my senses. It took me a few seconds to clear my mind. There was a sharp burning sensation in my neck and no feeling from the waist down. With my hands, I felt behind me to see if I still had my legs. My hand came back wet with blood and water. A large piece of metal had hit my canteen, and it exploded. I could stick my fist inside my canteen. Another piece of metal hit a stainless steel spoon in my right hind pocket, turning the spoon inside out. Many small pieces of shrapnel buried in my right hind cheek. A large piece of flesh was blown from my left leg just above the knee. Worst of all, a larger piece of metal entered my left leg about a foot above my left knee, and I found out later that a piece lodged deep in my

219

neck. My clothes below the waist were almost gone. I lay on my stomach and that saved my front. Also, the backpack I risked my life for yesterday saved my back. My clothes were gone and that was bad, but it made it easier for Bradley, the Platoon's senior corpsman, to administer first aid.

Squad Leader Bob Lane, Pappy Lavelle, Dick White, and Bill Wayne were also in the big bomb crater, and all were wounded. Young Dick White began shouting for a corpsman. I asked him about his wounds. He said he thought his heel was blown off. He also had a leg wound. When he yelled for a corpsman again, I told him to shut up. With everything else happening, his wounds were minor. I quit worrying about him. Each man in the pit told me their wounds were not life threatening.

The feeling came back into my legs, and I almost wished it had not. Bradley dressed my wounds then gave me a syrett {tube}of morphine through my dungaree jacket. We had to get on with the war.

On our left was the concrete bunker with the damaged roof. This is the one I thought the Jap officer ducked into early this morning. I watched it continuously out of the corner of my eye because we had our backs turned to it most of the time. I expected enemy action from it.

"Thank God, thank God" for the two men that handled our flame-throwers. They had carried them for two days and now part of a third. These flame-throwers were not only fully loaded but had been kept clean and ready to use. This is almost unbelievable considering the flame-throwers are heavy, bulky, and hard to keep out of the ash and dirt. Chuck Lindberg and Robert Goode accomplished this feat. Chuck was in charge of the Assault Squad, and it could not have been run better.

Lindberg was ready to go to work when he arrived. There was nothing for him to work on except the possible hole in the roof of the pillbox. I pointed to the hole in the roof, and Lindberg worked his way over to it. I hoped he did not expose himself to a back flash. If the hole was not completely through the concrete, the oil and flame would come back on him. The flame goes to oxygen. If there is none where the flame is pointed, it flashes back to oxygen in the open air.

When Lindberg reached the top, he stuck the nozzle of his flame-thrower into the hole. Flaming oil shot into the pillbox. The volcano-like eruption was almost spontaneous. Smoke came back out of the hole on top. Immediately, the explosions inside the pill box blew off the front concrete door. If the Japanese officer was in there, it was all over for him.

The potential danger of the now-exploding pillbox sitting there

220

behind us kept us from giving full attention to the big block house on our right. The big blockhouse on our right continued spewing out hand grenades. Japs inside the blockhouse evidently shot Rozek and Hathaway, and no help was coming from the rear.

I did not see Thomas, and I hoped they were too busy to shoot him. "I" Company was beginning to move up on our right flank. What was left of the enemy's firepower that killed Adrian and the machine gunners was focusing its attention on "I" Company's movement. The burning pillbox exploded every few minutes. Shell casings and flame would fly out of the door with each explosion. We lost contact with the second platoon on the other side of the exploding pillbox. It was dangerous to send anybody around there.

The enemy machine gunners that continually stuck their weapons out of holes in the mountain found good targets shooting at the Second Platoon on our left, and "I" Company was drawing fire on our right. We could hear them and make judgments about where they were. The Japanese had other targets and left us alone.

I heard someone yell. When I looked back and saw those turtle-like slow-moving tanks coming toward us. I could have kissed every tread on their tracks. I saw some Japanese mortar shells explode around them, but they kept coming.

Thomas was back! Thank God he helped tie "I" Company to our right flank — "What a Man!" One tank moved into our area. Thomas and Hansen quickly showed it the blockhouse that was giving us the hand grenade trouble. Lindberg exposed himself boldly and stayed near the tank. We were still dodging hand grenades, but we knew their limitation. They annoyed us to the point that we might do something foolish to stop them.

My thoughts quickly went back to two nights ago when the Japs rushed out of the back door of the big blockhouse. We had to be ready. I sent Goode to the backside where I knew there must be a concrete door opening out into the trench running along behind the line of pillboxes and blockhouses.

The tank moved to within a few feet of the blockhouse and lowered the muzzle of the French 75 millimeter cannon. It was only a few feet from the side of the blockhouse. When Goode was in place, the tank started firing at one spot with armor piercing shells. In what seemed like seconds I counted nineteen shells before they broke through. Lindberg quickly put his flame-thrower nozzle in the hole and fired two or three burst.

Only two or three minutes passed before the back door of the blockhouse flew open, and three Japanese ran out. All three were on fire

221

and partially covered with flame thrower oil. Why did Goode hold off from hitting them with his flame-thrower, I thought? When I quickly looked at him, I found him looking at me with a questioning look on his face. I gave him a look that he understood. He hit them with two or three flames of burning oil. The Japanese curled up like bacon. None of the other Japs tried to come out. The oil was still burning inside when somebody closed the door and sealed the hole on top.

The Platoon began working on the next blockhouse. I could not see it, but I counted the shots made by the tank, and it took twenty-one by my count. Thomas and Hansen had the men move on to the right; also, they started destroying smaller Japanese strong points nearer the base of the mountain. Only small problems remained in front and to the right. It was time to check our left flank.

I could hear action on the other side of the exploding bunker. Platoon Sergeant McGarvey and the Second Platoon were having their problems. The exploding pillbox was still on fire, but not as much as before. Shell casings were still flying out of the door with each eruption.

Because of the sniper fire and enemy machine guns that can appear almost like magic out of the mountain, I decided to risk passing the exploding front door. For me to go past the pillbox's backside was more dangerous, I thought. I would be exposing myself to the mountain. The pillbox afforded some protection if I could get past the door.

I cleared the door between explosions and was running with my legs wide apart to keep my wounds from rubbing. As I passed the door and my eyes cleared, orange trip-wires appeared everywhere. Trip wires to land mines, I thought as my mind was working overtime. With my legs already wide apart, I began to toe dance through them.

Quickly, I came face-to-face with a Japanese machine gun. The Japanese was only a short distance away and looking down at me. The sound of the bullets going by was different from the other times. He was not shooting at my head, because that sound was like the crack of a whip when bullets pass your ear. An enemy bullet passing by to one side would give a pop sound. This sound was different. From the expression on his face, I could see that the Jap gunner was intent on killing me.

Suddenly, I felt the bullets hitting the inside my left leg near the spot where a hot piece of metal had buried itself. His bullets were hitting close to my privates, which was the only place I still had some clothes. I quickly raised that leg and dived behind a small mound of dirt. The machine gunner continued trying to get to me.

Dirt was flying around me when Bradley, our corpsman, crawled up behind me, and started dressing my wounds again. My wounds were wide open and dressing was trailing in the dirt. Bradley asked me if these were new wounds, and I told him that I did not think so.

Later I learned that the machine gunner blew a large piece of muscle from the inside of my left leg, or Bradley did not record it the first time. It was not reported until I went aboard the ship. I was thinking that the hole was there. That was the reason I was running with my legs apart.

I heard another weapon firing near by. Quickly the enemy machine gunner switched his fire to another target. I raised and looked just in time to see a tall blond young man from the Second Platoon raise up. Hesse (Corporal Lewis M. Hesse) was standing upright and firing with his rifle. The Japanese machine gunner was firing at him.

When the Japanese quit firing, Private L.B.Holly, also from the Second Platoon and crouched near by, yelled, "You got him, Hesse," and Hesse said, "Yes, and he got me." Hesse folded up and laid down.

Bradley gave me another syrett of morphine through my clothes. He told me I should start back. I did not feel the first morphine shot, but I began to feel this one.

I could feel myself running out of energy. My wounds were beginning to take their toll. That was understandable. I had not eaten, drunk water, urinated, or defecated in two and one-half days. Maybe it was the shot of morphine that kept me going before, and this one would keep me going for a given length of time.

It must have taken at least twenty to thirty minutes to check the platoon and talk with Thomas and Hansen. We had cleaned the Japs out of our area. Thomas took over what was left of the platoon, and I started my long crawl back.

To the best of my knowledge we had seventeen casualties in that short battle, but only four deaths. The 3rd Platoon was now cut almost in half.

Chapter 13

THE CRAWL BACK AND GOING ABOARD THE COMMAND SHIP
ABOARD THE *ELDORADO*

I studied the area and selected a route through the Second Platoon. There was no use going back through the area the Third Platoon moved through earlier; I would skirt that area.

The Second Platoon's area I judged to be the less dangerous. It had more ground cover by being on the fringe area of the drop off to the ocean. I knew I could not run, and I knew I could not walk much longer. I passed Hesse. God bless him. A tag attached to his collar button-hole designated him for burial.

Just before I reached the open country I crawled into a protected area. There I found Lieutenant George L. Wilson and two senior sergeants. With field glasses and radios, they were observing. What else they were doing, I do not know.

Lieutenant Wilson was a good officer, and he was concerned about me. He ordered the two Sergeants to escort me back. I refused them for these reasons. There had been no replacements (fresh troops) sent down, and the platoon lost both men we had sent back. I had vowed that no one would touch me but a corpsman.

After our initial attack, only one man had made it down to our platoon. He came with the telephone wire. The enemy probably let him through just to spot a leader. We were not sure the lineman made it back. Headquarters did not send anyone else after the enemy mortar round hit the first roll of wire. Besides, more than one man out in that no-man's land might draw additional fire. Even with me ordering them to remain, the sergeants followed me to the open sand.

The ash and sand were hard to walk through even for someone healthy. It was not long before I was crawling most of the time. I saw Colonel Johnson watching me with his field-glasses.

A mortar shell hit near me. I put my head and chest in a slight depression and two more mortar rounds hit next to me. When the dirt cleared, I looked around to see what in the Hell they were shooting at. A dead man and I were the only ones near the explosions. The mortars did not fire again; however, I decided not to take a chance. Physically, I crawled directly over the dead man; that was the only protection in sight. The dead man occupied most of the small area.

Halfway over, I heard him groan. He asked for a drink of water, and I gave it to him. After looking him over good, I saw he was not going to make it if he stayed there very long. Most of his groin area was shot away; it looked as if he had a gut shot also. There was about two hundred yards left for me to crawl. I was not sure I could make it.

"If I can make it, I will send someone back for you," I told him, and I kept crawling. When I looked at the battalion defense line, I saw Colonel Johnson with a communication man, holding a radio, standing near him. Colonel Johnson was watching me with field glasses. I did not see anyone from "E" Company Headquarters, and they were near. In fact, I never saw anybody from "E" Company Headquarters except the man who carried the roll of telephone wire.

The colonel was sending a stretcher down for me. I saw them coming, on-the-double. Why they did not send one down for the other poor Marine I do not know. One thing I knew—I was not going to get on that stretcher. Captain Bo Bo Mears was on a stretcher when the Japanese mortars got him. Not as long as I could crawl would I allow them to carry me on one. I sent the stretcher on down for that poor man. This was his only chance, if he had one.

Over on my right was the light artillery group with 37 millimeter cannons. One of their men recognized me and yelled my name. He wanted to know If I needed any help. I told him "no." He asked if he could have my Tommy Gun. I told him that when I got my wounds dressed, I would be back. He said he would have it clean and ready for me when I did. The gun was getting harder for me to carry. I let him have the weapon.

It is true that I was looking out for old J.K.(me) on this crawl back, but when I did stop to rest, I looked back at the platoon area. The sergeant leaders would do a good job, and I knew it.

Pieces of human flesh lay everywhere. One piece of human intestine was several yards long. It was pointing toward the First Aid Station. All the stretcher carriers were headed toward that spot. I continued to crawl.

When I reached the station, I was put on a stretcher and carried down to the beach. There were hundreds there. The stretchers were end to end. God only knows how many there were with only inches between stretchers. This was a great target for the enemy, I thought.

I guess the enemy had enough targets where they were, and the nearby targets were more pressing. I felt totally naked lying there and looking at the war only a rifle-shot away. I wanted to crawl off to another place and get behind or under something.

We had Marines bringing Marines on stretchers, Marines leaving some with stretchers, and Marines caring for their buddies. Some

Marines in the stretchers were dead or dying. Landing crafts and small boats from all the ships at anchor were trying to penetrate the log jam situation at the water's edge so that they could pick up casualties. My body screamed for me to find protection. As I looked, Lieutenant Delbert O. Greenlee from Sioux Falls, S.D. came up to my stretcher. He had a wounded hand. It did not look bad, but it could get serious. He was undecided whether to go to a ship or back into combat.

I recognized a man heading in my direction. He was bending over each man and saying a few words. Some men asked for him, some never knew he was there, but for others it was too late. The man was Regimental Chaplain Paul(Padre) Bradley.I had long since forgiven him for what I thought was a mistake he made in camp back in Hawaii when he told the men about the fifty percent (50%) casualties.

Chaplin Bradley was giving "Last Rites" as fast as he could, and then he came to me. I said, "Not me, Padre;" He said "Wells" and then

226

asked about the seriousness of my wounds. I told him I thought they were all flesh wounds and imbedded shrapnel. He moved on quickly. This Chaplin was, and I am sure still is, a fine human being doing his job.

The two morphine shots corpsman Bradley gave me wore off, and I was now in pain. If I felt sorry for myself, all I had to do was to look around me. If there could have been a way in the world to have helped some of these men, I would have tried it. My heart just breaks now to think about it.

I thought it was bad to lie there on the beach, which we did for what seemed like hours. Finally, stretcher bearers loaded us side by side and end to end in the bottom of a landing craft. Two young sailors manned the landing craft.

Being flat bottomed, the boat did not ride the waves well. Everyone capable of being sea-sick was sick. If the wounded could, they would lean off the stretcher to vomit. The two sailors manning the boat paid no attention to the wounded. There was nothing they could do anyway. The only sounds were moans, groans, and cursing.

Apparently, our command assigned only one hospital ship to this operation, and it was loaded and gone. If there were more, they

227

were loaded and gone also. Every type of ship lying offshore took the dead and wounded aboard. I am not sure whether they used signal flags or flashing lights to designate a loading ship, but we would line up to be taken aboard.

The line would be long. Regardles of the length of line, regardless of the wounded's needs, we stayed in that long line and wallowed around until the loading ship was full. We would then rush to the next loading ship and line up to go through the same wallowing around in line until we charged to the next ship. Sick, sick, and dying, and still we lined up and waited. It had to be done the Navy way, and it was thought to be the best and most accurate. No doubt they thought they had moved the more serious off the beach first.

We lay in the bottom of the boat the rest of the day rushing from one ship to another lining up and then being turned away. The wounded men in our boat were not tended to in any way, not even given a drink of water, and that was bad. It was getting dark, and the loaded ships were leaving to go to a rendezvous area, miles away. No doubt this was war-time regulation. They would not be caught again, as they were at Pearl Harbor.

I heard the two sailors screaming, and when I looked I saw them standing up, stretched and waving their arms. This did not go on long until I saw them frantically grabbing life preservers. They had as many as two apiece, but they did not throw one life preserver to us. Some of the wounded and seasick were aware that there was a crisis, but no one stirred. I never saw anyone so frantic as the two sailors.

At the peak of their excitement, I looked up and saw a large ship so close that I believe the sailors could have reached out and touched it. The bow wake turned us up on the side, and I could see the ocean from the bottom of the landing craft. The passing ship was reaching top speed, and I am sure they never saw us.

The command ship of the operation, the USS ELDORADO, was the only ship remaining. How did I know it was the command ship? Its masts were so full of communication wire that the ship looked as if it had a hair net over it. Every other ship was filled and gone. We lined up. I think we were the third boat in line, and I lay on my back watching the unloading from the stretcher.

They would lower the pulleys and hook on to each end of the unloading boat. Then they would pull the boat up thirty or forty feet into the air and transfer the stretchers from the boat to the ship. The ship and boat would rock apart every few seconds or minutes and the crew would almost drop a stretcher. I am sure the crew had never performed this task before.

228

While I was watching, I saw a stretcher slip from the crew's hands and fall. The crew was not timing the rock of the ship. I do not know what happened to the man. Some crew member told me that it killed the wounded man, but of course I am not sure. He may have already been dead. Because they would transfer me soon, I made myself ready. When the time came, I not only told them how but when to make the transfer. If they dropped me, I was determined to take one or two of them with me.

Most of the sailors handling us were stealing everything that could be called a souvenir. They were desperate, I guess, for they had no way of getting souvenirs. The canteen that you could stick your fist into and the stainless steel spoon that was turned wrong-side-out was gone. I hoped that stealing did not effect the caring of the wounded.

My cursing was loud enough for the whole ship to hear. Dropping that man and the stealing enraged me. When they carried me into what looked like a stateroom turned into a hospital ward, I was still cursing loudly.

Inside everything was business-like. These Navy officers and corpsmen were doing their best to take care of the wounded Marines.

My loud cursing attracted the attention of a man in the very back and I heard this loud voice say: "Is that you, Lieutenant Wells?" and without looking, I said, "It sure is, Hathaway." What I am about to tell you now - bear with me. It really shakes me up. We are talking about one of the finest men, I ever knew.

Wayne C. Hathaway, a quiet spoken ex-Raider from El Dorado, Kansas. He was a quiet but sure man, and very dependable. Dependable is not a good word. Let us say, he was always there. What a man! If you remember, he received the Dear John letter back in camp. Others thought or pretended they did not care when they got a "Dear John letter" but not Hathaway. He cared. This morning, he was the one that knew we needed help and gave his life to try and get it for us.

On the ship the Doctors and Corpsman heard us trying to talk, and they could tell we cared for each another. They carried me over to him so that we could talk easy. He began trying to explain why he could not get men and shaped charges. I told him not to think about it and briefly told him how the battle had finally swung in our favor.

They brought me some food, and I could not eat it. The food would come right back up. It was then that they discovered that I had not eaten food or drunk water for three days. They learned that I did not urinate or defecate. They started force-feeding me with liquids and irrigating me in the other end. My system had taken up all moisture, and, I guess, food value. Only hard marbles washed out. I had almost killed myself by dehydration. They told me that if the Japs had not wounded me, I would have died, and soon.

Every few hours they gave me two or three shots of medicine. One shot, I learned, was penicillin. The doctors told me that it was their first use of this wonderful drug.

The doctor told me they would operate on Hathaway soon. He had serious internal bleeding. A Japanese shot him with an altered bullet that split into two or more pieces after it hit his body.

Every few hours I would get the corpsman to walk me. I remained determined to go back on Iwo Jima Island. I thought that nobody could run the platoon like I could. That is the way most young Marine officers think. The enemy will kill too many men if someone does not look out for them, I thought. From my experience, I did not trust part of the upper echelon.

I told the doctors I was going back ashore. Another man continued calling to the doctor, "Fix me up, Doc, I need to get back to my outfit." Since that was my thinking, I asked about him and others that might have the same thought. A doctor announced that everyone would be transferred to a hospital ship when one came. He also told me that the man doing the talking would be dead in a short time, because a shell had destroyed both of his kidneys.

Early in the morning I got a wake-up call. The corpsmen kept their distance until I was fully awake. They learned quickly not to walk-up and grab or touch me. When they touched me the first time without waking me first, I sent the needle flying and scared them. It was dark, and as far as I knew, they were Japanese. If I were awake, they did not have a problem.

I thought this call had something to do with the regular medical shots, but it was not. A corpsman helped me to Hathaway's bedside. Hathway was in serious trouble. He had attempted to leave his bed, they thought, for a bathroom trip. However, they were sure that in doing so, he had torn loose all that the doctors had done in an operation a short time earlier. The corpsmen admitted that they had failed to tie him to his bed after the operation.

They had found Hathaway's girlfriend's picture with her name and had been calling her name in his ear, but they saw no response. He would, however, react and be alert to the sound of my name. I did not tell them that Hathaway's girlfriend had deserted him. I spent a great amount of my ambulatory time with Hathaway. Later, I learned that this had an effect on the doctors and helped them to decide to allow me to return to Iwo when I requested it. The doctor told me that Hathaway was going to die. Also, the doctors told me that I had nearly killed myself with dehydration. I had lost something close to thirty-four pounds in three days. I resolved that in the next battle, I would eat a limited amount of food and drink plenty of water.

We were lucky to be on the Command ship. The ship did have a good medical staff; the small ships did not. I have already seen General Smith and Admiral Turner, the principal commanders of the invasion.

On the second night while the corpsmen were walking me, the highest ranking doctor aboard-ship invited me to sit with the General, the Admiral, and a Government dignitary. I learned later that it was Secretary of the Navy James V. Forrestal. They were watching a movie. The screen was set up in a secluded place. Lesser-ranked officers sat on the back side of the screen. They saw the picture in reverse. With all the bad news, I think now that they were doing the best they knew how to take care of the wounded and the Secretary of the Navy. They could do nothing else, but I will admit I resented them doing this and asked a corpsman to walk me to my bunk.

This ship was not expected to take on casualties and was not equiped to do so, yet there had been no hospital ship to take the wounded off. Men were dying and at least once a day the ship held burial-at-sea ceremonies. I saw them do this later, on another ship. The dead men were put in a sack with a weight in it. Corpsmen carried the dead to the open deck on a board-like stretcher with an American flag lying on top of the dead man. One end of the stretcher was hooked to the edge of the ship. After a short ceremony, they lifted the end of the stretcher, and the weighted sack went to the bottom of the ocean. This left the flag fluttering in the breeze as if it was waving "Good-bye."

The regular ships in the Navy were not prepared and did not have the knowledge or training to handle many of these wounded men. Blow flies had deposited their eggs on the men's wounds. The Navy doctors allowed them to stay. These maggots eat only dead flesh, we were told, and I think that was true. I inspected them closely. It was thought that the elimination of the dead flesh would help prevent Gangrene from taking hold. We thought Gangrene was the first stage of death for the wounded. This practice was used throughout the Fleet. It did not always work. Later, on another ship, I saw one young man die with gangrene, and he had maggots eating the dead flesh on his arm. He was sitting up talking, when suddenly he stiffened, turned white, and died. I liked this young stranger, and, with help, I went on the open deck and stood by for his burial at sea.

If any ship in the Fleet found any treatment working, they would pass the word on to the other ships. Until the hospital ship returned, the

231

combat ships tried anything that might work.

Someone circulated the information that the soft malleable wire that holds the straw on a common broom was the hardware that the doctors were using to put broken bones together. There was a mad search for brooms throughout the combat fleet.

Most wounds were never cleaned, but left just as they were. Corpsmen and helpers on the island wrapped clothes, dirt, and pieces of loose flesh in one large bandage. They covered the serious wounds with plaster-of-paris casts. This was on top of the above-mentioned things. Holes were cut into the casts. We could observe the maggots working. Infection was fought with sulfa and penicillin. Juices from the open wounds on the men's bodies soaked through the casts. These juices would rot and add that to the stench of the medication, and you can guess the condition of the sick-bay aboard ship.

On the fifth day of battle, my second day on the ship, the doctor and corpsmen said they expected a hospital ship soon. Also, they were getting patients ready to move. Hathaway's condition was worsening gradually. There was not much hope, but I did wish the hospital ship would just hurry.

Sometime before noon of the fifth day, there was a great commotion, and for the first time there was good news. The American flag was placed on top of Mount Suribachi.

I could tell, by talking to the doctors, that the day-to-day news was going out to the American people, and it had all been bad. Washington was on the hot-seat. The mothers, fathers, and the American people were not taking the deaths of their sons too well. Before the day was over, the high command had Platoon Sergeant Thomas out to the command ship to talk by radio back to the United States. He was in charge of the 3rd Platoon, and they had raised the American Flag.

General Smith allowed Thomas to spend about an hour with me and Hathaway. Hathaway did not know we were there. A reporter interviewed us, and I think he wrote something for the Marine Corps Leatherneck Magazine.

Sergeant Thomas told me that Colonel Johnson picked our platoon to go to the top of Mount Suribachi, secure it, and raise the American flag. First Lieutenant Harold G. Schrier, "E" Company's Executive officer went with them. I think Thomas was running the platoon better than I did. Is not that always the case?

Before the battle, our commanders led us to believe that we would win the battle of Iwo Jima in four days. Here it was the fifth day, and we were just getting started. Until the flag raising happened, because of the enormous loss of life, Marine morale was at the very bottom,

I spent an hour or more with Thomas before he returned to the outfit. This young sergeant was as fine as the finest. He would have gone far in the Marine Corps. I was proud of him. It was a privilege to serve with men like him.

The ship's personnel began moving quickly, and orders by the officers were crisp. The wounded were being made ready for transfer to a hospital ship.

Hathaway, and now Thomas, impressed the doctors, and the doctors and corpsmen arranged for me to hide in the Chief's quarters while they transferred the wounded. Hathaway made the transfer; however, I was told that he died a few days later.

The doctors loaded my B.A.R. belt with 20 tubes(seretts) of morphine and some sulfa drugs. The corpsmen and a doctor guided me to a passage way. They kept me there until a press boat was loaded and about to be lowered over the side of the ship. I strode across the deck and stepped into the back of the boat. Nobody said a thing. Nothing was said on the way to shore. I was going back to Iwo Jima Island.

Chapter 14

BACK TO THE ISLAND
MOUNT SURIBACHI

Well-organized work forces had taken over the beach area while I was aboard Admiral Turner's flagship, The Eldorado. The beach was not clear, but there was room to land the ship's boat. Loose equipment now lay in piles, and the piles were away from the landing area. I quickly got the feeling that the Marines and Seabees were organizing their work forces on the south end of the island. I dismounted (horse cavalry language) from the boat that brought me from the command ship and hobbled my way up the embankment.

While on the ship, Sergeant Thomas told me where to look for Easy Company Headquarters, so I started the long trek to the company area at the base of Mount Suribachi. Daytime enemy resistance had dwindled to almost zero on the south end of the island.

As I hobbled along, I passed mountains of loose equipment brought ashore, dumped, and then re-piled on higher ground. Most of the equipment would never be used during the battle. It belonged to the wounded and dead and had little or no markings to show ownership. It was a hodgepodge. My eye caught a familiar sight. There in front of me was a large pile of packs. These packs were the lower section and did not carry combat gear. I was short of everything; I could get what I needed here.

Normally, we laced these packs onto the bottom of the shoulder pack, but combat men do not carry the bottom part when landing in the assault waves. The lower packs are brought ashore later. I walked up to the pile and there in front of me was my own pack. The odds against this happening are unbelievable. However, this was like manna from heaven because in that pack was my air-mattress.

On my first trip overseas, I met three Marine officers who were proud owners of air-mattresses. Air mattresses were unheard of in the Marine Corps. These South Pacific Marine officers had the best, and the mattresses were rugged and made to last. I think the Australian Air Force formerly owned them. They were useful everywhere, especially while waiting for buses, trains,and military planes, as well as while in camp, etc. I wrote earlier about how I acquired the air mattress.

I never dreamed that I would use one in combat, but when I prepared myself, I put it in and left out what I called non-essential. I had guessed there would be plenty of regular equipment from dead, dying, and wounded, so I packed it in my lower pack. With fifty percent predicted casualties, I knew I would be killed or wounded - so why not take a chance. I did, and it paid off.

The fact that I walked up to this pile of packs and, without searching, picked out my pack with the good air mattress in it still mystifies me. The air mattress looked well protected, so I walked on. I heard my name called, and the man with my Thompson sub-machine gun ran up and handed it to me. It was clean and in excellent condition. I know this is difficult to believe, but it is true. Honorable and fine men! What a shame so many had to die!

Company Headquarters, at the base of the mountain, looked the same—well dug in. Our company-music (bugler) Frank Crowe from Haverhill, Massachusetts, greeted me. The greeting was refreshing. This young man was a top Marine and a first-class human being. He wanted to know, right then, if he could join the Third Platoon. The captain would not allow anyone from the Company Headquarters group to go to a rifle platoon, so that was out.

The long walk in the sand caused my wounds to pain me. I was trying to ignore it because I wanted to join the platoon on top of Mount Suribachi. Someone offered me a drink of whiskey. It was not Crowe, but some one else. I said, "Sure" and without looking at the bottle I ducked down behind some equipment and took a long swig. My breath came back to me sometime later. The whiskey was "Five Islands" whiskey, made in Hawaii from sugar cane.

I wanted nothing else to do with that whiskey. It would kill me if the Japs did not. There was plenty of morphine in my belt; I could use it in an emergency. As it happened, I never did use a single tube of morphine on myself.

Company Clerk Pfc. Donald J. Brengartner and Crowe told me that the Company and the beach near by were shelled every night by the enemy artillery and occasionally by heavy mortars.

The Second and Third Platoons of Easy company were still mopping-up on top of Mount Suribachi. Captain Severance did not want me to climb the mountain. Corporal Lindberg and Private Goode from the Third Platoon walked into camp to pick up supplies. These were the two men who did the beautiful work with their flame throwers at the base of the mountain.

Nothing had changed except that the Third Platoon had to "Come down" and not "Come back" to get supplies. It was a surprise both ways when we saw each other, and they insisted on taking me with them when they went back up the mountain.

The Third Platoon's having raised the flag and had a part in raising the second flag had nothing to do with my returning to battle. Put aside any thought that you might have that we knew that this flag raising would become historically important; that was the farthest thing from our mind. We could not see any further into the future than a few minutes - maybe one hour.

With the two of them almost carrying me at times, we reached the top. After greeting everyone, I found a spot, blew up my air mattress, and set up my command post only a few feet from the flag pole. Colonel Johnson found out I was back and ordered me to take charge of the mountain top. Warrant Officer or Lieutenant Nathan A. Lipscomb, who was in charge of the group on top, was ordered to come down and bring the Second Platoon of Easy Company. Lieutenant Schrier had gone down earlier. This left the Third Platoon on top to mop-up and get reorganized.

Colonel Johnson talked, over the radio, directly to me until we left the top of the mountain. He was the only officer from whom I received orders from that day until his death; after that, no one gave me orders—I did not know why.

Warrant Officer Nate Lipscomb was an old friend of mine. We had worked together with the Machine Gun Platoon in the early days of the Fifth Marine Division. He broke out a fifth of Old Crow whiskey, and we had one drink, by the flag, to celebrate on top of Mount Suribachi. The next time I saw Nate, we had another drink together in Abilene, Texas, in 1987.

I had not lost the feel for battle. I knew what most of the problems would be on top of the mountain. I remembered when we landed in the assault waves that we had seen the many blinking lights coming from the small caves around and on top of the mountain. Each location of blinking lights was an enemy machine gun in the mouth of a cave. Our Navy pumped shells into the mouth of these small caves, but that was all. The temporarily closed caves remained loaded with enemy soldiers and weapons. The enemy could dig out after dark, do their mischief, crawl back in, and then close the cave before daylight, so they were a problem.

After dark my first night on top of Mount Suribachi, I lay on my air mattress listening to the clear sounds coming from the island. The platoon was asleep and did not post a guard. The physical rest I got on-board ship and the potential danger all around us caused me to remain awake. Besides the enemy, the volcanic crater still smoldered, with steam rising occasionally. It was not dangerous, but I did not know that then.

I was in for another surprise. Just as everyone was asleep but me,

236

the mountain top lit up. The Japanese on the mountain were shooting flares around us. The enemy on the north end of the island was shooting flares also. It looked as if they were signaling one another. Suddenly, small explosions began bursting over our heads, and shrapnel whistled around us. If anybody else was awake, I could not tell; no one moved.

At a time like this, with wounds in my neck, legs and buttocks, I laid on my stomach, covered my head and neck and worried that my air mattress might be punctured. Colonel Johnson called on the radio and wanted to know, "What the hell is going on." I told him that I did not know. I found out the next morning that the Japanese were shooting at us with antiaircraft shells. The enemy was desperate. After the aerial display, I stayed awake most of the night worrying; nobody else did.

The next day we hunted all morning for the small cave openings that the enemy soldiers were using. The Japanese that fired the flares could not be found. They had resealed their caves.

Someone with authority sent a Marine or a Navy officer, I do not remember which, to the top of the mountain as a forward observer. He had the largest pair of binoculars I had ever seen. They must have weighed over twenty pounds, and they sat on a huge swivel. The officer was spotting the enemy for the Marine Corps guns; also he spotted for the ships at sea. When he was tired, I relieved him when I could.

His primary job was spotting the enemy's big weapons on the far end of the island. About eighty percent of the time the Japanese fired their large weapons in the late evening after our war ships had gone to their rendezvous for the night.

Because the enemy had the capability of moving their smaller weapons in and out of caves and hiding places, we suspected that they did the same with their larger weapons. They were probably pulled out of caves when firing and then quickly pulled back in for protection. From photographs we knew that the north end of the island was covered with deep canyons. The large weapon feared most was a launcher that hurled a large tumbling barrel of high explosives and scrap metal. Because of the noise it made as it tumbled through the air, the Marines called it "Screaming Jesus." Later we thought that its launcher also launched a Buzz-bomb with wings. We called it Buzz-Bomb because it flew with wings and left three or more streaks of fire when it left the north end.

Our United States flag flying on top of Mount Suribachi was guarded by the Marines who controlled the top of the mountain. It outraged the Japanese. The mountain was also an ideal observation post. Every evening the Japanese would do their best to knock out the flag and the observation post.

Our orders were to protect the flag and to kill or capture the remaining Japanese on top and around the lip of the mountain crater. Our next responsibility was to protect and help the observer spot the enemy's heavy weapons on the north end of the island.

In the daytime when our ships were in close and on the alert, our spotter had very little to do. At that time of day, enemy activity on top of the mountain was slow also.

The Japanese men were small and the holes that they crawled in and out of looked even smaller. I saw one later; in fact I crawled into it.

These night-roaming Japanese had never tried to hurt anyone. I think their primary thought was food and water. One man in the platoon told me that he thought they were unarmed. He caught one stealing water from his canteen. He yelled at him, and the Japanese left. I think I mentioned the absence of natural food and drinking water sources on the island. They were plaguing the enemy.

One night I slept soundly. When I awoke the next morning I found a Japanese calling-card lying in front of my face. That was all, just a card with a name on it. At first I thought the wind may have blown it there, but then I knew better. It became clear to me that the Jap let me know he was there. I still have that card.

The afternoon of the second day, I held platoon court. *Court* is really not a good word for it. I would set up a spot off to one side, far enough away that no one outside the two of us could hear. Sergeant Thomas let the sergeants come, one at a time, in order of rank. The men would be next. After that, Sergeant Thomas and I talked at length.

I do not recommend this type of thinking, but for months, we knew that many would be killed or wounded. We needed to know each other thoroughly. If there was any dissatisfaction in the Platoon, we needed to work it out. Things had not changed. I did not think they had; we were still family, maybe more so.

We had two men added to the Third Platoon. They came from the Mortar Platoon and added before the Third Platoon scaled the mountain. They proved to be First Class fighting men. They were Pfc. John. T. Schmitt and Cpl. Thomas J. Hermanek, Jr.

The sergeants and men knew that no matter what we talked about, I would never mention it to Thomas or anyone else. Some startling things came out. Well, not too startling. The sergeants reported that a few of the men were slow in jumping-off the morning we attacked the base of the mountain fortress. I pretended that it was bad. To be honest, I did not blame them. If there was ever a suicide mission, that was it.

I heard later that four different lieutenants in the battalion attacked the enemy and their men did not follow them and they were shot down. The men did not follow them. Three of the four were killed and one paralyzed from the waist down.

One of the young men that was pointed out to me by his sergeant as not moving out with the rest of the squad asked for forgiveness. I let his Sergeant make the decision; he would be fighting with him. Later, the same sergeant wanted to put the same young man up for one of the highest medals. The Sergeant reported that this young man attacked a large Japanese emplacement single-handed and almost destroyed it before the enemy wounded him. I told the Sergeant to let one cancel the other out.

At times we could relax, and they brought me up to date on what they did while I was out on the ship. They said that Colonel Johnson ordered them, with the rest of the company, to move between Mount Suribachi and a high ridge east of the mountain. In the dark they walked single-file and were never fired upon by the enemy. The high ridge on their left was the one we landed under the first day. Fighting was sharp the next morning but did not last long.

One story they told caused them all to laugh. A Japanese machine gun operating in the mouth of a cave kept all in front of it pinned down. One Marine near the edge of the Japanese fire lane quickly ran to the side of the mountain. After working his way down to the cave's mouth, he jumped over and jerked the machine gun out and away from the Japanese. The Marines out in front of the gun cheered.

Unarmed, the two Japanese ran back into the cave and the Marine ran after them. A few seconds later he ran out of the cave with the Japanese chasing him. Marines, making themselves ready to attack the cave, quickly killed the Japanese.

Thank God, the platoon's sergeants said the support weapons had become more coordinated. Destroyer ships would almost beach themselves while pounding the enemy's fortifications only a few yards away. They had high praise for the 37 millimeter guns and also the Marine tanks. They reported to me that 5th Engineers were sealing caves faster than the flamethrowers could do their work.

The platoon said that the Engineers were sometimes out in front of the lines sealing caves. First Lieutenant Eugene Adams, a good friend of mine, was in that group.

Large amphibian tractors supplemented our supply lines to the base of the mountain or anywhere else. They did not need a specified beach. I need to tell this story even though it may be out of sequence. Black men were in the Navy, but only at the end of the war were they picked for the Marine Corps. I was told that American Black men were

239

an unknown factor and we did not have time to experiment. The only black men that were around Marines were military stevedores, Fiji Island soldiers, and natives at Guadalcanal, South Pacific.

The large amphibian tractors (called Buffalos) were running supplies from ship to shore. Usually two black men manned them. At first the enemy left the supply units alone; they were hard to hit in the water and their weapons firing would quickly expose the enemy's gun positions.

However, we heard shells exploding in the water offshore. A large Jap gun was trying to hit a Buffalo bringing in supplies. Japanese shells were hitting the water so close that the heavily loaded, large amphibian was doing a slow dance in the water.

Excited, the two men jumped around trying to find protection and let the tank run itself. Finally, a shell almost raised the tractor out of the water. The two men bailed-out (jumped overboard) and remained floating in their life jackets.

Now, they were in real danger. Apparently the tractor had a built-in guiding mechanism, and the Buffalo was going in circles. Life jackets prevented the men from diving to get away from the tractor propellers or churning treads. The tractor passed directly over them with each circle, with the deadly moving parts missing them by inches. Thank the Good Lord, the wind or something moved the tractor to one side and the men were saved. On the beach, while they were unloading, the large enemy weapon turned and destroyed two or more of these large supply tractors before our weapons could silence it.

After losing five men the first two days of fighting and sixteen on the third day, we had twenty-four left of the original forty-five men. At the time I could account for only two deaths. Corporal Edward J. Romero, Jr. was caught in the Wild Charge at the base of the mountain, and Pfc. Donald J. Ruhl sacrificed his life for Sergeant Hansen.

Two men from the Mortar Platoon, Pfc. John.T. Schmitt and Cpl. Thomas J. Hermanek Jr.; eight stretcher bearers; the radio man; and Lieutenant Schrier made an eighteen (18) man patrol. They said that a Marine photographer went with them. Twenty years later I met this man in Virginia, U.S.A.. He was Marine Staff Sergeant Louis R. Lowery. We corresponded, and I have a Christmas card with a picture of his

First flag being carried up Mt. Suribachi.
Top to bottom: Cpl. Charles W. Lindberg, Pvt. Robert D. Goode,
Pfc. Thomas J. Hermanek Jr., Pfc. John T. Schmitt, and Pfc. Manuel
Panizo. (Schmitt, Hermanek, along with Earnest Mosley were replacements
to the platoon)

241

Sgt. Henry O. Hansen, Pfc. James A Robeson, Pvt. Phillip L. Ward, Pfc. James R. Michaels, Cpl. Charles W. Lindberg & Pvt. Robert D. Goode.

The enemy large covered weapon on right side was never used ....?

family.

Counting him, it made about a nineteen (19) man patrol with some stretcher bearers—not a forty (40) man patrol as some have stated. They fully equipped themselves and began climbing the mountain. Once on top they saw one large enemy weapon, out in the open, and still in its protective cover. They also saw several cave entrances. Why had the observation and attacking planes missed these, they wanted to know?

Soon after the Platoon reached the top of the mountain, a metal pole was found by Leader and Rozek. They thought it was some part of a water catching device. The flag was attached, and the first flag went up. Marine photographer Lou Lowery took some pictures on the way up and some on top. They said that Lowery dropped his camera when a Japanese charged from a cave throwing hand grenades. Chick Robeson killed the Japanese, and the wounded Jap was pulled back into the cave he came out of. The cave turned out to be large with several entrances. The entrances were soon hit with flaming oil from the flamethrowers of Lindberg and Goode. Then the caves were sealed.

3rd Platoon mopping up atop Mt. Suribachi.
Pfc. Clarence H. Garrett killing Japanese in cave below.

243

Some time later they reopened the cave and counted over one hundred dead Japanese; some had committed suicide. With their numbers and weapons, it was easy to see that they could have held off the Third Platoon. There were other caves with Japanese in them as well.

I cannot remember who told me the story on Snyder, but Snyder was there, and I remember the familiar grin on his face. The man said that soon after Robeson killed the grenade thrower, a Jap officer charged out of the cave, swinging a sword with a broken blade. It was like a bravo act, the teller thought. There was no one in reach for the Jap officer to cut. Before anybody could act, the officer jumped back in the cave. He did this more than once.

Snyder had a pistol, the same as I. He said that it belonged to Wheeler and that he got it from Wheeler on the third day of battle when Wheeler was wounded. The story goes that he told Wheeler that for Wheeler's sake he would kill a Jap with it and return the pistol to Wheeler.

There was a small mound of dirt just below the cave opening that the Jap officer charged from, so Snyder hid there and waited. The Jap officer ran out swinging his saber. Snyder surprised him by putting the pistol in the officers face and pulling the trigger. The gun snapped; it did not fire. This surprised both men. Before the Japanese officer could react, Snyder dodged away. Clarence Garret, from the cliff above the cave, put several rounds from his BAR into the Japanese officer. After that the platoon stripped the officer of all his worldly things, and threw him off the mountain for the Marines below to bury.

After searching out other caves, Robeson and Ward were returning to the flag area when they saw what looked like a large group of people near the flag. Chick Robeson told me that Ward said; "Looks like we drew a crowd." The group was preparing to raise a much larger flag.

The larger group was from Easy Company, mostly the Second Platoon, and I later learned they were joined by Marine photographer Genaust and a civilian photographer named Joe Rosenthal.

Third Platoon corpsman Pharmacist Mate Second Class John H. Bradley joined part of the Second Platoon to raise the larger Second Flag.

In the daytime, we searched with the field glasses looking for large enemy weapons on the island, and when not doing that, we searched the mountain top for caves and Japanese. I think that they only looked for water and food. They never bothered us.

When the spotter was not looking for weapons, I could watch the battle going on as if it was in my own back yard. With the powerful

244

glasses, I watched the fighting in great detail. I felt as if I could almost touch the Marines involved, especially in the fighting around the airfields. Most of the time the Marines and Japanese were fighting too close for us to be of use as spotter. The enemy was underground. By the time we could see the Japanese, the Marines were on top of them. The spotter and I looked for the larger enemy weapons.

The most spectacular thing I saw while watching was an American tank helping the Marines cross an airfield. The Marines had tried to cross the flat airfield, and the Japanese mowed them down like a mower cuts grass. Some of the wounded would try to work their way back, while the others moved very little or none. I watched the tank firing its big gun, and it looked as if it was circling or flanking a target. A monstrous explosion appeared to lift the tank completely off the ground. A puff of dirt came out from under the tank, and the treads on the tank went slack. The turret with the large gun attached left the tank. It rose at least another eight or ten feet into the air. A man sailed out of the tank with the turret. The man was very much alive. God only knows how he survived that blast. When he hit the ground he gathered his senses and tried to get out of the way of the turret that was coming down on him. He did not make it; the turret crushed him. To my surprise, I saw at least two men crawl from the bottom of the tank, and they appeared to make their escape.

I could not imagine the size of a weapon capable of doing this kind of damage to a tank. Later, I learned and had the opportunity of seeing this type weapon. An enemy anti-tank mine almost as large as a fifty-five gallon barrel was placed in the right spot to get the tank. I feel sure I am right on this.

I do not know how the Marines and Navy knew that the enemy would launch a buzz bomb, but I guess they did. The buzz-bomb launcher was the big thing. Besides the bomb, we suspected it also had enough power to hurl a large fifty-five gallon barrel-like projectile that I mentioned earlier.

Each evening, just before dusk, they would fire the buzz-bomb directly at the flag. This bomb was something similar to the one the Germans fired at London. It looked like the pictures that I have seen of the German bomb with wings.

Because the lieutenant observer was doing his best to spot the launcher, I stayed with him. At first our protective ships were gone for the night, so we did not have to wait long until we saw three or more spurts of fire on the other end of the island. The bomb had wings, and we knew it was powerful. The spotter did not protect himself, and I sat there and watched with him. I lit a cigarette and got six or eight puffs before the bomb sailed overhead. The bomb missed us and skimmed over the back lip of the crater.

Remember this mountain crater was only 500 feet high, and it was not very wide. By standing up we saw it land in the sea behind the mountain. When it exploded, a geyser of water shot at least 200 feet into the air. Now this was something to worry about.

To locate the launcher, we picked two prominent spots on each side of the mountain and located each one on an aerial photograph. A Platoon Sergeant was placed at each spot with a compass. Along with the officer spotting with the field glasses, we would triangulate with our compass readings. Remember? They were firing at us and there was no time to waste. If the enemy was able to hit the flag on the front lip of the crater, the bomb would destroy us.

The next evening we got set to zero in on the winged-bomb launcher. For some reason a battleship, I think it was the battleship *Texas*, decided to move from the east side of the island to the west side. In so doing they would pass behind Mount Suribachi at about the same time we expected the winged bomb.

The battleship was approaching the target area, and almost on cue, we saw the familiar three spurts of fire and watched the buzz bomb as it approached. We remained at our station near the flag and gave compass readings. Our Navy was ready and opened fire with all their weapons on what we thought was the winged bomb launch site.

About the same height as the evening before, the bomb passed over our heads. Its heading looked accurate to intercept the battleship. We stood up and watched as the bomb hit the water close behind the battleship. A loud explosion sent another geyser of water high into the air. The battleship went on an alert with bells ringing, sirens sounding, horns blasting, and sailors scurrying. Evidently the ships crew did not know what was taking place.

In looking back on the events that took place, I think the battleship *Texas* may have saved our lives on the mountain. We thought, at least, we were saved for another day. If they lowered their sights by a half-an-inch on their end of the island, the winged-bomb would blow the top of the mountain off where we sat with the flag.

After the ships left for the night, large containers of explosive began sailing through the air. They came from the winged-bomb launch area and were landing on the men below the mountain. The men claimed they looked like large oil drums tumbling through the air. When they hit the ground, a large area would shake from the explosion, and pieces of scrap metal would fly in all directions. Evidently they were not meant to be accurate. This made the explosions even more

246

terrifying.

We had heard these before and guessed that the winged bomb personnel were launching them. If this were the case, the Navy had not destroyed their ability to fire the winged-bomb, and the enemy would get another shot at us. Our only other hope was that the Marines would overrun their launch site before the enemy could hit us.

That evening the Japanese artillery that shelled the base of the mountain every evening raised their line of shelling, and I thought the shells might reach us. It was dark and luckily they stopped before they did.

As the battle shut down for the night, and without the roar of weapons, all sounds from the island and waters around us seemed to magnify. We were careful not to shoot each other at night, so we were not jumpy. The Japanese shooting flares on top of the mountain were not aggressive, like their brothers on the rest of the island.

When nightfall came, small boats would rendezvous offshore. These boats were caught away from their mother ships when darkness came. Their ships did not wait on them. We could hear the men talking, and because there was nothing to interfere with the sound, we could understand what they were saying most of the time. We could see lights occasionally when they lit their cigarettes. They thought they were secure.

We heard screaming and yells coming from the men in the boats. As terrible as it may sound, we could not help but laugh. We thought that they were finally getting a taste of the real battle. They were yelling like frantic men. Japanese were coming aboard their small crafts.

When the Japanese quit attacking the boats off-shore and finally came ashore, the Marines met them at the base of the mountain. "Get that son-of-a-bitch; There is one over there; Here comes a bunch - there are some more, etc." We heard every sound of the encounter.

Later, we found out that these Japanese were a Cult. They wore special garb and armed themselves with spears, knives, and swords. When they tried to come ashore, it was a slaughterhouse. Marines met them and killed them on the spot.

After this, yellow flares went up all around us on the mountain top. Yellow flares went up on the north end of the island as if they were signaling each other again. Colonel Johnson called me on the radio. First, he seemed pleased that we were on the radio - then, " What the hell is going on?"

I told him that we still held our position, and then I told him what we thought was happening at the base of the mountain. With the flares in the air around us every night and him not knowing what was taking place on top of the mountain, the Colonel said he was sending trained dogs up to sniff and hunt out the caves.

Two handlers with their dogs reported to me, and I turned them over to Sergeants Thomas and Hansen. Corpsman Bradley was having a hard time keeping my wounds dressed, and I refused to give myself

Dogs used atop Mt. Suribachi

shots of Morphine. When I did work with the men, I would stay on the path that rimmed the top lip of the crater.

A man reported that the dogs had found the mouth of a large cave and they wanted to know what to do. This baffled me, because they knew what to do—hit it with the flamethrower, seal it if they could, and take no chances.

They insisted that I come and take a look. I hobbled around to the backside of the mountain. A small trail worked its way to a large cave opening that overlooked the ocean. A narrow trail led to the cave mouth from both sides. From the cave mouth to the waters edge below was five hundred feet of a sheer cliff.

A large straw mat completely covered the mouth of the cave. My first thought was "Take no chance, just hit the cave entrance with a flame of burning oil." This was my decision that I formulated on the first day. These people would not surrender, so the best thing to do was to kill them quickly. To some degree that had changed. The enemy that roamed on top at night were not killers.

Also, the platoon told me that they killed over a hundred of the enemy when they first arrived on top. The Japanese had them out numbered and out gunned, yet only two or three exposed themselves.

The cave mouth that I hobbled over to see was impressive and so close to the edge of the mountain it forced us to stand close together, near the mouth, just to see the cave. Goode and Lindberg were ready. I was about to give the order to fire the flamethrowers—do not ask what stopped me, but something did.

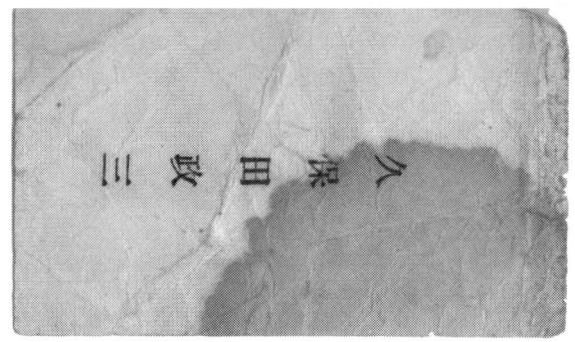

Seizo Kubota (interpretation)
calling card left by my face on Mt.Suribachi.

Maybe it was the calling card by my head that made me think twice. These Japanese were not like the ones below. My mind continued to scream at me, "Don't take a chance," but I did. I ordered a man, I do not remember which one, to climb to the other side of the cave and jerk the mat away.

We got set with our weapons and flamethrowers. The man jerked the mat away and there sat four large drums. They were almost the size of fifty-five gallon oil drums. Stamped on them were labels with Japanese writing.

I reported to Colonel Johnson that the dogs found no Japanese, but I reported what we had found. He sent up interpreters, and we learned that the drums contained high explosives. They were used as land mines and off-shore water mines. I guess they intended to roll them down on Marines below. If we had used our flamethrowers, that part of the mountain would have disappeared, and we would have

249

become a mist in the sky.

Chick Robeson, Corporal Lindberg, and others told me about the caves on top, and I knew about the ones around the sides. The caves must be connected, and we knew that we would never get all the roaming Japanese until they starved out.

We had visitors in the daytime. Most of them came from 5th Division Headquarters. One of them was Arthur Daniel Keefe, my close friend in Boot Camp, Officer's school, and Parachute school. He laughingly said that he expected to see me up there, and I could have said the same about him. He and the others always left before dark. That was heavy enemy shelling time.

That evening we were getting ready for the buzz-bomb watch. Although we had called in our compass readings the evening before and all our heavy guns did their best, we knew that buzz bomb probably still existed. Third Platoon sergeants were at their compass sites and ready for the compass readings, and the observer and I sat by the flag. Why I sat with the spotter, I do not know. The enemy shot the flying bomb at the flag.

We saw the three spurts of fire, and we knew the bomb was under way. I lit a cigarette and got a few drags before I saw it coming. Here it came, directly toward us. The lieutenant stayed on the phone. If I had stood up and jumped, I think I could have touched it as it passed over our heads.

It hit the backside of the crater and exploded. The mountain shook like jello, and pieces of the mountain flew into the air. A quick inspection near us revealed that the walls of the crater fell in and left raw yellow sulfur exposed to the air. I made a quick check of the men and saw that all was well. Colonel Johnson called and wanted to know immediately if we were still there. "Only by the grace of God," I told him. It was getting dark, and we must wait until morning for a full check of the damage.

Daylight came, and the disturbed Colonel was calling. He wanted to know if the mountain was about to explode. I looked behind me and saw that the exposed raw sulfur was letting off large quantities of steam. It looked to the men below as if the mountain was about to erupt. I assured him that it was not. The Colonel told me that we were being relieved and would go to the north end of the island.

The Third Platoon was soon ready to move off the mountain; we had very little equipment. All I had was the clothes on my back, my weapons, and the precious air mattress. Because my clothes were shredded on the third day, my clothes were part Navy, part Marine, and part Seabees.

250

When Private Goode heard the news, he stated, so everyone could hear, that he hated to go north and fight. I knew that the others felt the same, although they said nothing. My wounds were getting worse. We could not get medicine (sulfa) to them with the heavy scab on top. We were cut off from Penicillin, and infection was spreading. I was still walking.

My mind said, "Get off the mountain before dark." The dreaded Buzz Bomb, (flying bomb with wings) would surely knock the flag down that evening. We gathered our equipment and made our way off the mountain.

Pvt. Robert D. Goode firing into cave atop Mt. Suribachi

Sgt. Katy D. Metcalf & Pvt. Robert D. Goode destroying Japanese in caves while others in the platoon are preparing to raise the first flag.

252

Tying on the first flag atop Mt. Suribachi 1st Lt. Harold G. Shrier, Sgt. Ernest I Thomas, Sgt. Henry O. Hansen & Cpl. Charles W. Lindberg.

Photograph by Louis R. Lowery
The first flag raising over the still unconquered summit of Mount Suribachi
on Iwo Jima. (The second flag raising was immortalized by Joe Rosenthal
who photographed it for the Associated Press.) One of 35 photographs
taken by Louis R. Lowery in THE BLOODY BATTLE FOR SURIBACHI
by Richard Wheeler. (Thomas Y. Crowell)

PHOTOGRAPHER: Genaust 02/23/45

RAISING FLAG ON MOUNT SURIBACHI- Left to right: Private First Class Ira H. Hayes; Private First Class Franklin R. Sously, (KIA); Sergeant Michael Strank, (KIA); Pharmacist Nate 2/o John H. Bradley; Private First Class Rene A. Gagnon; Corp. Harlan H. Block (KIA).

Chapter 15

GOING TO THE NORTH END

When we reached the bottom of the mountain, we heard both good and bad news. The Marines on the north end of the island had overrun the buzz-bomb launching site; thank God, there would be no more explosive barrels or buzz-bombs.

The bad news was for me: "Colonel Johnson wants to talk to you," said Pfc. Leonard J. Mooney. He ran up to me when I reached the bottom of the mountain. In training, Mooney was our platoon radioman, and we thought he was a fine man with a good attitude. He handed me the radio receiver.

Colonel Johnson must have been a very busy man because all he said was, "Lieutenant Wells will remain in the rear," and then he clicked off.

Well, that was not good enough for me, and I had Mooney call him. I said, "Lieutenant Wells requests permission to go to the front with his men."

Right back, after a few curse words and a statement that the Japanese were killing previously wounded men unusually fast, he changed his tone to finality. "Lieutenant Wells will remain in the rear as I ordered." That was the end of the conversation.

If you think I was hungry to kill Japanese, you are wrong. I knew the Third Platoon men would do whatever I ordered them to do. I wanted to be sure of what we did and take every advantage we could. I guessed they would all be dead before long. You can think whatever you wish, but I thought that we could accomplish our mission of capturing the west side of the island by working together and not blindly charging the enemy.

After we had knocked out their big weapons and even before then, there was very little the enemy could do, unless we afforded him the opportunity. Our planes were soon making safe landings on our captured and repaired airstrips.

Since there were no natural food or water supplies on the island, in some areas the enemy was running out of food. The large enemy weapons, even the individual weapons, were fixed facing south. They had very little room in their fixed positions to change. As the men walked off, many of them from the company came by and had something to say. I remember Red Graan from Chicago. We were as different as the Good Lord can make any two people. For some reason we liked each other. He was in another platoon, but he took time to come by and wish me well. He was wearing an almost complete Japanese Officer's uniform. I guessed the enemy would kill him quick when they saw him, and someone told me later that they did.

I heard our men exchange words with the company they were replacing. The company returning from the front lines was Easy Company 27th Marines. Each was telling the other what to be aware of. Our group told the in-coming Marines that there would be enemy artillery shelling every evening—just at dusk. Some of them took heed, but many did not. To them the relaxed atmosphere at the base of the mountain looked like heaven. The new arrivals were leisurely walking around or sitting in groups basking in the sun.

Because I knew some 27th Marine sergeants, I felt that I should warn them again about the evening shelling that our company took each evening when they were there. I walked over and tried to warn the new arrivals. I told them that the volcanic ash absorbed most of the shock and shrapnel, but a little preparation, if only mental, would help.

They paid no attention to me and looked at me as if I were some raw recruit trying to give instructions. The 27th Marines were tired and bushed. They did nothing but sit down and begin eating some food that someone brought to them.

Corporal Jack First, one of our company supply men, offered me a part of his two-man dugout for my stay in the rear. He or someone else had found a small ditch and covered it with ammunition packing-crate boards and sand bagged the top and one end. We were safer there than we would be in downtown Dallas on Saturday night—with one exception. The Japanese living in the mountain near by were prowling every night looking for food and water, the same as they were doing on top of the mountain.

Corporal First did not build an escape hatch. I felt that one enemy hand-grenade, even a concussion grenade, would be the end of us. I blew up my air mattress lightly and prepared for the evening shelling.

The enemy shelling came on time, and I could not keep from feeling sorry for the men lying outside on top of the ground. I guess I slept off and on most of the night, but I could not keep from visualizing a Jap rolling a hand grenade in on top of us. I could mentally see him standing and waiting for us to show our heads as we tried to get out.

I believe it was on this island that I developed claustrophobia. Since World War II, when I enter a small bathroom with only one door, I can feel it. I leave the door open if I can because I get the feeling it could be a trap. Hallways without doors or with locked doors along the side or any place that does not have a quick escape route still make me nervous. The phobia is not severe, but I notice it.

The next morning I stuck my head out and looked toward the company that had just moved in. I saw shovels in the air and sand and ashes flying. They did not need to be told again; the enemy artillery shells would scare the Hell out of anybody. I did not check on them after that.

My wounds had scabbed over and infection had spread underneath. We could not doctor them. One of my wounds was a hole left by a piece of meat torn from the inside part of my left leg. Our doctors never had time to sew it. This made it hard to heal. I refused to use the morphine to kill my pain. Somebody directed me to the beach near the base of the mountain. There I found a specialized hospital.

The hospital was in a protected spot where a bulldozer had dug back into the dirt bank near the base of the mountain. The trench was large enough for canvas cots to sit end to end with a four-foot walkway at the ends and on the sides of the cots. It had a canvas roof and sides. It served as a hospital ward. Behind this setup was a small, completely portable surgical operating room.

Four men, sometimes more, with serious head wounds stayed in the larger tent. This setup was primarily for men with extremely serious head wounds who could not be moved to ships or planes. Most of the men had brains showing with only clear salve protecting the opening. A brain specialist was brought in to tend to these men.

The doctor was a brilliant man. He had help when he was operating in the small tent. He did not have help in the big tent where he acted more in the capacity of a nurse. These men with head wounds lay on their cots as if they were dead. There was no sign of life, except a slight movement of their chests when they breathed.

While at the hospital, I met a young, red-haired ambulance driver. It is hard to believe that we had an ambulance on Iwo Jima, but we did. The ambulance was a Jeep, the same type we had used in the Paratroops. The driver roamed the small island and was on call when there was a head wound.

His ambulance driving was rough, but he would carry me to the front line when I asked him. He knew the island and the enemy's fire lanes like the back of his hand. At times, I thought we were driving through the enemy's front line. We would go bouncing and drive almost into Easy Company Headquarters.

Once there was a man from our company lying dead not twenty feet in front of us, and no one could get to him. I think my young red-haired driver wanted me to show concern or fear. I would not let him know if I did.

258

I wondered what the Japanese thought. I know they could see us when we would drive up, but they could not train their weapons on us. The ambulance driver was a little wild, but if he thought I was going to say anything, he would have to think again.

Each time I went to the front, I asked Captain Severance if I could take over the platoon. He refused me. It must have been a standing order.

I spoke earlier of a foreign-sounding automatic weapon that fired at me on the afternoon of the second day, also for a short time on the morning of the third day. When I went looking and asking, I found it. The weapons men told me it was a British Hotchkiss machine gun, but later I learned that it was a Japanese copy of the gun. While I was looking, I went to the place where we had fought the pitched battle before I was wounded and found the machine gun that the "I" Company machine gunner used. In and on the water jacket, I counted 16 bullet holes or shell marks. You may wonder why I was so inquisitive. I thought that the battle for Japan was just starting. We needed to know everything.

Copies of the British Lewis and Hotchkiss machine guns.

I was still staying with Corporal First when High Command moved a company of antiaircraft personnel between us and the beach. They were armed with their regular weapons, which included 50-caliber machine guns. We wondered why they moved in. We saw only one Jap plane, and that was on the first day.

When they moved in, all casual movement at night ended. This included going to the bathroom. These people shot anything that moved, and that included each other. We heard that they killed or wounded several, but no Japs.

Soon after the anti-aircraft unit set its weapons in position, the Japanese shelled us heavily. We thought that we had all their big guns shut down, but we did not. They must have repaired one. One of their shells accidentally hit the Marine ammunition dump near by, and we thought the world was ending. Exploding shells went off in every direction. The fireworks in the late evening were unbelievable. The sounds were awesome, and this stimulated the Japanese. They continued firing.

Following the explosions, there was a strong gas odor in the air, and several gas detectors set off alarms. No one had a gas mask. Everyone had dumped them when we came ashore. Poison gas was the least of our worries. Some Marines dumped the gas masks and used the cases to carry hand grenades. I remembered seeing two or three gas masks, partially buried in sand and ashes, only a few feet from our dug-out entrance.

The gas odor got stronger, and one or more Navy destroyers almost beached themselves. Over loudspeakers they told us it was poisonous gas and asked us to come to the beach to be taken aboard.

The anti-aircraft personnel fired their 50-caliber machine guns at the first group of Marines rushing to the beach. I knew I was not going to run that gauntlet. I preferred the gas to our own scared anti-aircraft machine gunners, the best I remember the unit was an all black Army outfit. Jack First crawled out and headed toward the mountain. After looking for only a minute, I found three partially buried masks only a few feet from our entrance. I brought what I guessed to be the two best back to our dug-out. The first one I shook clean and tested. It seemed to be in working order, so I put the other one on Jack's side.

Jack returned later with his arms loaded with gas masks and seemed surprised that I had one on my head and was preparing to go to sleep. Morning came, and I found Jack lying beside me when I awoke. He had his gas mask on and was wide-awake. I tested the air and found that it had very little gas odor. We took our gas masks off, and Jack said that he had stayed awake all night. He also said I snored all night.

Someone passed the word that the gas was tear gas. I do not know what the Marine Corps was doing with tear gas on the Island. To my knowledge we never used tear gas in combat.

After that experience, I moved to a cot in the hospital ward on the beach. The doctor allowed it because I became his helper when he needed one. The roaming Japanese were not as dangerous as our own military that moved in between Corporal First's dugout and the beach. I had my wounds dressed occasionally and worked with the doctor there.

The patients who stayed in the recovery tent were extreme cases. One man had the front of his head shot away. He had a smile on his face, but we could not get any reaction from him. We stuck him with needles and yelled in his ear—nothing. The doctor told me that he had no way of knowing what kind of personality the man had before this wound, but if he lived he would always have that smile on his face.

The one that affected me most was a young sailor. He wore the uniform of a Marine corpsman. His wound was near the back of his head. When the wounded corpsman came to, he could not talk; he could only hiss and grunt. When he finally began saying words, they were all broken curse words. Every time we gave him medical shots, he cursed the doctor and me. Every few hours we gave shots to all the men with head wounds.

We did not know how long the corpsman lay in the field before some men brought him to the doctor. The miracle drug that was doing wonders for everybody was not working on the young sailor. The doctor said that he had Spinal Meningitis, and apparently the penicillin could not reach it. I do not remember how long we waited, but the doctor decided to try putting penicillin in the spinal cord. To his knowledge it had never been done before. I held the man on his side as the doctor injected a needle that looked as long as an ice-pick. I am exaggerating, but not much.

The reaction was quick, and he soon cursed better than before, but it was not long before he began losing what he had gained. We may have given him one shot or possibly two, I do not remember. He got weaker and weaker and died.

Late one evening they brought a man who could not stand up; an explosion had damaged his inner ear. He would fall each time he tried to walk. It was getting late in the evening when he was brought into the make-shift hospital. The Marines who brought him put him in a cot next to mine. This was in the back of the tent and away from the wounded.

After getting his attention, I told him to go to the bathroom before he went to sleep. I also told him that at night, he had to get my attention before he moved from his cot. The holed-up Japanese in the area had hit the panic stage for food and water and roamed every night. They were not extra dangerous—but who knows? I slept with my knife stuck in a small hole at the head of my cot.

In the middle of the night the wounded Marine tried to go take a piss. He fell across me, but luck was with him because he knocked my knife off the cot and I could not find it. I held him in a death grip. I was still searching for my knife when I heard him say some English words. He said words that a Japanese could not mimic. I gave him a cursing like he had never heard before. Can you imagine how I would have felt if I had killed him? I told him that if he had to go, to go in his clothes. I made him move one cot away. Thank God, they moved him to a ship the next day.

The operating tent behind our ward was used sparingly. One day, the doctor notified me that they had a special case. He had two helpers; I am not sure where they came from. The front of the small operating tent was left open, I guess, to get more light. They allowed me to stand there and watch.

A Marine was half sitting and half lying; his lower jaw was blown away. The socket bones looked to be intact. As I watched, they clamped blood vessels off as fast as they could. When they finished, he must have had fifteen or more scissor-like clamps sticking out of what looked to be his throat. I know I could not see everything, but I watched them tie veins off and pack his mouth area with cotton. Most of the skin that went over his jaw was still there and they sewed his mouth shut. Later, I saw and used a writing tablet to converse with this man in the hospital at Pearl Harbor, Hawaii

The day came when the Jeep driver and I went to the north end of the island and I was told that both Thomas and Hansen were dead. "Sick, sick, sick." I cannot describe the depth of my feelings. They told me that Platoon Sergeant Thomas was calling for tanks when a Jap bullet hit beside his head. Instead of ducking, he tried the call again and this time the Jap corrected his sight and hit Thomas in the mouth or just below. He died instantly.

Hansen was shot in the back with a dumb-dumb bullet. The Platoon was walking back to a better defense line and did not know that a Japanese officer and three men were hiding near by. I am almost sure they picked Hansen to shoot because he wore his pants tucked in his boots and carried himself like an officer.

Clarence Hipp told me that when Hansen was shot, there was no hope but they tried anyway. Bradley inserted a needle, and Hipp held

262

the plasma bag in the air, but Hansen showed no response. Suddenly, a Jap officer and three enlisted men rushed them. Hipp thought that they were the ones that wounded Hansen. Hipp dropped the plasma and fired at the Jap officer. The Jap officer was almost on top of them; he was swinging his sword.

Hipp's shot hit the Jap in the throat, and he fell dead. The Japanese men hit the ground. Hipp guessed they did because their officer did. Hipp said that Lindberg and others in the Platoon quickly killed the three Japanese soldiers. Hipp said, "You know Lieutenant, if I hadn't killed that Jap lieutenant when I did, he would have cut our ass off too short to shit." He grinned and said, "My gun jammed, or I would have shot Lindberg." Lindberg scooped up the Jap officer's saber, and Hipp thought the Jap saber belonged to him. I did not get Lindberg's story on this.

Before Hipp and Bradley could catch their breath, Private Robert D. Goode ran up for Bradley to doctor him. Hipp said that Bradley was in a state of nerves and could not hold anything to treat Goode. Goode thought that Bradley was shaking because of his (Goode's) wound. Goode told Bradley that it was nothing to be that concerned about; it was only a flesh wound-through the meaty part of the throat.

On my way back, I saw a dear friend of mine, First Lieutenant Walter R.(Bob) Browne, who ran the Second Battalion supply. He saw the depth of my feelings and talked me into spending the night in his makeshift lean-to. Browne poured me some sick-bay alcohol and grapefruit juice. Perhaps, I should have taken one of my morphine tubes, but I did not. I cried myself to sleep.

We were going to the front one day, and I recognized an area that I saw on the second day. This was the time I saw the man that was lying flat and would not raise an inch when I knelt down beside him and the dead red-haired Marine. He was the one who told me that if I stayed there a little longer, I would find out why he was lying so flat. The cautious Marine was still there; he had not moved an inch. He had built himself a fortification that rivaled those of the Japanese.

I am sure that I wrote about how peaceful it could be when we were close to an enemy fire lane. Strangers would never dream how deadly it was only inches from the men relaxing and drinking a cup of coffee. The ambulance driver and I arrived at the front one day, and Frank Crowe ("E" Company Music) rushed up to us. He told us about a dramatic scene that had just taken place. He said that a pilot from the airfield sauntered up to the front line and saw everybody relaxed and having coffee. They yelled at him and told him where the fire lane was, but he must have thought they were teasing him. Before anybody could

263

stop him, he moved out into the Japanese fire lane and stood there.

A Japanese shot him between the eyes. The bullet ricocheted from the back of his skull and entered the shoulder of an "E" Company man who was relaxing at one side of him. The only man happy about this was the wounded man. He had a ticket home.

I will never forget the time they told me that "The Little General," Sergeant Harold M. Snyder, was dead. "My God, My God," I thought, will this never end? They told me that he was shot on the side of the head and refused a stretcher; he said that he would walk back to the First Aid Station. He fell dead on the way. I was afraid we would have these great losses. I was thinking of the Marines on the island and not on the grand scale of defeating Japan. I understood that time was of the essence.

Corporal Charles Lindberg, in charge of the Assault Squad, received an arm wound and was gone. All wounds were serious, but to me wounds did not count, whatever the seriousness. At least the wounded were still alive. The line company men who were still alive were all wounded or seemed that way. Lindberg had a beautiful Japanese Saber, and he knew the hospital workers would steal it from him. He asked me to save it for him, and I did.

The two Lieutenants who were left in the company took over the remnants of the company platoons. The company informed me that Lieutenant Leonard Sokol died charging a cave with the pin already pulled on a hand grenade. He took Private Ralph A. Ignatowski from the Third Platoon with him on this charge. The men in the platoon said that the Japanese shot Lieutenant Sokol before he threw the grenade and he fell on it. The bullet and hand-grenade killed him, and this left Ignatowski alone with the Japanese. The Japanese soon killed Ignatowski. Before this, Lieutenant Sokol had suffered a bullet hole through the ear. I think Lieutenant Robert E. Schuelski was shot in the head and killed. I remember his pretty, little, and pregnant wife he left on the side of the road waving her arms off when we left California.

While I was at the front lines checking the men, getting my wounds cleaned, and having a cup of coffee with the men, a small plane flew over. It flew just above our heads. It sprayed a mist over us and the Japanese as well. The plane had evidently done this before. I wondered why the Japanese did not shoot at it. Then, I took a drink of my coffee. On top was a skim of oil. Someone said that the spray was to kill flies. We later learned that it was a new chemical called DDT. I drank it anyway.

Lieutenant James A. Myers crawled under a large net that covered me and a corpsman. We were lying under the net while the

264

corpsman was cleaning my wounds. Myers said that he was the Last Lieutenant Platoon Leader in the Fifth Marine division. The others were killed or wounded. I later learned that Myers was wounded soon after.

As we lay there on the front line under the medical tent, two 16-inch shells from a battleship hit near by. I am not going to try to describe it; it was too deafening and spine chilling. Everything went deadly silent, but we could still hear shrapnel singing. A piece finally landed on top of the net. It was spent but hot. We lay almost hypnotized as we watched it burn through the net and fall to the ground beside us.

That day when we returned from the trip to the front lines, we saw a small crowd gathered at the base of the mountain. I could not walk well, so I got the Redhead to drive close. We saw Japanese crawling from a very small hole in the mountain. As we drew near, we heard muffled explosions coming from inside the opening. The Japanese coming out of the opening had no weapons, and no one asked them to strip their clothes off. It looked as if there were six or eight of them. We were not interested in them; I was interested in the cave, and wanted to see if my theory was true. I believed the mountain to be a honeycomb of connecting caves. We knew we would confront this type of fortification all the way to Tokyo.

The Redhead left in a hurry and was soon back with a rope and large hand light that he got from a landing craft unloading supplies. We notified Marines at the mouth of the cave that we intended to go inside. I thought we might need the rope to mark our trail if the cave got complicated.

Shining the light in front of him, he crawled in and told me to follow him. He and I were soon bent over and walking side by side. He directed the light, and I had my Tommy-Gun trained down the corridor of the cave. We soon came to a hallway crossing our front, and our cave dead-ended into it. Red, without a weapon, scouted out the hallway to our left while I stayed there and protected his rear. Standing up and walking, we traveled down the hallway to an entrance into a small room. He shined the light in, and we saw three or four freshly killed Japanese. They had committed suicide by exploding hand-grenades to their heads. It was plain to see that those men were dead, so we did not mind leaving them behind us. We walked on and soon came to some stairs leading up and off to our left and some more stairs going down to our right.

A few steps down to our right, the stairs had a bamboo curtain crossing it. We listened and could not hear a thing. I got ready, and he jerked the curtain back. The stairs continued down. By then we felt secure and went down the stairs together. He held the light, and I kept the gun ready. On our left was a large room filled with new clothes and equipment. The socks had no heels, so one size fit all. I had no extra clothes; we both stocked up. We heard a noise above us, and I thought, "Oh! hell, we are in a trap."

Everything went silent, and then I heard someone say, "Did you hear that?" It was Marines. That was a relief. I let out a string of curse words so that there would be no mistake in their minds who we were. The rebounding and echoing of our voices made it hard to understand, but I got my message through. Their leader said, "We are getting ready to seal this cave forever; you had better get the hell out of here." It was the Marine engineers, and they meant business. They had robbed the dead in the small room. We were glad to get out. The cave system was even more elaborate than I had thought. Like all secure places, they can become traps. I had no desire to search another cave.

Washing and caring for wounds were impossible. My wounds were in terrible shape. Water was still scarce. The Navy converted salt water with a small conversion plant near the beach. This plant would handle only necessities. Personal hygiene meant taking a bath in the ocean; no one did. We would wash what we had to - no more. I talked to wounded men who said they did not take off their shoes through their stay on the island. My wounds needed serious attention, but I did not want to leave the island as long as Third Platoon men were fighting.

The island was bustling with activity. Small and large planes were landing and taking off like swarms of bees. Roads were being built, one to the top of Mount Suribachi, where the flag was still flying. We were told that this move baffled the captured Japanese. They had occupied this island for almost one hundred years, and nobody had thought to build a road to the top.

The day came when our officers declared the island secure. This declaration must have been for the people back home. "The Four Day Battle" had lasted almost a month, and the island was not secure.

I said farewell to the brain doctor, and the red-headed Jeep driver carried me to the front line for my last trip. Our company command post was behind some rocks, facing the enemy. Private Noe San Miguel met me. He was sad and excited; the Japanese had killed Pfc. Donald J. Brengartner, the company clerk. He had evidently exposed himself in a place that was safe the day before. No one had dared to move him. He lay dead in plain sight. His body marked the enemy's fire-lane.

I told Captain Severance that I wanted to talk to Sergeant Midkiff before I left the island. Sergeant Midkiff was the only Third Platoon sergeant not already killed. Severance told me that the Third

Platoon was on the beach at the extreme left flank of the Marines forward line. There were only three or four men left. To do this, I must run the gauntlet of two or three enemy fire lanes. San Miguel led me through these. I took a trail and moved as fast as I could down a steep cliff to the beach. My wounds allowed this, but I dreaded the climb back.

My God! How exposed could anyone be? Halfway between the water's edge and the cliffs was a small dugout spot with a few rocks around the edge of its forward and near side. Lying against the rocks was a dead, freshly killed Jap. Only a few feet away and toward the cliffs lay two more dead Japs. One of them lay on his back with one leg propped up.

I carried my knife in my hand and walked over to the Japanese on the ground with his leg propped up. He and the other Jap lay in the mouth of a canyon with sharp walls. I studied him closely. I satisfied myself that he was dead. Neither of the Japs moved.

As I walked up, the men rose and greeted me. If the Japanese in the cliffs near by wanted a target, they had one. No one moved the Japanese that lay at our feet. We stepped around or over him.

Besides Sergeant Kenneth Midkiff, Pfc. Manual Panizo, Pvt. Philip Ward, and Pfc. Graydon Dyce were there. We talked about the future, and how we would rebuild a combat unit for the Japanese homeland invasion. It is difficult to explain the deep caring for men and yet expend them, without a thought, if the situation demands it.

At ground level, two caves faced each other. We were told that they did this so that they could protect each other. Lieutenant Eugene J. Adams, a friend from Officer's School, and others from the 5th Engineer Battalion devised a way to solve this problem. They would set off explosives above one cave and the dirt would cover the mouth of the one below. Marines could move up and destroy the open cave and seal it. They would then open the other cave just enough to get a flamethrower nozzle in, and usually that would be enough. It would either kill Japs or run them out another exit.

I knew I could not stay long. Walking through the sand and climbing the cliff would be hard enough, but then I had to cross the Japanese fire-lanes fast. I have never understood why they did not kill me. After walking close to the Japanese and in plain view I climbed the cliff in front of the enemy. At the top of the cliffs, I did find enough energy to move fast across the deadly fire lanes. I made it. The ambulance driver was waiting.

He carried me to the check-in spot, and we shook hands and waved. They gave me a number, and I joined others lined up on the ground. They brought me a stretcher but I refused it. There were others

North end of island

who needed it worse than I did.

There was a Marine captain in the waiting line with a very minor wound. He took a stretcher. I knew this man; he flew a small spotter plane from a ship. A small piece of shrapnel had entered the bottom edge of his heel and came out the edge.

L. B. Holly rode bicycle in front of the enemy without interference.

Evacuated To Guam Island, Marianas Islands
Navy Hospital No.111

On the 16 March 1945, the day that Iwo Jima Island was declared secure, I was evacuated by air to a Navy Hospital seven hundred miles south of Iwo Jima. The Navy had rigged these cargo planes to hold stretchers that could be attached inside the plane. Each plane had a Navy Nurse with the crew.

Corpsmen carried the stretcher patients in first, and about six of us climbed a ladder and sat on the floor near the tail of the plane. My wounds were hurting, and I did not see how I was going to make it without being miserable. I think I needed to be on one of the stretchers.

Our nurse was a pretty red-head. The wounded Marine Captain could not keep his eyes off her. Everyone on the stretchers was asleep, except the Marine Captain. He knew my wounds were in bad shape, but he would not offer me his stretcher.

The nurse said she had meat for sandwiches, but the bread was

269

Ambulance plane transporting wounded back to Guam.

not sliced and she had no way of slicing it. Someone suggested that we use Lindberg's Japanese saber that I was carrying. The nurse invited me into the back of the plane, out of sight of the rest, where I sliced the bread with the Japanese saber. After I sliced the bread without wiping it off before cutting, she said, " Oh! Where has that been? I also noticed that she liked me. I do not know why; no one could look or smell worse.

Our reclining captain saw her attention to me and could not stand it. He offered me his stretcher for a short time so that he could visit with the nurse. I told him I needed it all the way or not at all. She continued playing up to me, and the captain offered me the stretcher for the trip. They woke me when the plane reached Guam.

Hospital ward smells are the same, whatever the military rank. At least thirty officers lay on beds lined up on each side of the long barracks walls. The many complicated wounds overwhelmed the poor doctor and his staff. I remember he had one nurse and several corpsmen.

The nurse was dictatorial, and she ordered me to stay in bed. The medical profession believed that staying in bed to give the wounds time to heal was the correct way. I did not agree and moved as much as I could in order to keep the blood circulating. I would hobble to a small library near by, get books, and read until lights-out. I would then go to the head and sit on a commode and read. I did anything to keep my mind occupied until I got sleepy.

The young red-haired nurse came by to visit, but I did not have the normal desire for female companionship that I did before the battle. I never thought much about this unusual lack of sexual feeling toward the opposite sex until thirty-five or forty years later. One of our Third Platoon corpsman on Iwo Jima, Pharmacist Mate third class Clifford R. Langley asked me if I felt a lack of interest in the opposite sex after the battle and if I enjoyed killing another man?

It dumfounded me that he would know about the difference. I had checked it off as unimportant because I get as single minded as a tight-wire walker when I am deeply involved in something.

Langley stayed in the military and nursed many combat victims. He knew what he was talking about. I told him that the only time I felt joy in killing was at the base of the mountain when the enemy was doing their best to kill us. Our Platoon situation was in doubt from the beginning that morning. As the battle raged at close quarters the situation was in doubt, and we finally destroyed them with the tanks and flamethrowers. The only way I could have enjoyed it more would have been to take off my boots and walk over them bare footed.

Langley said that he heard others talk about the deadening of sexual desires after the direct, close contact killing of the enemy. By the time I reached the States on the first day of July 1945, everything in that department was normal. I called Dorine, the dancing girl, and she came to visit.

In the Guam Hospital, the dictatorial nurse threatened me with a Court Martial if I did not stay in bed, and one night she had a corpsman steal my clothes. My enlisted friends, who visited often from the nearby wards, brought me some enlisted men's clothes, and I put them on and

271

slept in them so that no one could steal them again.

Some officers could not move, and others lay in their beds as they were told. Only a morgue could be that quiet; the silence was deafening. When a person is accustomed to constant loud exploding shells and changes overnight to total silence, it is hard for the system to accept.

I do not remember any of the officers speaking. They lay there and stared at the wall on the other side of the room. If I saw they had needs, I called a corpsman. I remember one officer who lay staring at the ceiling. A body liquid ran from his ear, and small black ants were feasting on the side of his face. I called a corpsman. There were others that I helped to the bathroom where at least we could talk.

Someone brought word to me that the Japanese had killed Sergeant Midkiff. It happened soon after I had talked to him. He was shot through the throat. I went into a deep depression. I had prayed to God for Him to save Midkiff. I felt sure He would.

My good friends, J.O. Reed and Amos Walley, the two young friends from Texas, Boot Camp, and Officers School, came by in a Jeep to visit. They saw the shape I was in and loaded me up in the Jeep. Without permission, they carried me to an Officer's Club and administered their kind of medicine, strong drink and caring friendship.

Soon, the day came when a cargo ship, reworked to carry wounded, notified the hospital to prepare the wounded for boarding. Many wounded were carried aboard for the trip to the hospital in Pearl Harbor. Reed and Walley carried me to the docks, and we swore to see each other for the invasion of Tokyo. The date was 25 March 1945.

Ship U.S.S. Napa to Pearl Harbor

On the ship all wounded were quartered together. I slept on a top bunk and below me on one side was a cot. On the cot was Pfc. Clarence Hipp from the Third Platoon of Easy Company, and at the foot of my bunk was Corporal Tommy Dale from the Machine Gun Platoon of "E" Company. Hipp had lost part of his hip and was in a cast that extended from the bottom of the foot to his waist. Dale had lost most of the flesh just above the knee on both legs, and he was in horrible shape.

Dale was delirious and moaning and groaning with pain twenty-four hours a day. Hipp was moaning with pain also. When they put the cast on Hipp's leg, they bent his toes back and stretched the ligaments in the back of his leg from the calf to the heel. Hipp thought that if about an inch of cast were removed, his heel would come back to its normal place and the pain would go away. I mentioned this to the

272

....talking out of cave.

doctor, who said "no."

Hipp and I talked about the 3rd Platoon after it went north. Hipp also told me that Sergeant Snyder had talked a Japanese prisoner out of a cave on Iwo Jima. He said that Snyder told the prisoner to strip naked and he did. Snyder had used the words we learned in Hawaii while training. A-da-ca-ni-nari,(take off your clothes) det-ti-coai (come out), cocha-coi (come here). He talked the prisoner into pointing out secret caves and let the prisoner go down and try to talk other Japanese into coming out. Each time when the new ones came out, they would have their clothes on and have a weapon. The platoon would save the naked man and kill the others. I was proud of them.

Someone passed the word to the Captain of the ship that he had a wounded officer on board his ship who had made quite a record on Iwo Jima. He sent for me to have dinner with him. I was still walking; the penicillin did its job in spite of me.

We ate separately from the rest of the ship's personnel, and before long I noticed something about the captain that did not ring true.

He carried an attitude about him that told me that he was not right mentally. He thought of himself as some great sea captain on a warship. It was a one-way conversation; I ate the fine food and listened.

When time came for me to leave, the captain stood up, shook my hand, and asked if there was anything he or the ship's crew could do for me while I was on board his ship. I said that I would like to interrogate the Japanese prisoners who were quartered below-deck.

Someone passed the word to me that we had many Japanese prisoners on-board our ship. It was against regulations to contact them personally. I was still trying to brush up on my Japanese language and learn all I could about the enemy.

The Captain called for the Navy lieutenant, who was in charge of the Japanese prisoners, to come to the Captain's quarters. The Navy Lieutenant reported in full uniform. When the captain told him of my request, he informed the captain that the Navy's regulations did not allow him to do this. The captain almost exploded with anger. He told the Navy Lieutenant that he, The Captain, ran this ship and that he gave the orders. I would have the right to enter the prisoner's quarters whenever I wished. I spent most of my waking hours from then on below deck with the prisoners.

I did not neglect the wounded. I disobeyed the doctor's orders and cut the plaster of Paris away from Hipp's heel and let his foot fall back in place. He was much relieved at first, but I guess it had been stretched too long. The pain came back. I tried to help Dale, but there was not much I could do. I am not going to tell what I did do. I still had my belt of morphine. Later, they amputated both legs. The doctor did not say anything about my trying to help. He did not want the Captain's wrath, I guess.

The doctor had just lost a patient. The young man that lay in the bunk at my head sat propped up most of the time and talked freely. One day he turned white and stiffened; he was dead. We knew the symptoms; it was gangrene. We held burial-at-sea ceremonies.

No matter how often I went below deck to talk to the prisoners, the ceremony was the same. The minute my feet appeared on the stairway, the prisoners jumped to their feet and their heads almost hit the deck when they bowed. They did not treat their officers with respect. To the Japanese, prisoners held no rank, and it was a disgrace for them to be Prisoners of War. The American military did not think this way and isolated the Japanese Officers. They had better sleeping arrangements; that was all.

Most of my below-deck time was spent with First Lieutenant Misugami. The name had something to do with water—like mine. He

274

understood, and he knew why I was there. The better I knew the enemy, the better I could do my job.

To the best of my memory, Misugami was wounded on Saipan Island. He was knocked-out by a minor head wound. The Marines thought he was dead, robbed him of his weapons, and stripped him almost naked. While he was walking around in a daze, the Marines took him prisoner. He had nothing to kill himself with before or after.

In our talking, it surprised him that we had captured Iwo Jima, but he did not think we could go any further north. I knew that he was limited in his knowledge of their national strategy. I was more interested in their language and way of life.

There was another Japanese lieutenant there. He was a smart-ass, and I did not spend much time with him. He spoke Russian, and that was the only way I could talk to a Korean prisoner.

The military did not know whether the Korean joined the Japanese freely or if he was a prisoner of the Japanese when the Navy captured the ship he was on. He spoke Russian, and so did the smart-ass Jap lieutenant.

The Korean said that he was taken as a prisoner by the Japanese and forced to work in a kitchen (galley). I knew that he had nothing to tell me and especially through that interpreter. The Japanese treated him as they treated each other.

I was not afraid of these people, but I always kept my back to a wall and allowed no one to go behind me. Their only weapons were single-edged razor blades. The prison guard counted out the razor blades to them and gathered them up after they shaved themselves. It irritated them, but they had to cut every hair on their bodies including around their privates.

The guards bodily inspected the prisoners after each shave. We were told that this made them cleaner and prevented infections. I think that the Japanese had cleaner and more sanitary habits than the Americans, but that was the way we thought then.

"The Navy and Marines have attacked Okinawa," the ship's loud speaker announced. Okinawa was west of Iwo Jima but still a long way from Tokyo, Japan.

Misugami would not believe it at first. He drew a map that showed how their navy, land forces, and the natives would defend the island. He said the natives were Japanese and friendly. Again he drew a map and tried to explain their air force, and how their planes would come from the islands near by. I think he was trying to tell me the mainland, Manchuria. He told me that these planes would dive into our ships (kamikaze) and that we would never make a landing. His officers

275

had indoctrinated him well.

Over our ship's radio we got our daily report. It finally soaked in, and Misugami believed that we were advancing into their homeland. The ship also printed a small one-page daily news letter. Evidently, we had reached the point in warfare where we did not have to maintain radio silence.

We were getting shipshape and making ready for our docking at Pearl Harbor, Hawaii. The ship's Captain was getting more overbearing with the crew. He wanted me on Quarter-Deck with him. He would order his officers around and treat them as if they were dirt under his feet. The crew knew that I had nothing to do with their bad treatment.

As we arrived at Pearl Harbor, a ship was leaving. Because of the distance between the two, the other ship thought it had the right of away. For some reason it made the Captain mad, and he ordered an increase in the ship's speed. The other ship's bells rang and signal lights flashed as we passed close to their fantail.

We docked behind a well-known aircraft carrier that had taken many direct hits. How it stayed afloat, I cannot guess.

No sooner than we had made fast to the dock than three or four Navy Officers came aboard. They acted "official" in every way. The ship's officers allowed no one to leave the ship. After a short time the Navy Officers came out on deck with the ship's Captain between them. They walked in a very tight group, shoulder to shoulder, and marched him off. He needed to be in a hospital. Someone must have radioed ahead. We landed at Pearl Harbor on the 31 March 1945.

Chapter 16

U.S. NAVY HOSPITAL NO. 10
Aiea Heights, Pearl Harbor, Oahu
Territory of Hawaii
9 - 19 April 1945

From the harbor, we were transported to the hospital by bus and ambulance. The more seriously wounded went to the main hospital, and the rest of us went to emergency units located in the canefield near by.

Wounded enlisted friends of mine from "E" Company and friends from other companies converged on my hospital ward daily to talk and search for other friends.

Many enlisted friends arrived at my ward escorted by members of the S.P. (Shore Patrol- Navy police). Because the situation usually arose from an ignored or broken hospital rule, most, but not all, of the problems were minor.

After an ordeal like Iwo Jima, Navy hospital chow and living quarters were as close to heaven as we could get. Mentally adjusting from the extremely harsh, brutal killing of other human beings into a totally relaxed atmosphere is difficult to do and much more difficult to explain or write about.

At the hospital, the Shore Patrol expected order to prevail and patients to obey all rules and regulations. These combat Marines deserved much more freedom than normally allowed. When a problem Marine reported that his own officer was also in the hospital, the S.P.s would quickly bring him to me for discipline. They sought any means to remove the responsibility from the Navy Shore Patrol. I would tell the man to be more careful in his dealings with the hospital. The Navy Hospital was excusing many things, and I hoped that they did not come down hard on these men.

This technique of getting out of trouble became so popular that men from other regiments appeared at my hospital ward. The staff knew that all these men could not possibly have served under me; however, by handling the problem this way, the responsibility lay on the Marine Corps and not the Navy.

The hospitals from Guam to California had been overflowing for weeks with casualties from Iwo Jima. Who would give harsh discipline to these fine men? The men were told that in a short time they would be well enough to be sent back to their Marine company or transferred to a hospital in the States for further treatment.

I could not blame anyone for breaking hospital rules. After all, I kept a fifth of whiskey in a cabinet at my bedside. The hospital would give us a morphine shot, but whiskey was not allowed. I was afraid of Morphine. My friends outside the hospital kept me well stocked with whiskey.

I never took a drink in the daytime. I did not have mental problems in the daytime because there were plenty of things to occupy my mind. At night, each hospital noise or the absolute absence of noise would send a shock wave through my body. I was alerted to an imminent danger that did not exist, but the situation was just as real as if it did.

At other times, nurses or patients would speak to me and I would not hear them, even though they were standing or sitting next to me. My mind was on a book or something else. At other times I would stop what I was doing and ask someone to repeat what they had just said. They would look blank and tell me that they had not spoken.

Because of the whiskey, the doctors and staff threatened me with a court-martial. One nurse tried to sneak up and take my bottle one night. She did not realize that at night I was extremely sensitive to strange noises. My reaction to her scared her so much that she and the staff refrained from trying to sneak up on me again for any reason.

When I drank at night, the aroma from the whiskey would over-power the hospital odors that always permeated the air. I could hear other officers sniffing the air. Regardless of what time it was at night, they could smell the whiskey.

Every afternoon, we arranged tables, chairs, and beds for a few officers to play a quiet card game. Propped up with pillows and facing the front of the ward made it easy for me to see anyone entering or leaving.

The above condition existed when Ira "Chief" Hayes showed up at the hospital ward with a group of Marine Officers, Marine Sergeants, and Marine Military Press. I said a few curse words, and the card players looked up and followed my gaze. The card game came to an immediate halt.

The Colonel leading this parade was abrupt with the nurse at the front desk, and when she pointed, he led the group straight to me. I could see why the colonel was assigned this job. He was in the habit of getting things done.

The entire group of visitors gathered around our table. This included the young man who drew Gizmo and Eight-ball comic strips in the Marine Leatherneck Magazine. His name was Rhodes. Later we

278

saw each other often.

Judging from my recent experiences, Ira Hayes was in more trouble than I could get him out of in a lifetime. His escorts were Marines and not the Navy Shore Patrol that we had been dealing with.

Ira and I were in the Paratroops together before the Marines disbanded us a year earlier. We ended up together in "E" Company. He was stocky-built and a very quiet man.

I rose to meet them. Ira Hayes had spent his youth in Arizona and me in Texas, both near the border of Mexico. Both of us spoke some Spanish. As he neared the card table, we greeted each other in Spanish. Ira Hayes always spoke slowly, and because of the slowness of the conversation between Hayes and me, the Colonel blurted out why they were there.

Back in the States Ira Hayes had become an instant hero. A picture of the flag raising on Iwo Jima had struck the hearts, minds, and spirits of the American people. Ira was in that picture.

The flag raising had its effect on the combat men on Iwo Jima. I was told that a civilian photographer could and did bypass most if not all censorship. They said that he showed his picture of the second flag raising on Iwo Jima. It was an instant success in the States.

The picture was self explanatory and something everybody, young and old, could see. It was not a long-winded story about men in a far-off island that most people at home had no reference point to visualize. The deep inside longing for victory by military service personel, factory workers, and families back home was brought into focus by this one picture.

The colonel let me know in action if not words what the Marine Corps expected of me. The Marine Corps and the United States Government had scheduled a Bond Tour. Hayes was an important part of that plan.

It did not take a genius to see that the United States remained in serious trouble. Two simultaneous wars were at their peak, representing four years of constant struggle. One war in the Pacific Theater and another in Europe had drained the U. S. Government of funds. Morale had reached an all-time low, and the United States' loss in men and material in Europe and in the Pacific was beyond our imagination.

At the present time, the Marines and other forces were fighting a fierce battle at Okinawa, an island north of Iwo Jima. The United States government and the U.S. Armed Forces had to face the fact that the next major battle in the Pacific would be the Battle of Japan. This would not be small island hopping. Estimated casualties to American troops exceeded one million. We were already informed of this. There would be many millions of casualties on the Japanese side.

To the combat veteran troops, we referred to the battle of Japan as "The Big Show." There was no illusion about the job ahead; even the youngest understood.

The Colonel in charge of this group expected me to convince Ira to make the Bond tour. Pharmacist Mate Second Class John H. Bradley from the Third Platoon and Private First Class Rene Gagnon (Company Runner) formally of the Third Platoon of Easy Company were already in the States making the tour or getting ready. The other men in the second flag raising were killed on Iwo Jima.

The United States, our Nation, was waiting to honor the heroes of Iwo Jima. It took me a few minutes to piece things together. The evidence showed that I, a lowly little First Lieutenant, had more power than the United States Government, U.S.Marine Corps, and the Colonel. No wonder he had a deep, authoritative look on his face. If he thought that look impressed me, he was wrong. However, the Marine Corps did.

The pressure from above that this young Indian was forced to take was enormous. However, he was from an Indian Reservation, and reservations were independent nations. We were told that Reservation Indians could not be forced to belong to the United States Armed Services. We were told that legally, the Reservation Indians were still prisoners of war.

Ira's family, when he was away from the Reservation in Arizona, was "E" Company 28th Marines, and the men there were like brothers to Ira. So, back at camp on the big island (Hawaii) was Ira's adopted family.

The island of Hawaii was the place the Marine Corps sent the remnants of "E" Company 28th Marines to recuperate, rebuild, and train for the next campaign. The Marine Corps brought Ira from the big island, Hawaii, to see me at the hospital on Oahu Island. It is difficult to believe that one lone Indian could have that much power.

Most of the company's men understood Ira's feelings about leaving the company and going out among strangers. People in the States were strangers to this young reservation Indian. His loyalty to others in the company made matters worse. There were men in the Third Platoon that he felt were more worthy because they were in the first flag raising. Ira was in the second flag raising picture. Flags waving, bands playing, and movie people jazzing it up may affect the people on a "Spirit and Money" raising Government Bond Tour, but the combat veteran had rather have silence and a cold beer. The combat veteran knew what the Marine Corps expected him to do in the forthcoming battle.

The Marine Corps and others had promised Ira three things: All expenses would be paid, he could see his family, and if he was not satisfied with the Bond Tour, they would bring him back to "E" Company.

In my western way of thinking, I truly believed that I was saying and doing the right thing. I encouraged Ira to take advantage of the situation and go see his family before we attacked Japan. Pressure from above did not affect my decision. I do not think it did. I had withstood that pressure often. We, the troops, were the ones that fought the wars.

When we were in training, Ira spent most of his liberty time in camp. He was not a liberty-hound like the rest of us. I had the feeling that he was not comfortable away from his family and Indian friends on the Indian Reservation or his adopted friends in the Marine Corps.

Ira's beardless face put him in the category with other full-blooded Indians and many of our teenagers in the company, who did not have a beard. Marines must carry shaving equipment in their combat gear whether they had beards or not. This was Marine Corps — by the book.

"There is no razor in this Marine's combat pack," said Colonel Robert H. Williams, former Paratrooper and veteran of the South Pacific, as he was inspecting "E" Company one hot day in our training camp. I was a Second Lieutenant Company Executive Officer in charge of the inspection. He pointed this out to me with a stick he always carried. Colonel Williams was a "by the book" officer. I said, "You remember Chief Hayes, don't you Colonel?" He said, " Oh! Yes, Chief, how are you?" We continued checking equipment. He respected Ira because Ira was a well-known Paratrooper and warrior.

Ira used a small piece of coiled spring wire to pull the few hairs that grew on his face. He would bend the spring and let it close on the hair, and with a jerk, he was shaved.

On my word, Ira Hayes went to the States, and the Marine Corps press told me later that Ida Lupino (the movie star) kissed Ira Hayes and many people offered him money in the form of War Bonds, whiskey, and women. This was foreign to his way of life, and it hurts me deep inside that I was a part of what happened to Ira. Through the Marine Corps press, word reached me almost daily that Ira did not fit on the tour. At times he would not meet with the others, and they would find him at a local bar. The Government sent him back to his friends on the Big Island of Hawaii. The Marines had promised that they would, and they did.

Ira's untimely death occurred as he was returning to his home on the Reservation. I learned later after Ira's death that, for his sake, I should have stayed neutral at the hospital when the Marine Corps brought him to me. I can excuse myself by saying that I had no idea that we had an atomic bomb and that the war would be short lived.

The fact that Ira forced the Marine Corps to bring him to see me should have told me that Ira did not want to go back. I should have respected that. Ira's eyes expressed sincerity, and I felt that he trusted me. I will take my share of the blame.

I will always consider Ira Hayes' trust in me as the highest honor that one warrior can bestow on another - that one individual can show another. Ira knew whom I represented, and when Ira Hayes insisted that he get my sanction before he returned to the United States to help our Government, he taught me a greater depth of understanding. They made a movie about Ira "Chief" Hayes. I did not see it and do not intend to.

Someone brought word to me that Sergeant William G. Harrell from "F" Company wanted to see me. He was in the main hospital, so I knew his wounds were serious. He was laughing when I hobbled up to his bed. Harrell lay there with pillows propping him up. He held a long cigarette holder in his mouth. Ashes from his cigarette had dropped on his chest and burned small holes in his short hospital gown. The nurses and I tried to keep them from hitting his chest.

President Roosevelt had used a long cigarette holder like the one being used by Harrell, but President Roosevelt had two hands, Harrell had none. Quickly, I saw that Sergeant Harrell's laugh was not real.

Harrell and I were in "D" Troop Cavalry at Texas A&M College together, and in Marine Corps training we spent time together. So, when 21 April 1945 came around and we were still in the Hospital at Pearl Harbor, Hawaii, we realized it was "Aggie Day." Aggies (Texas A&M men) meet every year at this time, wherever they are. I managed to meet with them near the hospital and told them about Harrell. I returned to the hospital and found that Harrell had two dozen roses by his bed. To my surprise, I did also.

While hobbling up to see Harrell one day, I saw a small handicraft workshop that the Navy had for recuperating patients. My curiosity caused me to enter. Standing in front of me was the young man without a jawbone. I had watched the "head" doctor and his helpers sew his face together at the makeshift hospital on Iwo Jima. I told him that I had watched the operation. He had a note pad with a pencil, and we communicated for about thirty minutes.

Years later, I think I saw his picture on Look or Life magazine, and I also think I read that they made him a jaw from part of his shinbone. The magazine showed a heavier set man, but I am sure it was

282

the same.

Also, years later, I learned that Sergeant William G. Harrell received the Congressional Medal of Honor for his work on Iwo Jima. When Harrell died several years ago, Arthur Stanton notified me. Arthur was the Easy Company Marine we tried to carry on a drunken ride from the Army hospital at Pearl Harbor. He said he had read it in the paper. In 1993, I met Harrell's second wife, Mrs. Olive Harrell, and his two sons. One son, Bill, served in the Marine Corps and lives on the West Coast. The other son is Commander Gary Harrell USN and, at this time, (1994) is assigned to the Pentagon in Washington, D.C.

After the episode with Ira "Chief" Hayes and the many enlisted men that came by, the hospital staff quit harassing me about the rules I broke. The Marine Corps editorial staff in Honolulu, Hawaii, did everything in their power to see that my wishes were carried out. I never had so much attention in my life. The young man that drew "Gismo and Eight-ball," a cartoon series in the Marine Corps magazine, helped me get an article published in the Marine Corps Gazette. All I remember is that his pen name was "Rhoads." My article showed how we could militarily take highly defended strong points of the Japanese defense without losing many men. The article was published the same month that the Atom Bomb was dropped.

The Word (gossip) went through the hospital wards like an old women's sewing circle. I could not believe what I was hearing. Someone passed the word that the Marine Corps was looking for volunteers to fight on Okinawa. The battle was raging, and they wanted all the experience they could get. Some Marines may have gone.

In the middle of May 1945, many of the wounded and I were shipped to the States on the USS ADMIRAL C.F. HUGHES, from Pearl Harbor T. H. to Marine Barracks, US Naval Dry-Docks, Hunters Point, San Francisco, California.

Chapter 17

Uncle Sugar

8 May, 1945 detached to:
MARINE BARRACKS, US NAVAL DRY-DOCKS, HUNTERS POINT, SAN FRANCISCO, CALIFORNIA

We sailed to San Francisco and were transported to a make-shift hospital near the Bay. They placed me in a room with Captain Phil E. Roach. He was our executive officer when we first formed Easy Company in California in 1944. Before the war, he was a star football player for Texas Christian University at Fort Worth, Texas. Phil was at least two years older than I, and we came from rival schools. To be honest, I always liked Phil. He was a fair and determined man.

When I moved in the room with Phil, he was not friendly. He made an acid remark, and I told him that it would please me if he did not say another word to me, only I used the Marine Corps language to make my message clear. After that, we completely ignored each other.

The Navy shipped us by train to a Navy hospital in Norman, Oklahoma. This was nearer our homes in North Texas. Phil and I kept our distance until one day after a card game, he rolled his wheelchair up to me and said, "I hear you are one of the Above-and-Beyond-Boys." To be honest, I had no idea what he was talking about.

The Hospital announced in a small handout paper that an Awards Ceremony would be held. Nothing was said to me, and I went into Oklahoma City on liberty. Very few Purple Heart medals were given in ceremony because there were too many to give. The officials laid them on our pillows or handed them to us in the hall. A friend reached me by phone and told me to get to the hospital quick. I was expected there in full uniform. I reached the hospital in time to put on fresh clothes, but not enough time to shave. The Navy Captain, head of the hospital, would be presenting awards.

Phil and I were both there, him in his wheelchair with me standing beside him. The program was a big mystery to me.

My name was called out by Captain E.C. Carr, Medical Corps, U. S. Navy Medical Officer in Command, Naval Hospital, Norman, Oklahoma.

Presented to: FIRST LIEUTENANT JOHN KEITH WELLS, UNITED STATES MARINE CORPS RESERVE. Who is awarded

284

the Navy Cross for services as set forth in the following CITATION. (picture and citation in back)

Phil Roach received the Silver Star. Phil called me that evening and asked me to push his wheelchair to the Officers Club. We became the best of friends, and I pushed his wheelchair almost everywhere. We formed a deep friendship. In early 1950, the Fort Worth Star Telegram newspaper reported that Phil died of a bone disease instigated by his war wounds. I felt a deep hurt inside; he was a good man.

The piece shot out of my left leg took longer to heal than my other wounds; it was well now. The imbedded shrapnel in my left leg, buttocks, and neck would remain there. I was ready to leave the hospital and start training for the battle of Japan.

We received word that the Marine Corps was forming a new Marine Tank force on the East Coast. It would be ready for the invasion of Japan. If my memory serves me right, the tank outfit was called the Sixth Tank Battalion or Regiment. I made some contacts. After all, I had never tried that field, and the tanks did impress me on Iwo. I needed a new beginning with new faces, and new things to learn.

Before I could go any further with this project, the United States planes dropped atomic bombs on Japan, and the war ended. The young Japanese will never know how lucky they were. The thousands killed by the Atomic bomb were nothing compared to the millions that would have been killed if we had made the invasion as planned.

The Marine Corps sent me to Marine Barracks, U.S. Navy Ammunition Depot, McAlester, Oklahoma to await orders. Almost everyone I knew was getting out of the military. Clearly I had decided to stay in the Corps, but I did not want to be in tanks in peace time, I thought I would expand my knowledge of warfare. I requested and filled out papers to attend Flight School to become a Marine Pilot.

The flight physical was not hard. They did not take into account the embedded shrapnel. Lieutenant Colonel Mooy, Marine Barracks, Naval Ammunition Depot, McAlester, Oklahoma, sent my request in with a footnote that upon completion of flight school, I expected a one-year waiver on my age to attend the Naval Academy at Annapolis, Maryland. I thought I would "Shoot the Works." If the request did not work, I would go on inactive duty and finish my education.

Big Decision

As Thanksgiving 1945 approached, the Marine Officers attended a party on the Navy base. The party was beginning to develop when someone called me to the phone. First Lieutenant Robert K. West U.S.M.C.R. Great Falls, Montana was calling.

We were together in Boot Camp and Officer's School. He was third in our graduating class in Marine Officer's School at Quantico, Virginia. Bob West was assigned Sea-Going duty aboard a Navy Cruiser, the <u>Salt Lake City</u>, and the Cruiser served at Iwo Jima.

The Marine Corps had released Bob from active duty, and he was at home. He and his father, Robert Karl West, who was a leading attorney in Montana, had planned an elk hunting trip in the mountains west of Great Falls, Montana. They wanted me to go with them.

All my leave time was used, so Lieutenant Colonel Mooy covered for me. An army officer from McAlester drove me to Oklahoma City to catch a plane. I was soon in Great Falls, Montana.

We left early the next morning and drove about fifty miles west. There we met Bob Neal, a recently released Marine sergeant, who was wounded on Saipan Island. He had guided elk and deer hunters before the war. I felt at home with this fine man. We used him and his pack horses.

We helped him pack both our equipment and some of his. He would leave most of his equipment in the mountains for future hunts. We left his place near Augusta, Montana, and went to or near the Bob Marshall Wilderness area. Bob West and the locals called the area "The Bob," which was in the Lewis and Clark National Forest. We would pack our equipment on pack horses and make camp above the Gibson Reservoir. Basic camping equipment had been left there before the war under a well known tree at the head of the Sun River drainage.

With Bob Neal and his pack horses, we packed about twenty miles into the mountains. We followed a chiselled-out trail in the face of a sheer cliff rising above the Gibson Reservoir. The pack horses carried our food, a sleeping tent, and sleeping bags. Our rifles fit on the saddles of our riding horses.

When we reached the camp area, we saw nothing of the camping equipment previously left there. Sergeant Neal was sure it was there, so we began digging.

We dug up and used a ragged cook tent and a metal cook stove. This stored equipment had not been moved for four years or longer. In case of emergency we had two horses penned, by leaving hay in a blind canyon and using old trees to block them. We stayed nine days.

I killed my elk the evening of the first hunting day. Bob shot one and followed him by his trail of blood. I gutted my elk and took the back-strap to camp for us to eat. It was a good thing we took the meat. Large bears got into the kill that night. Bob later killed a large buck deer.

286

It was uncanny how well I could see both small and large game. Even as a young boy I had this ability, but now it was more finely tuned.

It was hard to believe that I was really there, and isolated from the rest of the world. I had time to think. For the past four years I had nothing to think about but war. Now, the exact opposite was true. While I was still among the clamoring crowds, a decision seemed easy. If the majority of men were getting out, then I would stay in the service.

Here, I was isolated from the noise of a multitude of people, where the sun does not set but dies in the early afternoon. The stillness, the camp fire, and the long hours gave me time to think.

"What was I trying to do with my life? Was I trying to become the most destructive man in the world?" I thought it would not be easy for me to stay on active duty in the Marine Corps with no wars to fight. Thank God, I had no inner desire to kill or manhandle anyone. Something inside me said, "Get out of Marine Corps active duty and go back to school. If there is another war, they will call you."

The days were short and the evenings and nights were long. I could easily become addicted to this quiet life. Too soon, in the still air, we heard the pack horses coming with Bob Neal's horse in the lead. As we worked our way back down the icy, slippery trail, I felt as if a heavy load was lifted from my shoulders.

When Bob's family put me aboard a plane and we said farewell, we knew it might be many years, maybe never for some of us, that we would meet again. With that resolve, we said "Goodbye" at the Great Falls Airport. I never met finer people than R. K. West and his family. In 1993, Dr. R.K. West, now a retired medical doctor in Fresno, California, came with his wife to Texas to visit Kathryn and me. A book could be written about this fine man. He served many years on the ship Good Hope. Now in his retirement, he teaches resident doctors one day a week and donates time to a medical clinic whose patients are unable to pay. This was his third trip to Texas in forty-three years. What an honor it was to have him and his wife here.

I caught a plane at Great Falls to go to Denver, Colorado. There I hoped to catch a "hop," a free ride on a military plane, back to Oklahoma. At the military air base in Denver Colorado-I think it was Lowery Air Force Base-I met my friend John Kimbrough from Texas A&M. He was in charge of the very thing I needed, a plane ride out. He was the great Jarring-John-Kimbrough on the Texas A&M football team in the late thirties and early forties. Texas A&M was the Number One Team in the Nation. We were laboratory partners in an agriculture course. I was lucky he remembered me.

John told me where I could get something to eat while I waited.

287

I had not been there long when a very young man in civilian clothes walked up and announced that he was a wounded Marine.

Marines were a scarcity in the central United States, which made me stand out among the Air Force personnel. He said he had recently been in battle on Iwo Jima and was wounded there. I asked him what outfit he was in, and we finally worked it down to "E" Company 28th Marines. It was hard for me to believe what I was hearing. When I asked him what platoon, he said 3rd Platoon.

I told him that I commanded that platoon on Iwo Jima, and he looked up at me and asked, "Are you Lieutenant Wells?"

He then told me that he came to the platoon while I was getting my wounds dressed, and that they told him about me, but he was wounded before I returned to the platoon.

John Kimbrough told me that my plane was about to leave. I boarded and soon was at McAlister, Oklahoma, and reported in to Lieutenant Colonel Mooy. He said that my orders to go to flight school were there. I told him that I had changed my mind, and he wanted to know what I intended to do. When I told him Inactive Status, he said, "Go eat breakfast." When I returned, he handed me my papers.

Within one month I was in Texas Technological College near my home. Texas A&M was still military and an all-male institution. As much as I thought of that school, I could not go back there.

I had hardly found a spot to live in Lubbock, Texas, when I received a letter from a woman in Washington D.C. She said that she had kept my war records and she could not believe that I was leaving active duty in the Marine Corps. What did I intend to do in life. I wrote one sentence back to her: "I intend to start life over again."

This story of my records might have ended here, but forty seven years later, my wife and I were invited to Washington, D C. There I was handed those records. Someone had saved them from being micro-fisched and destroyed with other World War II records.

I do not know who you are but, if you are still living - "Thank You a million times."

I am sure it was through Richard Wheeler's historical writing that I was invited to speak for three hours before the top Generals of the Japanese Defense Force and over one hundred of their Staff Officers. My wife and I were entertained privately by Lieutenant General Yoichi Hayashi, Commandant, JGSDF Staff College and his Staff on 10 June 1983.

In two and one-half years at Texas Tech I graduated in Petroleum Geology and went to work in the oilfields and tried to forget war. The large oil corporations were not for me. If I had wanted a job with a

288

large corporation, I would have stayed in the Marine Corps. I decided to work for myself.

Volunteer youth work, Boy Scouts, YMCA, and church work have been the greatest cure, if you want to call it that. I do not forget my wife, Kathryn, our three children-Connie, John, and Wesley - our eleven grandchildren, and many friends. With their help, I have had a wonderful life.

Corporal Richard Wheeler, of the Little General's squad, did the most to preserve the history of our Platoon. Soon after the war he sent out questionnaires to all of the survivors. I would not fill out mine because I did not want to remember. After many months, my wife talked me into answering Wheeler. She said, "That could be his life's work." Several questionnaires followed. I learned that the cross check was for accuracy, and Wheeler finally got a portion of his book published in <u>American Heritage</u> for June, 1964. It was almost twenty years after he started work on it. The following year, Thomas Y. Crowell and Company published <u>The Bloody Battle for Suribachi</u> by Richard Wheeler. Wheeler has become a famous historical writer, and we have stayed in touch all these years. The Platoon can never thank him enough.

He visited us in Abilene, Texas, in 1975. Some of the Platoon and men from First, Second, Third and Headquarters Platoons of "E" Company have visited here many times. I have the deepest respect for all of them.

I do not know whether it is egotism or what it is that burdens a man that has responsibility, but it is there inside. The burden is deep, especially when there are many lives lost. The Marine Corps passed the word that the proper thing to do was write the families of the dead. I did that until I received two letters from mothers; each thought that I was to blame for their son's death. I stopped writing.

To some of you, these men are not real. They are out of a book or in motion pictures. To me, time has faded a few things, but there are times when the ones that were killed on Iwo are as real to me as if they were with us now. After almost fifty years its deep hurt has changed to a much deeper feeling.

One of our platoon's youngest consoled me. He is older now, but I remembered years earlier when we were training in California. When I asked for volunteers for the machine-gun platoon, I saw a small hand sticking up. It was a very small teenage boy. He could not carry the weapon, but he volunteered.

I watched that little boy grow and develop into a man. He took over the Browning Automatic Rifle on the first night on Iwo Jima and used it like an expert until he had most of his right hand shot away while

289

he was firing it. As we stood there staring off into space amd thinking, the little boy, now a man, Chick Robeson read me like a book. He knew what I was thinking, "All the young men killed." He let me know that they fought for the same country that I did.

He said,

"Don't let it bother you, Lieutenant; that's what we came for."

Afterword

If it were a piece of fiction, Keith Wells' story would be known as a bildungsroman, for the narrative traces a young man's growth and expanding range of awareness with the horrors of war. In that sense it parallels Remarque's All Quiet on the Western Front, certainly one of the classic stories about war and its effect on those directly involved in it. Wells was definitely involved in this one, particularly in preparing to do his duty for God and country on the small island of Iwo Jima and, if necessary, beyond to defeat the enemies of his country.

Wells' work is anything but fiction. It is not even fictionalized fact common from media correspondents about such a conflict. His is the story of a bonafide war hero, more in the vein of Audie Murphy's To Hell and Back instead of the fictional The Naked and the Dead by Norman Mailer. Wells' story is epic in scope, for the battle detailed here was only the Pacific war in microcosm, just as is the relatively brief time of the battle for Troy depicted in another war classic, Homer's Iliad.

Although the focus of the narrative is the three days of combat on Iwo, the story details the events beginning with Wells' days as a student in the Corps of Cadets at Texas A & M University through Boot Camp, Officer School, Parachute School, the final days on Guadalcanal, and preparation for the battle of his life on Iwo Jima. It also includes his decision not to become the greatest killer of all times but to leave the Marine Corps to become a geologist to search for the riches of the earth, not cover it with the blood of his country's enemies. This narrative enables the reader to identify with the soldiers as people, not as stereotypes in stories such as the Iliad or the Medieval Romances of Western Europe, classics such as The Song of Roland and El Cid, in which countless thousands died in a treatment so objective that the nameless, faceless masses were merely stick figures littering the landscape, not, as Wells saw it, pieces of bodies oozing blood into the sand and volcanic ash of a foreign land.

From his youth Wells seemed destined for this time--February, 1945--and this place--Iwo Jima. There he and the men he had trained for the job rose on the morning of the third day and led a charge that has echoed through the annals of the finest hours in Marine Corps history. Without supporting fire, one man led by example a group of warriors, in the finest sense of that term, who breached the line of fortifications at the base of a literal fortress, the honeycombed inferno known as Surabachi with its blinking lights of death pointed at the Marines trying to wrest it from its Japanese defenders. Wells was the right age, barely twenty-three, and he had the experiences in life and the benefit of

291

training to do this job and do it well. The fact that the character of Stryker played by John Wayne in the Hollywood film version of the battle, <u>The Sands of Iwo Jima</u>, is based in part on Wells is a credit to his role in the battle. It also highlights his ability as a leader of men in the most trying of human activities, combat, in which the purpose of the "game" is killing real men if it is required to accomplish the mission and staying alive to do so, unless the job requires the ultimate sacrifice a man can give.

These men were real. They had feelings, felt fear, and had hopes of life after the war. When required to do so, however, they gave their lives for the job they had been sent to accomplish. Many died on the bloody sands of Iwo. They and their comrades and their families are recalled here, partly in hope that this kind of violent conflict need not be repeated.

Wells' narrative style in telling this story is as down to earth as he and his men were in this battle. It is appropriate for his story. This narrative of a show of "guts" by highly trained members of one of the elite fighting units in the world is told in Wells' own words, sometimes raw, never apologetic, always with verve and eagerness to tell the story not as interpreted by a historian who has sifted through the documents and interviewed survivors. This is instead the story of one who was there and was one of the principal players in a deadly game to fight the enemy on his own ground and defeat him.

Dr. Lawrence R. Clayton

This picture is a composite of two Marine patrols.

The first patrol was the Third Platoon Easy Company, with two men replacements from the morter platoon. They raised the first American flag atop Mount Suribachi Iwo Jima Island. Marine photographer Louis Lowery took the picture.
About four hours after the first flag was raised, a second patrol from Easy company brought a larger flag. The larger flag was raised as a joint effort.

1st Lt. John Keith Wells receiving Navy Cross
Norman, Okla. Naval Hospital, 1945

THE SECRETARY OF THE NAVY

WASHINGTON

The President of the United States takes pleasure in presenting the NAVY CROSS to

FIRST LIEUTENANT JOHN K. WELLS,
UNITED STATES MARINE CORPS RESERVE,

for service as set forth in the following

CITATION:

"For extraordinary heroism as a Rifle Platoon Leader of Company E, Second Battalion, Twenty-eighth Marines, Fifth Marine Division, in action against enemy Japanese forces on Iwo Jima, Volcano Islands, 21 February 1945. When ordered to attack across open terrain and dislodge the enemy from a series of strongly-defended pillboxes and blockhouses at the base of Mount Suribachi, First Lieutenant Wells placed himself in the forefront of his platoon and, leading his men forward in the face of intense hostile machine-gun, mortar and rifle fire, continuously moved from one flank to the other to lead assault groups one by one in their attacks on Japanese emplacements. Although severely wounded while directing his demolition squad in an assault on a formidable enemy blockhouse whose fire had stopped the advance of his platoon, he continued to lead his men until the blockhouse was destroyed. When, an hour later, the pain from his wound became so intense that he was no longer able to walk, he established his command post in a position from which to observe the progress of his men and continued to control their attack by means of messengers. By his courageous leadership and indomitable fighting spirit, First Lieutenant Wells contributed materially to the destruction of at least twenty-five Japanese emplacements, and his unwavering devotion to duty was in keeping with the highest traditions of the United States Naval Service."

For the President, .

Secretary of the Navy.

295

REPORT ON FITNESS OF OFFICERS OF THE UNITED STATES MARINE CORPS
(To be submitted in accordance with Art. 237, U. S. Navy Regulations, 1920, and Art. 10-22, Marine Corps Manual)

WELLS, John Keith   (021592)   First Lieutenant   U. S. M. C. R.
    (Name—Surname first)   (Rank)

Ship or station Co "E", 28thMar, 5thMarDiv, FMF, c/o FPO, San Francisco, Calif.

Period covered ____3____ months, from ____1Jan45____ to ____31Mar45____
To be answered by officer reported on:

1. Regular duties ____Company Officer.____

2. Additional duties ____None.____

3. Wife's address ____None.____

4. Name, relationship, and address of person other than wife to be notified in case of emergency ____Mr. Del Earnest____ Wells, (Father), Lakeview, Texas.

         JOHN KEITH WELLS   1stLt U. S. M. C. R.
         (Signature)   (Rank)

To be answered by reporting officer:
    THOMAS B. PEARCE, JR.   Major   MCR
5. Reporting officer ____(Name)____   (Rank)   U. S.

6. Method of rating.—When rating this officer, consider carefully and keep in mind the following definitions, taking into consideration his length of service, the opportunities afforded him which might have a bearing on his performance of duty, his personal characteristics, and professional qualifications:
    UNSATISFACTORY.—Inefficient; below minimum standard.
    FAIR.—Satisfactory; passably efficient; up to minimum standard.
    GOOD.—Average qualifications; efficient, but to a less degree than "Very good."
    VERY GOOD.—Above average; efficient; well qualified.
    EXCELLENT.—Highly efficient; qualified to a high degree.
    OUTSTANDING.—Superior; exceptionally efficient; qualified to a preeminent degree.
    NOT OBSERVED.—To be used in all cases where the reporting officer has had insufficient opportunity to observe the officer reported on during the period covered by this report to permit a rating as to performance of a particular duty, personal characteristics, or professional qualifications.

JUN 19 1945

7. Before making out this report, decide in your own mind on an actual officer in the grade of the officer now being reported on who, in your opinion, based on personal knowledge, is the outstanding officer of his rank in the Marine Corps; or Decide in your own mind the character attributes and professional qualifications which the ideal officer in the grade of the officer now being reported on should possess.

8. Considering the officer reported on in comparison with your ideal (7), and having in mind the instructions under (6) "Method of Rating," indicate your estimate of him by marking "X" in the appropriate space below.

Performance of duty (based on fact):	Not observed	Unsatisfactory	Fair	Good	Very good	Excellent	Outstanding
(a) Regular duties						X	
(b) Additional duties	X						
(c) Administrative duties	X						
(d) Executive duties	X						
(e) Handling officers						X	
(f) Handling enlisted men							X
(g) Training troops						X	
(h) Tactical handling of troops (unit appropriate to officer's grade)							X

FILE FITNESS REPORT CASE

Report after Iwo

9. To what degree has he exhibited the following qualifications? Consider him in comparison with your ideal (7), and indicate your estimate by marking "X" in the appropriate space below.

	Not observed	Unsatisfactory	Fair	Good	Very good	Excellent	Outstanding
(a) Physical fitness (physical stamina; endurance under hardship, adversity, or discouragement)					X		
(b) Military bearing and neatness (dignity of demeanor; neat and smart appearance)			X				
(c) Attention to duty (industry; the trait of working thoroughly and conscientiously)						X	
(d) Cooperation (the faculty of working in harmony with others, military or civilian)						X	
(e) Initiative (the trait of taking necessary or appropriate action on own responsibility)					X		
(f) Intelligence (the ability to grasp readily situations and instructions)					X		
(g) Judgment and common sense (the ability to think clearly and arrive at logical conclusions)					X		
(h) Presence of mind (the ability to think and act promptly and effectively in an unexpected emergency or under great strain)						X	
(i) Force (the faculty of carrying out with energy and resolution that which is believed to be reasonable, right, or duty)					X		
(j) Leadership (the capacity to direct, control, and influence others and still maintain high morale)					X		
(k) Loyalty (the quality of rendering faithful and willing service, and unswerving allegiance under any and all circumstances)						X	

10. Has he any characteristics—temperamental, moral, physical, etc.—which adversely affect his efficiency? __No__
If yes, briefly describe them _____

11. During the period covered by this report, has the work of this officer been reported on either in a commendatory way, or adversely? If so, indicate subject matter and date __None__

12. During the period covered by this report was he the subject of any disciplinary action that should be included on his record? __No.__ If yes, and if not previously reported to Headquarters, attach separate statement of nature and attendant circumstances.

13. In case any unfavorable entries have been made by you on this or on a previous report, were the deficiencies noted brought to the attention of the officer concerned? __None__ If yes, what improvement, if any, has been noted? _____
If no improvement was noted, what period of time has elapsed since the deficiencies were brought to his notice? _____

14. Considering the possible requirements of the service in war, indicate your attitude toward having this officer under your command. Would you—
(a) Particularly desire to have him? __X__ (c) Be willing to have him? _____
(b) Be glad to have him? _____ (d) Prefer not to have him? _____
If (d), explain briefly. _____

15. (To be answered only when reporting on officers serving under revocable commissions.) Do you recommend retention in the service after expiration of revocable period of commission? _____
(Yes or no; if negative give reasons)

16. REMARKS: (To be used for additional pertinent information or comment, if any, not covered elsewhere in this report)
__Recommended for Navy Cross for action on Iwo Jima.__

17. Indicate your estimate of this officer's "General Value to the Service", using the ratings specified in (6) _____
__Excellent.__

18. Having in mind the special fitness of this officer and the efficiency of the naval service, I certify that to the best of my knowledge and belief all entries made hereon are true and without prejudice or partiality.

Thomas B. Pearce Jr.
THOMAS B. PEARCE, JR.   Major   U.S. MCR.
(Signature)   (Rank)

17 April, 1945   Commanding Officer, 2nd Bn, 28th Marines.
(Date)   (Duty)

Report after Iwo

REPORT ON FITNESS OF OFFICERS OF THE UNITED STATES MARINE CORPS
(To be submitted in accordance with Art. 127, U. S. Navy Regulations, 1920, and Art. 16-22, Marine Corps Manual)

WELLS, John Keith _____ (021592) _____, _____ 2dLt. _____ U. S. M. C. R.
(Name—Surname first) _____ (Rank)

Ship or station "E"Co,2ndBn,28thMar,5thMarDiv,FMF, Camp Pendleton, Oceanside, California.

Period covered ____3____ months, from ____1Apr44____ to ____30Jun44____
To be answered by officer reported on:

1. Regular duties __Company Executive Officer__

9. To what degree has he exhibited the following qualifications? Consider him in comparison with your ideal (7), and indicate your estimate by marking "X" in the appropriate space below.

	Not observed	Unsatisfactory	Fair	Good	Very good	Excellent	Outstanding
(a) Physical fitness (physical stamina; endurance under hardship, adversity, or discouragement)						X	
(b) Military bearing and neatness (dignity of demeanor; neat and smart appearance)					X		
(c) Attention to duty (industry; the trait of working thoroughly and conscientiously)						X	
(d) Cooperation (the faculty of working in harmony with others, military or civilian)						X	
(e) Initiative (the trait of taking necessary or appropriate action on own responsibility)						X	
(f) Intelligence (the ability to grasp readily situations and instructions)						X	
(g) Judgment and common sense (the ability to think clearly and arrive at logical conclusions)						X	
(h) Presence of mind (the ability to think and act promptly and effectively in an unexpected emergency or under great strain)	X						
(i) Force (the faculty of carrying out with energy and resolution that which is believed to be reasonable, right, or duty)						X	
(j) Leadership (the capacity to direct, control, and influence others and still maintain high morale)						X	
(k) Loyalty (the quality of rendering faithful and willing service, and unswerving allegiance under any and all circumstances)							X

10. Has he any characteristics—temperamental, moral, physical, etc.—which adversely affect his efficiency? __no__
If yes, briefly describe them. _____

11. During the period covered by this report, has the work of this officer been reported on either in a commendatory way, or adversely? If so, indicate subject matter and date __no__

12. During the period covered by this report was he the subject of any disciplinary action that should be included on his record? __none__ If yes, and if not previously reported to Headquarters, attach separate statement of nature and attendant circumstances.

13. In case any unfavorable entries have been made by you on this or on a previous report, were the deficiencies noted brought to the attention of the officer concerned? __none__ If yes, what improvement, if any, has been noted? _____
If no improvement was noted, what period of time has elapsed since the deficiencies were brought to his notice? _____

14. Considering the possible requirements of the service in war, indicate your attitude toward having this officer under your command. Would you—
(a) Particularly desire to have him? __yes.__ (c) Be willing to have him? _____
(b) Be glad to have him? _____ (d) Prefer not to have him? _____
If (d), explain briefly. _____

15. (To be answered only when reporting on officers serving under revocable commissions.) Do you recommend retention in the service after expiration of revocable period of commission? _____
(Yes or no; if negative give reasons)

16. REMARKS: (To be used for additional pertinent information or comment, if any, not covered elsewhere in this report)
_____Recommended for a regular commission._____

17. Indicate your estimate of this officer's "General Value to the Service", using the ratings specified in (6) __Excellent__

18. Having in mind the special fitness of this officer and the efficiency of the naval service, I certify that to the best of my knowledge and belief all entries made hereon are true and without prejudice or partiality.

JUL 2 4 1944

CHANDLER W. JOHNSON _____ LtCol _____ U. S. MC
(Rank)

27 June 1944
(Date)

Commanding 2ndBn, 28th Marines.
(Duty)

Enter 2nd Fitness Report

NAVMC—652 DF

REPORT ON FITNESS OF OFFICERS OF THE UNITED STATES MARINE CORPS
(To be submitted in accordance with Art. 127, U. S. Navy Regulations, 1920, and Art. 16-22, Marine Corps Manual)

WELLS, John Keith _____ (021592) _____ , _____ 2dLt. _____ U. S. M. C. R.
(Name—Surname first)   (Rank)

Ship or station "E"Co,2ndBn,28thMar,5thMarDiv,FMF, Camp Pendleton, Oceanside, California.

Period covered ____3____ months, from ____1Apr44____ to ____30Jun44____
To be answered by officer reported on:

1. Regular duties ____Company Executive Officer____

9. To what degree has he exhibited the following qualifications? Consider him in comparison with your ideal (7), and indicate your estimate by marking "X" in the appropriate space below.

	Not observed	Unsatisfactory	Fair	Good	Very good	Excellent	Outstanding
(a) Physical fitness (physical stamina; endurance under hardship, adversity, or discouragement)						X	
(b) Military bearing and neatness (dignity of demeanor; neat and smart appearance)				X			
(c) Attention to duty (industry; the trait of working thoroughly and conscientiously)						X	
(d) Cooperation (the faculty of working in harmony with others, military or civilian)						X	
(e) Initiative (the trait of taking necessary or appropriate action on own responsibility)						X	
(f) Intelligence (the ability to grasp readily situations and instructions)						X	
(g) Judgment and common sense (the ability to think clearly and arrive at logical conclusions)						X	
(h) Presence of mind (the ability to think and act promptly and effectively in an unexpected emergency or under great strain)	X						
(i) Force (the faculty of carrying out with energy and resolution that which is believed to be reasonable, right, or duty)						X	
(j) Leadership (the capacity to direct, control, and influence others and still maintain high morale)						X	
(k) Loyalty (the quality of rendering faithful and willing service, and unswerving allegiance under any and all circumstances)							X

10. Has he any characteristics—temperamental, moral, physical, etc.—which adversely affect his efficiency? _No_
If yes, briefly describe them _____

11. During the period covered by this report, has the work of this officer been reported on either in a commendatory way, or adversely? If so, indicate subject matter and date _No_

12. During the period covered by this report was he the subject of any disciplinary action that should be included on his record? _None_ If yes, and if not previously reported to Headquarters, attach separate statement of nature and attendant circumstances.

13. In case any unfavorable entries have been made by you on this or on a previous report, were the deficiencies noted brought to the attention of the officer concerned? _None_ If yes, what improvement, if any, has been noted? _____

If no improvement was noted, what period of time has elapsed since the deficiencies were brought to his notice? _____

14. Considering the possible requirements of the service in war, indicate your attitude toward having this officer under your command. Would you—
(a) Particularly desire to have him? _Yes_   (c) Be willing to have him? _____
(b) Be glad to have him? _____   (d) Prefer not to have him? _____
If (d), explain briefly _____

15. (To be answered only when reporting on officers serving under revocable commissions.) Do you recommend retention in the service after expiration of revocable period of commission? _____
(Yes or no; if negative give reasons)

16. REMARKS: (To be used for additional pertinent information or comment, if any, not covered elsewhere in this report)
Recommended for a Regular Commission

17. Indicate your estimate of this officer's "General Value to the Service", using the ratings specified in (6) _____
Excellent

18. Having in mind the special fitness of this officer and the efficiency of the naval service, I certify that to the best of my knowledge and belief all entries made hereon are true and without prejudice or partiality.

JUL 24 1944

CHANDLER W. JOHNSON   LtCol U. S. MC
(Signature)   (Rank)

27 June 1944
(Date)

Commanding 2ndBn, 28th Marines.
(Duty)

299

Major Yoshitaka Horie-Liason officer to Gen. Kuribayashi

Lt. General Tadamichi Kuribayashi-Commander on Iwo Jima island

COMMANDING JAPANESE STAFF, IWO JIMA

Above Right: Seated fourth from the left is Lt. Genera Tadamichi Kuribayashi. He commanded the defence of Iwo Jima island. Seated next to him on his left is Rear Admiral Toshinosauke Ichimaru twho commanded the anti-aircraft weapons on Iwo Jima. Seated on Gen. Kuribayashi's right is Major Yoshitaka Horie, who was stationed on Chichi Jima over 100 miles away. He was Iwo's emergency supply officer.

Reception given by Major Wells: General Kuribayashi's two daughters is standing next to them. Mrs. Kuribayashi and an enlisted Iwo survivor stand next to Major Wells. Kathryn Wells is next with Major Horie's son. Major Horie is on the extreme right.

302

J. Keith Wells, speaking before Officers of Japanese Defence Force with Y. Horie as interpreter. 1983 Toyko, Japan.

Staff officers Japanese Defence Force 1983 Tokyo, Japan.

303

J. Keith Wells being presented a plaque by Gen. Yoiche Hayashi, Japanese Defense Force 1983 Tokyo, Japan

Iwo Jima hero Keith Wells, who led the most decorated platoon to ever come out of a single engagement in the history of the U.S. Marine Corps, was honored at Quantico during a recent visit there.

Maj Wells, Col Gaboury, Col MacDonald with 2ndLt Schenberger and Col Conway (CO, TBS) at the inauguration of MCROA's Keith Wells Award for Military Professionalism.

Iwo Jima hero Keith Wells, who led the most decorated platoon to ever come out of a single engagement in teh history of the U.S. Marine Corps, was honored at Quantico during a recent visit there.

Almost 50 years ago, on 21 February 1945, then 1stLt Wells was cited "for extraordinary heroism as a Rifle Platoon Leader...in action against Japanese forces on Iwo Jima" and earned the Navy Cross. He was the leader of the third platoon, Easy Company, 2ndBn 28thMar, 5thMarDiv, that raised the first American flag on Mount Suribachi, Iwo Jima after one of the fiercest battles of World War II.

Between 19 and 23 September 1994, now Major Wells (Retired) visited Quantico, Virginia to inaugurate a MCROA award and to lecture students at the Marine Corps University about combat leadership. At the Basic Class 3-94. He told the class that "If you're not careful you can get a strong mind set if you do everything by-the-book. The enemy reads the book too!"

Later, at Company C's Graduation, MCROA presented its initial award recognizing *"Excellence in Land Navigation"* to 2ndLt Matthew R. Schenberger.

While speaking at another engagement, of his platoon's assault on the Japanese emplacements at the base of Mount Suribachi, he said, "It wasn't the normal way we did things, but if we had, we'd still be planted there. In combat, men need to be ready to change."

Major Wells was also honored in a public ceremony at Quantico's Iwo Jima Monument. BGen Richard, Asst Deputy C/S for M&RA (Reserve Affairs), HQMC presented him with a replacement for his Navy Cross and Col Bradley MacDonald thanked him for sharing his experiences with Quantico's Marines.

This article was taken from; *THE WORD* Marine Corps Reserve Officers' Association Nov/Dec 1994

Gen. Anthony Lukeman presenting Shadow box of Medals Washington, D.C., 1992

Gen. Joy & Major Terry Barnes looking on Shadow box of Medals Washington, D.C. 1992

John Keith Wells & wife Kathryn with shadow box of medals presented in Washington, D.C. 1992

Sargeant Ray Winklehausen handing John Keith Wells his complete records. Saved by unknown person or persons.

Keith Wells, Clem Crazythunder's Little brother, L.B. Holly and three Arapaho Indian friends were the pallbearers at the funeral of Dan Friday on the Indian Windriver Reservation, Wyo.. Dan won honors in the South Pacific, was wounded on Iwo Jima and was with Easy Company. Clem Crazythunder an Ogallala Sioux served with the Paratroops in the South Pacific and was killed on Iwo Jima.

Richard Wheeler is the author of Iwo and The Bloody Battle for Suribachi. Both books were reprinted in 1994 by the Naval Institute Press. Wheeler is the author of many first class Historical books. Richard Wheeler was a Corporal in the first squad of the Third Platoon of Easy Company 28th Marines. He was wounded on the third day of battle in the early morning attack at the base of Mt. Suribachi.

Pvt. James A Robeson &
Cpl. Charles W. Lindberg 1944
Camp Pendleton, Ca.

Pvt. James A Robeson &
Cpl. Charles W. Lindberg
32 years later

Boeing B-29 Superfortress

Army North American P-51D Fighters

From back to front: Navy PBY "Catalina", Army North American P-51 D Mustang Fighters, Army C-47 Skytrain Transport, Army Northrop P-61 "BlackWidow" Night Fighters

Japanese zero

THE SECRETARY OF THE NAVY

WASHINGTON

The following Assault Troops of the FIFTH Amphibious Corps, United States Fleet Marine Force, participated in the Iwo Jima Operation from February 19 to 28, 1945:

9th Marines; 21st Marines; 3rd Engineer Battalion (less detachment); 3rd Tank Battalion; 3rd Joint Assault Signal Company (less detachment); Reconnaissance Company, Headquarters Battalion, THIRD Marine Division; Liaison and Forward Observer Parties, 12th Marines; Pilots and Air Observers, Marine Observation Squadron 1; 23rd Marines; 24th Marines; 25th Marines; Companies A, B, and C, 4th Tank Battalion; Companies A, B, and C, 4th Engineer Battalion; 1st Joint Assault Signal Company; 1st, 2nd, and 3rd Platoons, Military Police Company, Headquarters Battalion, FOURTH Marine Division; Companies A, B, and C, 4th Pioneer Battalion; 10th Amphibian Tractor Battalion; 5th Amphibian Tractor Battalion; Reconnaissance Company, Headquarters Battalion, FOURTH Marine Division; Companies A and B and Detachment, Headquarters Company, 2nd Armored Amphibian Battalion; 7th Marine War Dog Platoon; Pilots and Air Observers, Marine Observation Squadron 4; Liaison and Forward Observer Parties, 14th Marines; 1st Provisional Rocket Detachment; 26th Marines; 27th Marines; 28th Marines; 5th Engineer Battalion; 5th Tank Battalion; 6th War Dog Platoon; 5th Joint Assault Signal Company; 3rd Amphibian Tractor Battalion; 11th Amphibian Tractor Battalion; Companies A, B, and C, 5th Pioneer Battalion; Reconnaissance Company, Headquarters Battalion, FIFTH Marine Division; 1st, 2nd, and 3rd Platoons, Military Police Company, Headquarters Battalion, FIFTH Marine Division; 3rd Provisional Rocket Detachment; Pilots and Air Observers, Marine Observation Squadron 5; Liaison and Forward Observer Parties, 13th Marines; Companies C, D, and Detachment, Headquarters Company, 2nd Armored Amphibian Battalion.

For the President,

Secretary of the Navy

Page two of two pages

312

Index

315